INFORMATION
COMPUTER
COMMUNICATIONS
POLICY

9 Software:
An Emerging
Industry

ORGANISATION FOR ECONOMIC CO-OPERATION AND DEVELOPMENT   PARIS 1985

Pursuant to article 1 of the Convention signed in Paris on 14th December, 1960, and which came into force on 30th September, 1961, the Organisation for Economic Co-operation and Development (OECD) shall promote policies designed:

- to achieve the highest sustainable economic growth and employment and a rising standard of living in Member countries, while maintaining financial stability, and thus to contribute to the development of the world economy;
- to contribute to sound economic expansion in Member as well as non-member countries in the process of economic development; and
- to contribute to the expansion of world trade on a multilateral, non-discriminatory basis in accordance with international obligations.

The Signatories of the Convention on the OECD are Austria, Belgium, Canada, Denmark, France, the Federal Republic of Germany, Greece, Iceland, Ireland, Italy, Luxembourg, the Netherlands, Norway, Portugal, Spain, Sweden, Switzerland, Turkey, the United Kingdom and the United States. The following countries acceded subsequently to this Convention (the dates are those on which the instruments of accession were deposited): Japan (28th April, 1964), Finland (28th January, 1969), Australia (7th June, 1971) and New Zealand (29th May, 1973).

The Socialist Federal Republic of Yugoslavia takes part in certain work of the OECD (agreement of 28th October, 1961).

Publié en français sous le titre:

**LES LOGICIELS :
L'ÉMERGENCE D'UNE INDUSTRIE**

This report was prepared for the Committee for Information, Computer and Communications Policy, following a decision at its first session in March 1982. An Ad Hoc Group of experts from Member countries was formed and met twice, in June 1983 and March 1984 (the experts are listed in Annex 1). A questionnaire on government software policies was produced as part of the project and 19 Member countries sent in replies. The final report, and the sector studies on which the Group of experts based its work, have been produced by Mr. Rauf Gönenç and, on the legal aspects, Miss Martine Briat, of the OECD Secretariat.

The ICCP Committee examined the report at its October 1984 meeting and suggested that it be published under the responsibility of the Secretary-General of the OECD, who has agreed.

TABLE OF CONTENTS

PREFACE

Obviously not intended to be very technical, this report draws attention to the highly specific economic features of the software industry and the main ways in which governments can act to encourage its growth. As such, the report should contribute to reflection and decision-making in an industrial field which, though crucial to the development of so many branches of economic activity, remains somewhat unexplored, probably because it is new and its output rather intangible.

The reader should bear in mind that the software industry is probably thriving too vigorously not to out-date the report's statistics quickly most of which in any case are not from government or official sources and must be used cautiously. It seemed however essential to include them for illustration and as a guide to orders of magnitude.

Part II of the report sets out to identify the main points on which governments can take action, especially to reduce the bottlenecks in the software industry with their spill-over effects on so many industries downstream. Such action can take a wide variety of forms, from providing training and encouraging research to solving problems regarding legal status and intellectual property for software products. These points suggest topics for further work, both in the ICCP Committee and elsewhere.

J.P. Brulé
Deputy Chairman
Committee for Information,
Computer and Communications Policy
Chairman of the Ad Hoc Group of Experts
on Software

SUMMARY

What are the trends in technology, industrial organisation and government policies in the field of software? This report studies these questions which, though highly technical, are now of critical importance as OECD economies and societies make the transition towards the general diffusion of information technology.

Software, defined as "sets of data and instructions capable of causing information technology hardware to perform particular functions"[1], is at the heart of all types and sizes of information technology applications. Computer and word processor systems, industrial automation systems, data banks, communications and telecommunications systems, electronic fund transfer systems, industrial products based on micro-electronics, air, sea and road transport control systems and the various national defence systems all operate via their software.

The central role of software in information technology applications became more visible in the early 1980s. At that time it was realised that the spectacular advances in the hardware components of these technologies would only become economically and socially useful if supplemented by the right kind of software to make them functional and accessible to the majority of economic and social actors. The realisation that serious technical and economic problems might be holding back the development and distribution of this software component was what first gave rise to fears of a possible "software bottleneck".

And yet, surprisingly, awareness of the software problem is still largely confined to computer communities in Member countries. In most parts of industry, public administration and government, the opportunities, challenges and possible difficulties of applying information technology are still largely perceived in terms of the efficiency, costs and social implications of the hardware involved. This means that they define information technology strategies, policies and policy instruments mainly in terms of hardware, with a tendency to regard the software question as an adjunct or, in any event, a secondary aspect of the technological transition on which they have embarked.

This incomplete perception of the complementarity between hardware and software is not only liable to make both industry and policy makers at once over-optimistic (as regards possibilities and costs of the new information technologies) and over-pessimistic (as regards their impact on employment and economic growth). It may also make them slower to realise that software needs to be treated as a technology and industry in its own right, and consequently slower to set the right kinds of framework and policy to encourage its proper development.

For that reason, the OECD's Committee for Information, Computer and Communications Policy considered that a project in this field would be useful. The attached study, prepared under the direction of an international group of experts (see Annex I), considers the main aspects of the question. It reviews the main technological and organisational trends in software and considers the emergence of a "service industry" in this field. It identifies the key policy issues for governments and looks at the policies which some of them have already introduced. Thus, it is hoped, it will contribute to an enhanced economic and policy awareness of the importance of software, exploring not only the difficulties but also the potential of this "hidden face" of information technology.

TRENDS IN TECHNOLOGY AND INDUSTRIAL ORGANISATION

The survey brings out three categories of phenomena which, until recently, have characterised the technology and industrial organisation of this field, and which underlie the set of problems known as the "software bottleneck".

Software production is an engineering discipline still in the formative stage

Software production is an activity which is for the moment more of a craft – and an art for some – than a real technology. Software design still relies mainly on the intuitive and experimental skills of specialists, who make but little use of theoretical and practical tools to increase the capacity, productivity and reliability of their work. Among the different phases of software production, it is mainly programming that has so far seen substantial technical progress, with the introduction of many high-level languages. There has been little progress in the introduction of software engineering tools and methods to improve software definition, specification, design, quality and maintainability.

The fact that software design techniques are still at the formative stage places objective limits on the performance that can be expected from current software, in particular for complex applications. Furthermore, since software design is very largely an intellectual task which uses little automation, software production is at present extremely costly.

Software production still has an uncertain economic status

A second set of difficulties stems from the fact that software design is not yet perceived by most users as a production activity like any other. It is therefore not systematically subject to economic evaluation. In fact, the main decisions in software planning and engineering are taken by technical teams who dispose of and apply relatively few economic optimisation criteria and methods. Since the great majority of software is still produced within the organisations that use it or incorporate it in their products or services, and is consequently not subject to market competition, it often seems to be a privileged activity, self-evaluated and self-validated.

This situation may hamper the dissemination and efficient use of technical solutions available, given the state of the art. In particular, it may discourage user firms and departments having their software needs met externally, i.e. using the expertise and products of specialised suppliers. The latter take advantage of the considerable economies of scale typical of software production and competition among them increases the quality of the services and products they supply and forces prices down.

There are uncertainties with regard to the way in which intellectual property law, accountancy law, and tax law apply to software. It is not yet entirely clear how software products will be protected by copyright and patent. However, there is an increasing trend that software is protected by copyright. Whether software can be considered as an asset or not, whether expenditures on software should be considered as current operating expenditure or an investment, and whether software sales should be treated as sales of goods or services all have important legal and economic consequences.

Markets for software production factors and software products are still forming

The organisation and economic optimisation of software production are also limited by the precarious nature of the factor and product markets in this field. Markets for factors such as skilled labour and software engineering tools and markets for products such as professional services and software products (packages) are at present subject to considerable uncertainties, supply/demand imbalances, geographical compartmentalization as well as information and access problems . These phenomena, which are due to the immaturity of these markets, impede their functioning as channels for technology transfer and means of achieving economic optimisation.

As regards the skilled labour market, the problem is first that of imbalance between supply and demand. The shortage of skilled staff, in the first place quantitative, is aggravated by a qualitative problem concerning the skills demanded and offered on the labour markets – internal and external to firms and organisations. The rapid pace of change in users' technical requirements, in hardware and software environments, call in fact for continuous and rapid updating in the skills of specialists, to the extent that they are supposed to employ the technical potential offered by the state of the art. However at the same time, the quantitative pressures on the labour markets make this qualitative adjustment more difficult. The variety and rapidity of technical progress also give rise to difficulties in defining and certifying professional skills, which hamper the establishment and operation of the labour markets.

The markets for software engineering tools, on the other hand, show an imbalance in the opposite direction, demand being still very low, mainly due to the delay in adjusting the skills of potential users. These markets are also subject to uncertainty, information problems and difficulty on the part of users in evaluating products. They are also very compartmentalized geographically, supplier firms being generally small in size and concentrated in certain countries and certain regions.

The markets for professional services and software packages are subject to rapid technical change on the supply side and substantial uncertainties on the demand side. These uncertainties are brought about by the proliferation of alternative solutions and products offered and by the more and more interdependent and less and less reversible nature of software investment within firms and organisations – which may make them reluctant to undertake big investments. Furthermore, imbalances between supply and demand can be seen in certain up-market professional services, where the very small supply has developed only in certain privileged geographical areas. This kind of disequilibrium is less important in the case of software packages, whose reproduction on a large scale and distribution over a large geographical area, though not spontaneous, are incomparably less costly. Some excess of supply over demand can even be seen in certain software package markets.

Technological and industrial organisation in the software field in the OECD area is at present progressing considerably. This progress is to be found in each of the three problem areas mentioned.

Significant progress in software engineering

Substantial progress is now beginning to appear in software engineering techniques, in the form of "software development systems". These concern the programming, testing, debugging and program documentation phases of software production, and bring significant

12

improvements in productivity and reliability. The overall systems definition and specification phase, the most critical and difficult stage, however has so far benefitted least from this progress. Integrated approaches to the planning and management of the entire software life cycle – including maintenance – represent another major methodological advance in software engineering.

Software Expenditures and Activities Are Being Rationalised

Faced with exponentially rising costs of the development, maintenance and conversion of their software systems and in response to the various complaints of end-users, more and more firms and organisations are reorganising their data processing functions. One of the main aims is the rationalisation and transparency of data bases and software libraries (the "Infocentre" concept) and a trend is emerging toward the establishment of "internal computer service markets", possibly subject to competition from outside suppliers. The availability and the relative cost of software packages compared with custom software also encourages users to buy an increasing share of their software requirements on the outside market. In this context a tendency to transform data processing departments into profit centres is certainly in the cards, but comes up against various technical, organisational and legal difficulties.

The software industry is maturing and growing rapidly

Despite the rapid changes to which it is subject and the uncertainties of its markets, the software industry is visibly maturing. This can be seen by the increasing size of software firms, their less precarious nature, their expansion on the international scale, the growth of a software publishing and distribution sector and a tendency toward concentration in many segments of the market. Information is also becoming more systematic and the introduction of many basic standards – for the most part de facto – is to some extent reducing user uncertainty. The division of labour between hardware manufacturers and software firms is also becoming a little clearer in many sectors of the market and their complementarity is now better organised through co-operation and marketing agreements. All these factors are helping software firms to increase rapidly their investment, employment and sales, and – even though over half of data processing expenditure remains within user firms and organisations – the software industry is now one of the fastest growing sectors in the OECD area.

ROLE AND ACTION OF GOVERNMENTS

These processes of technical progress, rationalisation of software activities and the maturing of the software industry cannot be handled entirely by the autonomous and independent action of the firms and organisations concerned. They also call for the availability of a range of external factors: new scientific and technical knowledge; new professional skills; diverse infrastructures, appropriate standards; and the financial, legislative and legal frameworks and practices necessary for the unfolding of these processes. While other actors are also involved – particularly very large firms, technical societies, learned bodies and trade associations – governments have an important responsibility in the availability of these factors. This is the subject of the second part of the report "The Role and Action of Governments" (Part II).

Research policies

Software research, including artificial intelligence research, has to date been mainly the responsibility of public bodies. However, the public resources actually devoted to this activity are still limited. University laboratories, research centres specialised in computer science and laboratories connected with the defence field are all involved in this area of research, and better co-ordination between them is now being sought. There are also a number of private research centres associated with the big computer manufacturers which are contributing to the advancement of basic scientific knowledge. At present the main research policy issues in this field are: how to increase the resources devoted to software research, while traditional scientific disciplines continue to receive the lion's share of public research funds (in a context where total research funds are under pressure); how to encourage young professionals to embark on research careers at a time when they increasingly prefer industrial careers; how to achieve better co-ordination of research activities, both nationally and internationally, in view of the high critical threshholds necessary for scientific advances in this field; how to improve interaction and technology transfer between research and industry, at present considered inadequate in most countries.

Training policies

The existing gap between the number of professionals actually qualified in information technology and the demand for such professionals is a top policy issue in all OECD countries. Because of present trends in these technologies, this gap is greatest, and widening fastest, for various categories of software specialist.

Most governments have announced they are now preparing active policies to make good the shortfall. Chief among these are naturally the governments of those countries where education and vocational training are mainly a public service. Countries with mixed systems are also concerned, needing to determine to what extent their present system is managing to adapt to the challenges of new technologies. In both cases, there are several major issues crying out for government attention: the huge resources (equipment and training personnel) required to enable information technology to aspire to an important place in the secondary and higher education systems; the difficulty of adjusting course content to rapid technical progress; the difficulty of forecasting trends in technology and future needs of the economy with a view to drawing up medium-term training programmes; the value of co-ordination between independent training establishments in designing their curricula; the value of assessment, certification and possibly some standardization of the multitude of professional diplomas issued by the different types of training establishments; evaluation and organisation of the interaction between the teaching of computer techniques at primary ("computer literacy"), secondary and technical levels and its teaching as an engineering discipline in higher education.

It is also argued that if greater progress were made in the development of systems which allowed end users to write their own software, the demand for professional software designers would ease off and the backlog of underdeveloped applications would diminish rapidly.

Government software procurement

Software procurement is important for governments from two standpoints. First, information processing is taking on increasing importance in public services and the performance, quality and cost of the associated software warrant priority attention in procurement policies. Second, government departments, including defence departments, constitute an enormous software market and their procurement policies, technical choices, standards, etc. can have a significant impact on the software industry in general. Consideration is now being given in many countries to the rationalisation of government procurement objectives and methods – efforts that so far have been concerned for the most part with hardware.

Standardization issues

Standards play a vital role in information technology, especially in the software field. Their importance is growing with the introduction of integrated and distributed computer and communications systems involving a great number of hardware/software and software/software interfaces. These interfaces depend on the "homogeneous network" concept where all of these components are structured according to the specifications of a given manufacturer, or on the "heterogeneous – or open – network" concept when they can be supplied by different manufacturers and service firms. The latter solution brings about, in most cases, more technological progress and more price competition, whereas the former does not always guarantee that a single manufacturer's various hardware and software components are totally compatible. Other standardization issues in computer systems are the acceleration of innovations which brings risks of obsolescence and incompatibility if the interfaces between various components of systems are not standardized; and the increasing number of specialised packages which can function only in standard "environments". The growth of international trade and investment also requires recognised international standards.

While most of the standards used in information technology have so far been "de facto" ones, stemming from the dominant positions of a small number of hardware manufacturers, a growing need is now developing for "de jure" (consensus) standards, involving the wide participation and co-operation of large and small hardware and software producers and end users – in particular if "open networks" are to be promoted. It is difficult to organise and implement this kind of standardization nationally, and even more so internationally, because of the numerous commercial interests involved and rapid technical progress which leads to the frequent launching of innovations on the market. Nonetheless, substantial progress has been made, notably in the validation of new versions of programming languages and especially with the gradual acceptance of the multi-layer network architecture OSI (Open System Interconnection) developed by the International Organization for Standardization.

Role of telecommunications infrastructures

In conjunction with the spread of integrated and distributed information systems at local, national and international levels, the role of telecommunications is assuming increasing importance. Telecommunications policies in terms of technical specification and geographical coverage of the network, availability of value-added services – in particular data transmission services – tariffs and standards are thus becoming critical factors for the introduction of integrated software. The majority of OECD countries have recently been making considerable efforts to adapt their telecommunications services to these new technical needs and opportunities. There is still need for improvement in many countries, in particular to meet the needs of smaller users and less well-served regions. More effective co-operation is also needed at the international level.

Implications for software of industrial policies in hardware

Industrial policies in the field of hardware in several OECD countries increasingly have an impact on software. Hardware of different origins is in fact increasingly differentiated according to its system software, its catalogue of application packages, and the "stock" of service firms specialised in producing custom software for it. Government policies in support of "national" hardware industries thus now amount to support for its specific software environment, and hence may work to the disadvantage of alternative software environments. In the same way, tariff or non-tariff barriers to hardware imports affect the technical choices and costs of service firms using or specialising in this imported hardware, and hence the quality and price of the services they offer on the national market and their competitiveness in the international market. These factors have led many governments to look for ways to make their software industry less dependent on industrial policies in hardware, in order to allow it to optimise its technical choices and grow on the basis of universal advances in hardware.

Growth problems for software firms and government support

Software firms are faced with substantial growth problems in many OECD countries. The fact that these firms are new, or in their initial growth stage, causes them financial difficulties. The innovative nature of their services or products raises the problem of the potential local market they can anticipate; and the "intangible" nature of their products makes it difficult for their clients, their financiers and governments to evaluate their assets and products. In this respect venture capitalists play a key role in the financing and piloting of young software firms, but only in those countries where the venture-capital industry has shown significant development.

In several Member countries, governments support software firms:

i) By including them in the "industrial" sector and seeing that they benefit from support measures in relation to creation, investment and R & D on the same footing as other industrial firms;

ii) By developing assistance schemes specifically designed for this sector, notably through public loans or government participation in funding the heavy and risky investment involved in software package development;

iii) Through the software procurement policy of public agencies;

iv) Through general export promotion policies via financial and logistic aids.

Government efforts to clarify the law on intellectual property, fiscal law and accountancy law as applicable to software are also of importance in the development of software firms.

Foreign trade regulations applicable to software

The growth in their development and marketing investment and the increasing specialisation of their markets (and hence of clients) are pushing software firms to internationalise their activities rapidly – particularly in the smaller countries. Similarly, users in all countries try to find suppliers whose products and services are most appropriate to their needs, whatever their country of origin. In this context, the international trade regulations applicable to software are taking on increasing importance.

So far regulations have been broadly liberal in the OECD area. This seems to be due more to uncertainties in the identification of trade and investment flows in this field, rather than to an explicit international consensus on the advantages of this liberalism and to consequent trade policies. Consideration has in fact recently been given in many countries to the advisability of imposing customs duties on software and the ways in which this could be done. At the same time, governments are aware of the technical problems involved in any attempt at taxation – due to software flows within multinational firms, software transfer through telecommunications networks and the sales made by software firms' foreign subsidiaries – as well as the considerable economic cost of any protectionism in this area. But more active international co-operation now seems necessary concerning international telecommunications and the intellectual property protection of software for further development of international trade and investment in this field. Procurement policies of public agencies could also be reassessed, if an international consensus emerged on this point, in order to encourage further international trade and co-operation.

Legal aspects of software

The legal problems raised by the emergence of a software market do not only reflect the uncertainty of the economic status of software. Lawyers are also concerned by the polymorphous aspect of software. Thus, although for the moment there is a tendency to protect programs under copyright law and consider them as intangible goods capable of existing without any material support, there is uncertainty regarding the best legal method of protecting certain types of program. If Member countries were to adopt divergent approaches to solve the problem of legal protection of software, this would certainly create barriers to international trade and investment in software industry. Problems are found also both in evaluating the effectiveness of protection through copyright and in defining the subject matter of a contract when it covers the communication of software to a third party. The way in which software is treated under tax and accountancy law is subject to similar uncertainty. It is sometimes considered as hardware, sometimes as a good distinct from hardware which may be considered as an asset, and sometimes as an "intellectual service" which cannot be counted among the long-term investments of a firm. Insurance companies seem to have the same problem, since software may be covered by policies protecting a user's assets, on the same footing as equipment, and there are also policies protecting the user from any damage which using a software package may cause.

Part I

TECHNOLOGY AND INDUSTRIAL ORGANISATION

INTRODUCTION

Most applications based on information technology – programmable electronic systems – are structured around and operate via their software components. These consist of a combination of data and instructions, many being algorithms, carried in the form of binary electronic signals that are "readable", "interpretable", and "executable" by the system's control units. As electronic systems become more sophisticated, diversified and widespread, their software tends to become more complex, more diversified, often more cumbersome, and to be produced in a constantly increasing number and variety of locations in industrial structures. As a result, software is assuming increasing importance in the "technical systems" of the OECD area and its production is becoming an industrial activity, with its own economic organisation.

With the rapid technical advances in the hardware components of electronic systems and the spectacular way their costs have been brought down, the software side is clearly, today, the main constraint on their potential applications. It also adds to their cost and impedes their diffusion throughout our economies and societies. This "software bottleneck" is illustrated by Figure 1, probably the best-known figure in computer literature of recent years[2].

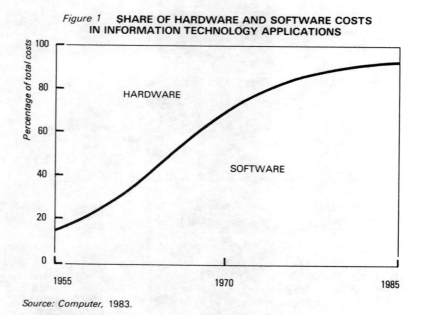

Figure 1   SHARE OF HARDWARE AND SOFTWARE COSTS
IN INFORMATION TECHNOLOGY APPLICATIONS

Source: Computer, 1983.

20

Chapter I

DATA PROCESSING SOFTWARE

Data processing capacity installed in OECD countries has grown extremely fast. Table 1 shows the growth of the market and of the world stock of general purpose computers between 1977 and 1987 (forecasts from 1983), over 90 per cent of this growth being in the OECD area.

Table 1. **Worldwide general purpose computer market and stocks, 1977-1987**[a]

	Production		Installations	
	Number	Value (million $)	Number	Value (billion $)
1977	17 800	12 500	111 500	77.7
1978	10 800	14 740	113 000	88.6
1979	10 200	15 710	105 500	98.2
1980	19 900	16 610	110 300	108.1
1981	20 200	15 120	109 400	110.3
1982	18 300	18 630	115 700	120.5
1983	16 500	21 690	118 400	131.9
1984	18 000	19 940	121 900	137.4
1985	29 400	24 600	133 600	148.1
1986	29 500	28 840	146 900	162.1
1987	28 600	27 900	159 100	172.0

a) Forecasts for the period 1984-1987.
Source: IDC, 1983.

This growth in the stock of general purpose computers has been accompanied by even stronger growth in the numbers of minicomputers, small business computers and microcomputers. These three categories, which occupied a limited place in the world market and computer stock until the late 1970s, are tending to dominate in the 1980s. Figure 2 illustrates the process, through a value breakdown of US computer production from 1978 to 1987 (forecasts from 1983 onwards), reflecting a pronounced volume of microcomputers.

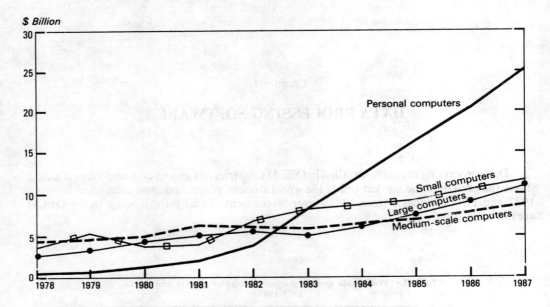

Figure 2   COMPOSITION OF US COMPUTER SHIPMENT VALUE, 1977 TO 1987

Note : Small computers: computers in the $ 10 000 to $ 100 000
price range in 1984;
Medium-scale computers: computers in the $ 100 000 to $ 1 million price range;
Large computers: computers priced over $ 1 million, including supercomputers.

Source : IDC, 1984

A.   TECHNOLOGICAL TRENDS: THE MAIN TYPES OF SOFTWARE AND THEIR LIFE CYCLES

1.   Main Types of Software

DP software can be classified in the first instance within three broad groups: systems software, applications software and integrated software systems. The first two were already used in conventional data processing, but have evolved considerably in their technology recently. The third category is more directly associated with the emergence of distributed computing, though it also includes various special combinations of the first groups and represents the state of the art in software technology.

a)   Systems Software

This refers to the combination of programs required to make optimum use of the computer and its peripherals. In the first case it includes *operating systems* which handle the

22

resources of a computer system, i.e. control the relationships between the central processor, peripheral memories and user interfaces. They regulate and monitor the implementation of various programs according to how much processing time and memory capacity they require. Next come *compilers and interpreters* which translate programs written and stored in the different symbolic languages (COBOL, FORTRAN, Pascal, etc.) into sets of operational instructions that can be interpreted and performed by the computer. Systems software also includes *data-base management systems* which organise whole files or individual data stored in the memory, controlling access according to the needs of running programs, and *utility programs* and *debugging aids* which are used for general housekeeping tasks such as copying files from one medium to another and program development testing.

Three new types of system software have recently appeared on the market as a result of progress in software technology: "programming environments", "programming generators" and "data-base query systems". A *programming environment* is a programming aid system including various development tools, some general, some specific to the field of application concerned (see "Software Life Cycles" below). It represents an advance on conventional programming languages and some are described as "fourth generation languages" (Ramis, Focus, etc.). At the same time it can include data-base management functions (Mantis, UFO, IDMS, etc.) or even operating systems functions (Unix). The *programming generators* may be considered as a sub-category of programming environments. They are designed to significantly improve the productivity of applications designers and programmers. A program generator converts a "procedure definition" written in a system-dependent notation into a program in the source form of a conventional programming language. Classes of program generators are report writers, macro generators, decision table processors and structured language facilities (ADS, Genasys, ALL, Delta, etc.). A *data base query system* is software that gives the user direct access to information contained in the data base, according to various criteria and, possibly using instructions close to ordinary language, for which it may make use of artificial intelligence techniques (Intellect, Clio, etc.). Several fourth generation languages also have extensions performing this type of function (Focus, Dataspan, Data Connection, Linc, Mapper, etc.). Thus a data-base query system constitutes a user interface for a data-base management system.

One important technological variant in systems software is to incorporate it in the hardware, in the form of *firmware*. This is usually done in "read only memories" forming part of the physical structure of a computer, where the software concerned is recorded once and for all. It can also call upon other specific processors or circuits. Firmware technology has so far been used in complex instruction sets for mainframes, in resident compilers, in language machines (Ada machines, Lisp machines, etc.) and in some operating systems (SSX for the IBM 4321, Unix for AT&T's 3B series). Further technological advances in firmware, and the corresponding strategic decisions on the part of data processing manufacturers, might at some point in the future put unbundling (dissociation of hardware and software) into reverse for some DP systems.

b) Applications Software

This term covers all programs whose purpose is to solve the computer user's own problems. The most important contribution of computing to the user is its capability to memorise and treat extensive information and to implement complex algorithms using such information; applications programs utilise these principles to meet various needs of the users. The systems can be either man-made coherent conceptual systems (e.g. business accounts) whose internal logical definitions are used to obtain certain output data on the basis of certain input data; or they can be models representing some external reality (e.g weather conditions) where an attempt is made to anticipate behaviour in response to various parameters on the basis of a formal represenatation of their internal relations. So most applications software consists of programs defining a modelled structure intended to explore the pathways defined within the structure.

There is a great variety of applications software, corresponding to the wide range of possibilities for applying computer processing and modelling. The International Software Directory [Computing Publications, 1983] classifies 107 groups, under five major headings:

1. Accounting, administration, production, distribution;
2. Banking;
3. Design, modelling, simulation, statistics;
4. Insurance;
5. Others.

Datamation's Applications Software Survey uses another classification with six headings:

1. General accounting;
2. Personnel pay and management;
3. Corporate management;
4. Production management;
5. Banking;
6. Insurance.

Recent advances in software technology, associated with the new opportunities opened up in hardware (faster speeds, higher memory capacities) and in particular by microcomputers/work stations, have generated four new types of application software: "decision-aid systems", "expert systems", "semi-custom applications packages" and "one-shot programs".

A *decision-aid system* directly enables the end user not only to recover data but also to solve some of his assessment and forecasting problems. It comprises programs designed to explore different scenarios (futures under different assumptions), mainly in the financial field. The familiar Visicalc spread-sheet can be regarded as a precursor. Several other products are already on the market (FCS, Interactive Financial Planning System, Stratagem, Express, Nomad 2, Ramis 2, Empire, etc.), claiming to be decision-aid systems.

Expert systems use artificial intelligence techniques. They are designed to simulate the intellectual processes of a human expert in a particular discipline, and to infer responses to different problems. This technology, though still very young, is highly promising in many professional fields, at first for the professionals themselves, then gradually, even for their clients. A certain amount of expert system software has already been developed and gone into actual use in Member countries (Mycin, Puff and Sam in medicine, Prospector and Litho in geology, Decos, R1 and Dart in computing itself).

One crucial point must be made about these new types of user-friendly software: insofar as they involve analysis of natural language, they raise very important problems of translation. This is because algorithms for analysing natural language are wholly dependent upon the particular language for which they have been written (mainly English) and cannot be converted in order to analyse other languages. Software relying extensively on such algorithms is very complicated and sometimes impossible to translate, and therefore the user is limited to working in the original language. It will be important to observe progress in fundamental research here over the next few years, especially for the non-English-speaking countries.

The term *semi-custom software* is usually applied to applications software which are adaptable to particular organisations, situations and problems. It consists either of modules or of specific tools with which easily to change the configuration to meet new needs. To some extent it represents a kind of synthesis between conventional application software, software libraries and development systems, but there is little as yet on the market.

The *one-shot program* is designed and written to meet just one requirement, with a lifetime of only one or a few runs. One-shot programs are proliferating in firms and organisations alongside the spread of micro-computers and fourth generation languages.

One technological variant of certain applications software has been a tendency towards embedding it in the hardware. Sometimes it is incorporated as *"firmware"*, (e.g. for Tandy's Model 100 micro-computer and Convergent Technologies' Workslate with built-in word processing and financial planning software). Another way is to use a custom hardware configuration (processors, memories, peripherals etc. of its own) in the case of a dedicated, permanent and large scale application (e.g. library management, airline reservations, various banking systems, etc.). This type of custom hardware/software configuration is called a *vertical turnkey system.* Its market is growing rapidly in the OECD area but has not, so far, affected the broader tendency for hardware and applications software to be designed and marketed separately.

c) *Integrated Software Systems and New Categories of Software*

Beyond these important but "localised" advances (limited to particular fields) in the different types of software, the most important technological trend for the 1980s is the emergence of integrated software systems. These are so designed that the different systems and application software components match one another, sharing data and transferring results among the various programs on just a particular site or on a number of sites communicating with one another. In the latter case, integrated software systems represent the changeover to distributed computing.

This tendency towards integration gives rise to four types of system: the integrated system on a central mainframe, the integrated system on a micro-computer, the distributed system involving a central mainframe and micro-computers, and office automation systems. A fifth type of software, communication software – and particularly local area network software – plays an infrastructural role in promoting the last two applications.

Integrated software on a central mainframe has actually existed since the earliest days of computing, but has evolved technologically to become more user-friendly, less expensive and consequently much more popular recently. In this kind of integrated system, a new application is not designed solely around systems software and its own files, but refers to and integrates with other applications programs with which it shares a centralised data base. Communication among applications programs relies on distributed architecture. This approach was launched by specialist systems software companies and is utilised in products they have recently launched [Cullinet's IDMS, ADR's Fourth Generation system, NCSS's Nomad, Cincom's TIS, Information Builders Inc's Focus. IBM has adapted to the new technology and announced its first relational data-base management system: DB2].

The *integrated micro-computer software* is based on the same principles. Made possible through the extension of micro-computer memory capacities, it meets the needs of the typical end-user who wants to develop an all-purpose data base and to be able to transfer results, texts and graphics among different programs. There are three kinds of systems:

  i) *Product families* with standardized interfaces though often not usable simultaneously (MicroPro's Wordstar, Calcstar, Datastar and Infostar family;

Perfect Software's Perfectwriter, Perfectcalc, Perfectfile, Perfectlink family, etc.);

ii) *Window managers* which enable several programs to be run simultaneously, giving the user a continuous interface with the various "windows" on the screen (Visi-on, Desq, Starbust, Windows, and more recently IBM's Topview, etc.);

iii) *Multifunction systems on micros* with several applications programs that can be run simultaneously via windows (Lotus's 1-2-3 and Symphony, Ashton-Tate's Framework, Context's MBA, Executec's Series One Plus, Software Productions International's Open Access, etc.). Some of these systems can offer communication with other micro-computers.

A tendency can be observed for some hardware manufacturers to build this kind of integrated software into the hardware, including some easy-to-use embedded development tools (especially Apple's Lisa and Macintosh products). This solution has not so far demonstrated any greater technical efficiency than unbundled configurations, but may bring some cost reduction in the software concerned (on a per unit basis) through the large captive market it creates.

The *integrated central mainframe/micro-computer software* has come to the fore with the rapid spread of micro-computers in large companies and organisations which, after early enthusiasm for decentralisation, now strongly feel the need to co-ordinate, communicate and share computer resources. These systems are still embryonic: rather than supporting genuinely distributed software systems, their aim is to enable messages, data and programs to be transferred between the central mainframe and peripheral micro-computers. Technical advances are giving a larger role to the micro-computer, which will gradually grow from a simple terminal to a decentralised processor. The most advanced of these systems have been developed in large firms and organisations that are both highly decentralised and highly co-ordinated. But certain standard interfacing products are also appearing on the market (MSA's Executive Peachpak II, Informatics and Visicorp's Visianswer-Answer/DB, CCA's PC-204, McCormack & Dodge's PC Link, Cullinet's Personal Computer System and the most recent, IBM's PC 3270, etc.).

It is worth pointing out that these developments, contributing to the formation of large-scale integrated and distributed computer systems, are also partly perceived and described in the industry as "office automation". This is because the main technological vector for office automation, the word processing technique, was from the outset a dedicated computer system with built-in software performing a combination of highly specific functions (e.g. the Wang system). Later, technical advances in hardware and software have been increasingly extending those functions towards the storage, processing and transmission of all types of alphanumeric data, i.e. conventional data processing functions. At the same time there has been a certain cleavage (unbundling) between hardware and software, especially with the diffusion of portable word processing and graphics software. The most advanced word processing systems now have many of the features of the small and medium-sized administration and management-orientated "multifunction systems".

The advent of the intelligent terminal, followed by the microcomputer, has practically consummated the marriage of the two techniques, office automation and data processing, so that word processing, tabulation and graphics are now becoming the main application for microcomputers. The outstanding success of such software as Visicorp's Visicalc, MicroPro's Wordstar, Context's MBA and latterly, Lotus' 1-2-3, reflects this tendency. Another point to note is IBM's creation in 1983 of an Office Products Division, designed around and run by the Personal-Computer (IBM-PC) team.

d)   Network Architectures and Local Area Networks (LANs)

These applications of distributed and integrated computing are demonstrating the need for network architectures to provide a framework for their future growth . Although it is possible to develop networks without a reference architecture to underpin the design, the drawbacks of such ad hoc design are increasing overall cost and increasing difficulty of system interconnection.

For some time, the major computer manufacturers (IBM, Digital, Burroughs, Honeywell and others) have offered proprietary network architectures applicable to their own product lines and to equipment which is plug compatible with their products. In addition, several local area network (LAN) product vendors (such as Wang, Prime and Zilog) have offered networking architectures appropriate to LANs. However, the International Organization for Standardization has determined that, although there may be technical differences between the operation of local area networks and wide area networks, architecturally they are similar.

The International Organization for Standardization has developed a standardized network architecture which provides a framework for the orderly development of networks using heterogeneous network components (i.e. incompatible network components usually from different manufacturers). The reference model for "Open Systems Interconnection" has been approved as an international standard. This reference model provides an architectural description whereby systems are decomposed into seven layers according to the services to be performed. Standards for the protocols and services relating to these seven layers are, in several cases, well advanced and some Member countries (notably the United Kingdom through its INTERCEPT strategy) are encouraging manufacturers to develop products in conformance to these emerging standards. In the area of wide area networks, several ISO and CCITT standards exist to facilitate interconnection. In local area networks, the IEEE 802 Committee has developed a widely accepted standard (or more correctly, a group of standards) which establish certain of the technologies as acceptable standard methods for LAN communications (Token Bus, Token Ring and CSMA/CD).

Strong pressure from the user community has led to an increasing recognition on the part of vendors, that interconnection of heterogeneous networks and products is a valid user requirement. The major manufacturers have played a large role in the standards development work on Open Systems Interconnection. Most major vendors have indicated a commitment to it. It is likely that their individual product lines and individual proprietary architectures will evolve towards compatibility with the international standards. However, certain experts feel that IBM's strategy concerning its own network architecture's (SNA) compatibility with the OSI model is not yet clear, and that the success of the OSI model will depend essentially on this decision.

e)   Note on the Impact of Technical Progress in Hardware

Before completing this review of software trends, attention should briefly be drawn to the probable impact of current progress in hardware. Two kinds of impact, corresponding to consecutive phases over the period, should be considered.

In the next few years, hardware advances such as very large scale integration, large capacity microprocessors and memories, bubble memories, optical discs, and optical fibres can be expected to encourage the current new software trends by improving the scope for both local processing and real-time and distributed computing. The fact that the leading companies in hardware technology (Intel, ATT, IBM among others) are at the same time the most vigorous promoters of the new kinds of software reflects this process of convergence.

27

Looking a little further ahead towards the 1990s, the pattern is very difficult to predict. The main question is whether some new basic computer technology will really be available between then and now and if so, whether it will impose itself on the market. If the Von Neumann principle (single CPU, sequential programming) were superseded, as has already been heralded for several years, and its successor became an industrial reality (with parallel architecture computers, data flow machines etc.) the probable consequence would be a further technological reorganisation on the software side. If not, the software approaches emerging now in the 1980s would probably have been accepted once and for all, and be in widespread and popular use by 1990.

f) Note on The Japanese Fifth Generation Computer Project

This project aims to develop a radically new type of data processing to exploit the most recent technological advances in the various software fields, not only in Japan but in other countries too. This project was launched under the auspices of the Ministry of International Trade and Industry in 1980 with an estimated budget of $500 million over ten years, with leading Japanese manufacturers contributing scientific staff. The emphasis is less on highly ambitious technology, which the rather modest resources would not have permitted, than on exploiting synergies between four hitherto separate research fields:

   i)   Artificial intelligence;
   ii) Very high-level programming languages;
   iii) Distributed computing, and
   iv) Very large scale integration (VLSI) in circuits.

The practical outcome of this project was not determined in advance and it is currently the subject of three different interpretations: a very powerful super-computer; a multi-processor computer simultaneously running a great many programs; or a machine that processes not only individual data but also formalized knowledge. This latter interpretation seems to be closest to the intentions of the project's initiators (see Annex IV, Figure 9). In any case, this is the only research project co-ordinating the different ingredients of tommorow's computing to have been publicly announced in Member countries.

2.   Software Life Cycles

In this section the broad features of organisation, methods and techniques in the production of software, together with the main technological advances relating to the various phases are reviewed.

The production process, both for systems software and for applications software, is a succession of different stages requiring increasingly differentiated skills, methods and techniques. These stages fall into one of four broad groups:

   i)   System definition and specification;
   ii) Programming;
   iii) Testing and debugging;
   iv) Maintenance.

In contrast with other industrial activities maintenance is an integral part of the production process, continuously adapting software to new needs and new situations, and therefore includes miniature stages of definition and specification, programming and testing. The whole production process continues practically up to the end of the software's lifetime and can be

28

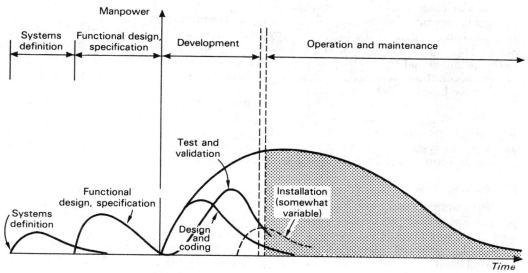

Figure 3 **THE SOFTWARE LIFE CYCLE**

Source: Computer Services Association.

shown as a life cycle (Figure 3). In the case of software packages, this is achieved through successive "releases" of the same package, each of which upgrades and enhances earlier versions.

a) Definition, Specification and Analysis

In the first stage, the aim is to produce an overall representation and an unambiguous logical formulation of the problem to be computerised. This stage involves the future users of the system, end-users in the case of applications or data-base software, computer specialists in the case of systems software, who describe their requirements and constraints, and the computer design engineers who translate these into a formalized unambiguous language. Several difficulties often arise at this stage, stemming from the differences in approach and the different concerns of the two parties. If these difficulties are not properly cleared up at the outset, they inevitably surface later on, in the form of logical inconsistencies in specification or programming, or in a final product not corresponding to the needs of the user. (See Annex IV, Figure 3)

The second stage is the detailed specification for the software, with its inputs, its logical structure and its output. Produced by an "analyst" it provides the basis for flow-charts which constitute the skeleton of the software. In the case of relatively simple designs a verbal (written or spoken) description of the task may be substituted for such formal flow-charts.

Although this is the most critical phase in the software production process, little technical progress has so far been achieved in definition, specification and analysis. This is because of

29

the intellectual and organisational complexity of this phase, which relies extensively on creativeness, trial and error, and constant consultation with users, hardware suppliers and suppliers of other software components, all making it hard to formalize or automate. A number of "specification languages" are already on the market, but are not yet regarded as very efficient. At present the hopes of many researchers in this field lie in the direction of artificial intelligence techniques, with a view to "sifting out" the forms of knowledge necessary in the definition and specification task, to structure these in data bases, and to use them to obtain specifications automatically from a summary description of the final system desired (knowledge-based software engineering).

Another recent trend, less ambitious and shorter-term, is the proto-typing method for definition and specification. In this approach a kind of "to and fro" movement is set up at the beginning of the software life cycle, formulating finished system prototypes iteratively from summary analyses and specifications, and acting as designer/user conversational tools to achieve an unequivocal analysis of and specification for the system.

b) Programming

Programming is the best known and best documented phase in the software production process. That is probably because it attracted the most attention, sometimes too much, in most data processing projects during the 1960s and 1970s as the most costly phase of software production, when the importance of the definition, specification and maintenance phases could not be clearly perceived beforehand. It also better lends itself to systematisation than the design-type phases. Programming is therefore the phase in which the greatest variety of technological progress has been and is still being achieved.

In this phase, the flow-chart is transformed into a program when a "programmer" translates the procedure as defined by the analyst into a set of instructions that the computer can execute. The language used by the programmer to communicate with the computer may range from a low-level assembly language, in which the programmer uses mnemonic instructions which correspond to the basic instruction set of the computer, to one of the high-level languages in which a single (often English-like) instruction generates a whole series of machine instructions or sub-programs. Programs written in a programming language are known as "source programs" prior to their translation into machine instructions (or codes).

There are many high-level programming languages. Those most commonly used today were developed, some in the late-1950s but most in the 1960s, through several concerted actions within the computer community (mainly in the United States). The most important are COBOL for management applications, FORTRAN for scientific applications, PL/1 for both, RPG and BASIC for simple applications, and APL for complex scientific and engineering applications. Figure 4 shows trends in the use of each of these languages in the United States.

A recent survey – by Nomina Information Services – of computer programmers in Germany showed that 48 per cent used COBOL, 35 per cent Assembler, 35 per cent RPG, 10 per cent BASIC, 9 per cent FORTRAN, 6 per cent PL/1 and under 2 per cent other languages.

A 1981/82 survey in Japan showed that 40 per cent of the programs in service and being maintained there were in COBOL, 32 per cent in FORTRAN, 10 per cent in Assembler, 4 per cent in PL/1 and 14 per cent in other languages.

A 1984 survey of 1 400 minicomputer users in the United Kingdom showed that 30 per cent used COBOL, 19 per cent BASIC, 19 per cent RPG, 13 per cent FORTRAN and 4 per cent Assembler.

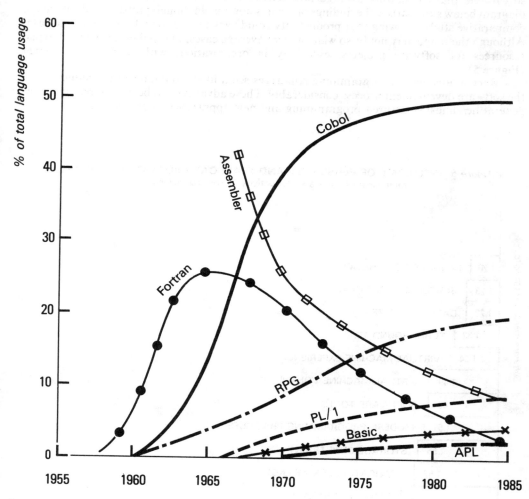

Figure 4   USE OF MAIN LANGUAGES IN THE UNITED STATES

Source: IBM.

The programming stage can be very demanding, in proportion to the complexity of the system, notwithstanding the considerable advances in productivity introduced by the high-level languages. According to B. Boehm, in *Software Engineering Economics* [Prentice-Hall, 1981], whereas a small program may include an average of 2 000 source instructions, an intermediate program may include 8 000, an average program 30 000, and a large program 130 000 source instructions. Assuming that an average programmer can write about 15 "delivered" source instructions[3] per working day, it is understandable why this stage of software preparation is so costly.

Here should be emphasized the enormous diversity in programmer productivity, which is so variable that calculating average productivity has in fact no practical relevance. The diagram below summarises the findings of what is now an old though probably still significant comparative study, showing that productivity could vary in a ratio of 1:26 in extreme cases. Although the range may not be so wide in more average cases, this makes it very hard to plan resources for software projects, especially in organisations with high staff turnover. (Figure 5)

Recent advances in programming languages seem likely to improve the productivity of the software development process considerably. These advances can be considered under two general headings: structured programming and new approaches to programming.

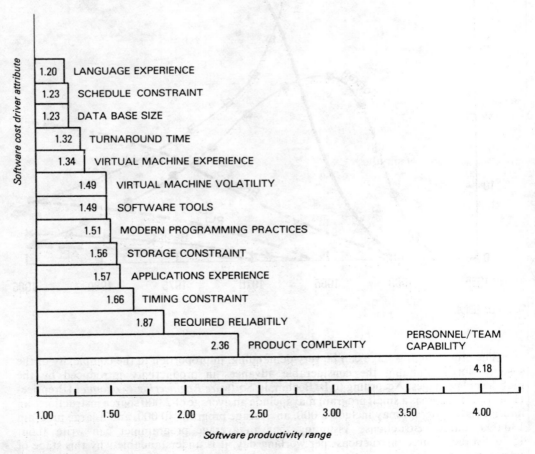

Figure 5 **INFLUENCE OF PERSONNEL AND TEAM CAPABILITY ON SOFTWARE**
multiplicative software productivity factors cœfficients

Source : B. Bœhm/D.o.d.

Structured Programming

In fact, structured programming is already an old concept, introduced towards the end of the 1950s. But the worsening software bottleneck in the 1970s together with recent hardware progress (which has made powerful compilers possible and economical), have brought it back to the forefront. It consists of trying to break programs down into functional, independent blocks. This considerably facilitates the division of labour during the programming phase, as well as error detection and identification during the test stage. It also encourages a simpler, better structured definition of systems by making this compulsory at an earlier stage.

Languages specially constructed around this concept permit the implementation of structured programming. The first of these was Algol, jointly specified between 1958 and 1960 by an international committee. But Algol was designed for scientific and military applications, lacks interfaces to make it accessible to larger numbers of programmers, and has spread to a somewhat limited extent. Two languages deriving from it are probably the main channels for generalising structured programming throughout the computer world; Pascal and Ada.

Pascal was developed in 1968 at the Eidgenossische Technische Hochschule (ETH), Zurich. It was very rapidly adopted by the scientific community and thus became a standard in university computing. It is interesting to note that today it is belatedly entering industry, not under the auspices of any government organisation or large computer manufacturer, but with the support of a whole generation of young computer specialists arriving from the universities. The main problem with Pascal is that there is no authority to control or validate its many diversions or extentions. This considerably impedes its own portability and that of the applications software and the support aids based on it (and undermines the universality of Pascal-related qualifications). The International Organization for Standardization defined a standard Pascal in early 1982, but that appears to have been rapidly overtaken.

Ada has had a very different history. The United States Department of Defense, with all the disadvantages of simultaneously using 400 different languages and dialects for its radar, guided missile and weapon control systems (costing $3.5 billion for software each year), decided in 1974 to develop a very high-level standard programming language for its embedded applications, as it had done with COBOL in the 1950s for management applications. A French team from CII-Honeywell Bull was commissioned in 1977 to develop such a structured language. The first version of Ada was ready in 1980. That version has since been subjected to countless analyses, reflections and concerted action (an estimated 7 000 comments have been presented from 900 institutions in 15 countries). Overall, the collective thinking seems to have proved very favourable to the new language, and the American National Standards Institute (ANSI) published the official description of Ada in February 1983. It has since been submitted as a Draft Proposal to the International Organization for Standardization (ISO) as a language to be used not only in military but also in sophisticated industrial applications [see below for software engineering tools being designed around Ada].

The EEC Commission has decided to back the introduction and distribution in Europe of Ada, which it regards as a language of European origin. Under the Community Multi-Annual Programme in the field of data processing, the Commission supports a number of Ada activities. The current projects utilise ECU 7.5 million, or half of the budget initially available under the project support mechanism of the programme. A major part of this has been used for two projects, the Portable Ada Compiler Family undertaken by a French/German consortium, consisting of Bull, Siemens and Alsys, and the Portable Ada Programming System by a Danish/Italian consortium consisting of Olivetti, Christian Rovsing and the Danish Datamatics Center. A total of 10 smaller Ada-related projects (mostly feasibility studies) are also supported. Further projects, notably for a Formal Definition of Ada, and for competitive designs for a full-scale Ada Programme Support Environment (APSE) are being called for under the current extension of the programme. The Commission also sponsors the Ada-Europe group where European experts meet regularly to exchange ideas and information about new developments in the Ada field.

Industry has reacted quickly and favourably to Ada in many OECD countries and the language is now in the public domain. Several hardware manufacturers and software houses are already offering or preparing of offer Ada compilers for different types of hardware. A number of compilers, produced both by specialised companies, and by hardware manufacturers, have been validated, among which also some European products. More validations are expected to occur in 1985.

Ada also has many critics: some consider that industrial applications have become too highly developed and too diversified to accommodate a single reference language and are against any giant universal language in principle. Others consider that the extra benefits of Ada over Pascal do not justify undermining the solid university infrastructure, built with so much difficulty around Pascal. Still others fear that Ada may already have been made obsolete with the arrival of non-procedural programming.

New Approaches

Three new approaches are aiming rapidly to overtake conventional procedural programming methods, whose structured languages represent a high degree of rationalisation. These are "logical" programming, "functional" programming, and "object-oriented" programming.

Logical programming is based on the logical description (of the nature and relations) of the system to be computerised. The Japanese fifth generation project aims to develop this approach, relying on a language jointly developed at the University of Marseille and Imperial College, London in the early 1970s, Prolog.

Functional programming is based on high-level functional instructions. This approach is considered to be particularly suitable for the development of expert systems, which manipulate largely non-numeric lists, information and symbols. A functional or "applied" language called Lisp was developed for such "artificial intelligence" applications in the late 1950s, by the Massachussetss Institute of Technology. Lisp has recently been winning a growing following, due the practical promise of these techniques (see above). The market for Lisp machines, i.e. special-purpose processors designed for fast list code execution/interpretation and marketed by specialised manufacturers (Xerox, Symbolics, Lisp Machines Inc., etc.), is growing accordingly.

Object oriented programming aims to work on objects defined by their internal states and their relationships with other objects. This form of programming is expected to be particularly suitable to the systems that are highly dependent on their external environment, relying in particular on graphic interfaces with the programmer. It is also expected that relatively novice programmers will be able to manipulate complex objects through their well-defined and often simple interfaces. Simula is thought to be the first language of this kind, from which Xerox has developed Smalltalk, a promising language/operating system.

All three of these new approaches, based on new programming languages, are in fact aiming to do far more than achieve productivity gains in the writing of programs. The aim is a complete remoulding of the four-stage production process (definition, specification, programming, testing) by trying to generate automatically finished programs from a direct description of the desired system performances. Are they about to achieve this? Opinions differ, and the question remains open for the moment.

One important point must be made about the new structured and non-procedural programming languages: the programmers who have mastered these trends, either to use them or to assess them for the future are a distinct minority of the present stock of programmers in Member countries. This is because only recent university graduates will be familiar with structured programming; whereas non-procedural programming, although a key issue for many computer installations (which are currently being committed to software options that will be difficult to reverse), still seems to be an enigma for the great majority of programmers.

c) Testing and Eliminating Errors

The next stage is to carry out the various forms of testing, to identify and eliminate errors. This generally takes quite a long time and can tie up considerable resources. Regularly confronted with the impossible task of going through tens of thousands of instructions with a fine toothcomb to detect the source of this or that error, software designers are trying to alleviate the operation by improving the reliability and quality of work during the preceding phases. This aim is difficult enough in itself and, according to some observers, has been further impeded over the 1970s by the decline in the average skills of programmers (due to the exponential rise in their numbers).

d) Maintenance

A 1978 study by the National Bureau of Standards showed that only 33 per cent of investment in software over its lifecycle was for creating and testing it, as against 67 per cent for maintenance. Investigations into the allocation of computing resources by business and government users have also disclosed the enormous maintenance burden (Figures 6 and 7). It is regarded as one of the main causes of the software bottleneck, since it limits the resources available for the development of new, more efficient programs better geared to user needs. An estimated 75 per cent of United States computing resources for 1980 were absorbed by maintenance activities, leaving only 25 per cent for development activities.

Maintenance activities in fact take many forms. They are largely attributable not to shortcomings in the finished software, but to alterations in its external environment: hardware changes, systems software changes, new user requirements etc. (Figure 8). However, many experts estimate that if more effort was spent during the early stages of the life cycle, less would have to be spent on the maintenance stage.

e) Progress in Integrated Software Engineering

In view not only of these manifold difficulties, but also of the variety of important technical advances, though isolated within the various phases of the production process, a new approach is emerging to the organisation and management of the whole range of processes (including maintenance): "integrated software engineering".

This new approach has two major components: formal methods and computerised tools (computer-assisted software engineering).

Methods

It was at the end of the 1960s that the need was first discussed for systematic, formalized methods of designing and managing large-scale software development projects. The very expression "software engineering" was introduced during a high-level NATO conference in 1968 . But the concept has only now begun to come into popular use.

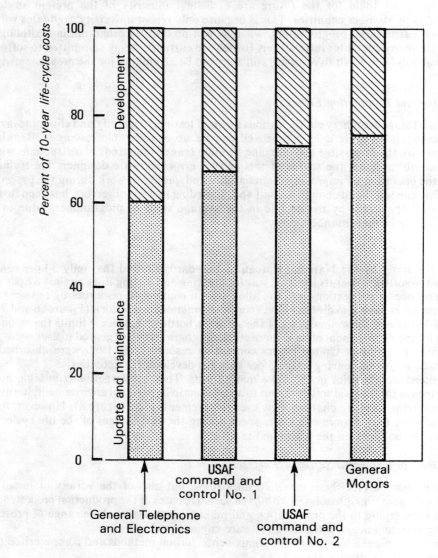

Figure 6 **SOFTWARE DEVELOPMENT AND MAINTENANCE COSTS IN LARGE US ORGANISATIONS, 1976**

Source: B. Boehm.

Figure 7 SOFTWARE DEVELOPMENT AND MAINTENANCE COSTS IN 487 US BUSINESS ORGANISATIONS, 1978

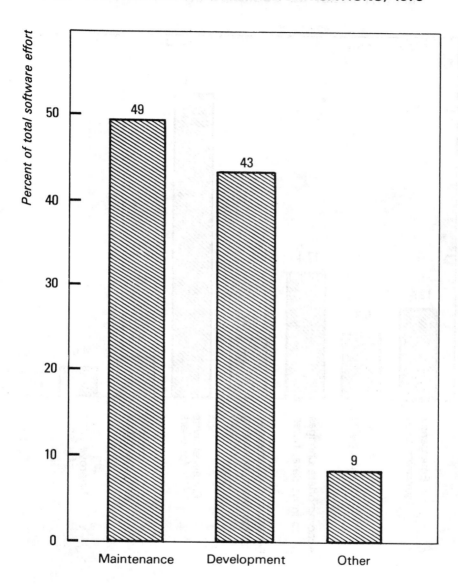

Source: Lientz-Swanson/B. Boehm.

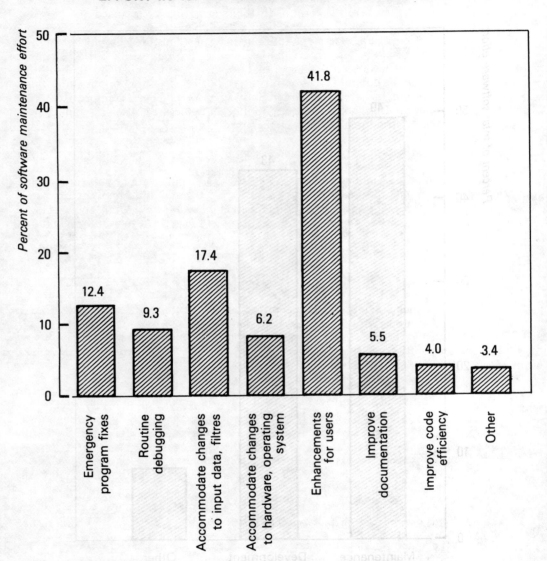

Figure 8 **DISTRIBUTION OF SOFTWARE MAINTENANCE EFFORT IN 487 US BUSINESS ORGANISATIONS, 1978**

Source: Lientz-Swanson/B. Boehm.

Software engineering methods in fact cover a range of methods to optimise different types of projects. It consists of procedures to predefine the main phases of a project, their respective functions, how they are linked, what resources and time they require. Software engineering methods often take the form of PERT diagrams to be specified and adhered to.

The most widespread and commonly used of these methods, at least in the English speaking world, appears to be GOALS, Goal-Oriented Approach to Life-Cycle Software. More recently, methods have been developed that are more sophisticated and closer to the functional structure of the different types of software; among the most important of these are Higher Order Software Inc.'s Higher Order Software Methodology, Stanford Research Institute's Hierarchical Design Methodology, Softech's Structured Analysis and Design Technique, Ken Orr's Structured Systems Development, and Jackson's Methodology. Some of these methods rely on specific software to facilitate their use and thus come under the heading of computer aids in software engineering.

One methodological innovation in software production is to build in an on-site quality control function. Already commonplace in US Defense-related applications, software quality control is now beginning to spread to other countries too. According to the UK Computer Services Association (CSA), the quality control function is exercised by strictly applying a set of principles from a quality control manual specific to each project. The task of the manual is to check that:

- Software is properly specified, and the specification is properly controlled;
- Proposed changes are properly reviewed and authorised before being implemented;
- Standards are adhered to;
- Testing is adequately specified and witnessed;
- Software is properly released and integrated;
- A software error reporting procedure exists and is used;
- Common software is controlled;
- Software is properly documented;
- Maintenance does not reduce the level of quality of the system."

The quality control function will also probably play a major role in standardization:

"Quality assurance can play a major part in promoting common standards throughout a wide area – for instance, all projects on a site, or company-wide standards. Staff will become familiar with the required standards; they will not have to change standards when moving from one project to another; project specific standards can be reduced to a minimum; development proposals can include or reference the site standards, and can agree to comply with them at little extra cost."[4]

Computer-Assisted Software Engineering (CASE)

Software engineering computer aids are themselves software systems, often even combined software/hardware systems, designed as an infrastructure for program creation. They are also referred to as software workshops, office automation for the programmer and recently, computer-aided software engineering – CASE

Up to now, software engineering aids have introduced no radically new functions in comparison with existing "manual" formalized and non-formalized methods. But they make for convenience and considerably improved productivity in the management of the various phases in a project (especially such peripheral aspects as follow-up, documentation, testing, and library management). They include functions to assist in design and analysis, programming, testing, documentation processing, project follow-up, measurement and program library management. According to B. Boehm, a software engineering specialist, appropriate use of these aids can yield productivity gains of up to 10 per cent at the design specification stage, 20 per cent at the analysis stage, 60 per cent at the programming/partial test stage and 80 per cent in the integration/final test stage.

Several software engineering aids are already available on the market, costing from a few thousand dollars for a software package to 100 000 for a multi-station turnkey system[5]. The total market for such tools has developed rapidly in recent years (Table 2). The most prominent are Information Builders' Focus, Bell laboratories' Unix-Programmers Workbench, Xerox's Mesa, DEC's Application Development Environment, Boeing Computer Services' Argus, ADR's Autoflow, Spectrum Inc.'s Spectrum in the United States; Philips' Maestro, CGS' Multipro, Cerci's Vulcain, Systems Designers' Mascot, and INRIA's SOL project in Europe. However, certain experts estimate that many of the tools now in the market place are in fact "over-rated". The computerised versions of specific software engineering methods, which are still marginal, probably represent the frontier of the state of the art in this field.

Table 2. **Independent program design/development software market**
US suppliers, worldwide sales, $ million

System size*	1982	1983	1984
Large-scale	57	83	126
Medium-scale	68	121	198
Micros	5	11	26
Total	130	215	350

* See Figure 2 for scale definitions.
Source: IDC, 1985.

In this connection one system still under development is attracting considerable attention: APSE (Ada Programming Support Environment). This is a set of aids currently being developed as part of the United States Defense Department's STARS (Software Technology for Adaptable Reliable Systems) project, to support programming in Ada. Several observers expect this program to create a support environment of outstanding quality, which will obviously have a considerable bearing on the future of the language. (Table 3)

At the same time, various software engineering aids are being developed for specific fields of application, with the aid of expert systems and software module libraries.

Expert system aids are particularly intended to provide the layman with a means of generating programs simply by describing his requirements. In this sense they share some of the aims of the new programming languages but remain confined to specific application fields [two examples already available of this type of aid are Business Information Analysis and Integration Technique (BIAT) and STSC's Long Range Planning (LRP), in which the user directs program generation by answering questions from an expert system]. This technique may prove highly useful in the future by, among other things, enabling the ordinary public to program microcomputers.

40

Table 3. **ADA programming support environment (APSE) tools**

Level	Tools
Minimal APSE (MAPSE)	Text editor Prettyprinter Translator Linkers Loaders Set-use static analyser Control flow static analyser Dynamic analysis tool Terminal interface routines File administrator Command interpreter Configuration manager
Full APSE	ADA program editor Documentation system Project control system Configuration control system Performance measurement Fault report system Requirement specification tools Design tools Program verification tools (as available) Translators Command interpreters

Software module libraries represent another approach. These rely on the fact that a number of software "components" are systematically rewritten and used in a great many programs (a United States study suggests that on average only 15-20 per cent of a program is original creative work, the remainder being made up of variants on common routines). Software module libraries aim to provide users with a collection of such routines (modules) to be incorporated as units in their programs. For the moment, these libraries are still specific to different types of application, and might otherwise become so enormous as to be unwieldy. Examples of these aids are Raytheon's Readycode (COBOL management software modules), McCormack & Dodge's AFS (Advanced Financial Design System Methodology) and IMSL's Library of Scientific Software Modules.

One very important problem associated with the state of the art in software engineering is, like the new programming languages, that the great majority of users do not know enough about them or how to use them. Recent observations in the United States, which is, after all, the source of the majority of innovations in this field, show that users are submerged by information and suggestions on the subject of software engineering, but that most are incapable of assessing the potential value. The level of sophistication of users in software engineering in the United States industry varies tremendously. Accordingly, the reaction of many users is one of rejection, with a tendency to ignore developments in the state of the art. Another factor confirming this picture from another angle has been the emergence of consultants (or consulting firms) charging extremely high prices for simply *evaluating* methods and aids available.

The difficulties of disseminating software design tools have recently been reviewed in various Member countries. In the United States, consultants Pressmann and Associates have

41

identified several similarities between the situation of CAD/CAM (computer-aided design/computer-aided manufacturing) in the early 1970s and that of CASE in the early 1980s. In their view, the similarities are:

i)   Everybody favours the new technology philosophically but few use it;
ii) No comprehensive, integrated solution exists;
iii) Systems focus on the wrong tasks and often completely ignore the important tasks;
iv) Technical professionals are often unaware of available systems and are unfamiliar with methods for evaluation;
vi) Smaller vendors, some of whom offer superior products, have difficulty overcoming a lack of name recognition.

In the United Kingdom, a recent Department of Industry study identified the main obstacles to the spread of software design tools as:

i)   Lack of integration for most software tools;
ii) Costs still very high, in spite of strong downward trend;
iii) The difficulty of justifying them beforehand, on the basis of a calculable return on investment;
iv) Lack of an integrated technical and economic approach to software life cycles on the part of most company managements.

Lastly, a survey by the Gesellschaft für Mathematik und Datenverarbeitung in 1983 has shown that the market for software engineering tools will probably remain limited in Germany over the next few years because:

i)   The smaller firm prefers to buy packaged software (see below) rather than develop its own applications in-house;
ii) The medium-sized firm prefers a development tool specially adapted to its own area of activity; and
iii) The larger firm's computer system is too "inert" to change over easily to the new software engineering techniques.

The Impact on Maintenance Activities

Whatever the immediate difficulties with these integrated techniques, they will increasingly affect software production processes, at least partially and gradually. They will then have an important impact on maintenance activities, which will evolve from being most laborious, but routine and subsidiary, to become an integral part of systems engineering and management. This transformation will make maintenance both less laborious and more sophisticated.

Firstly, advances in software engineering will reduce "adjustment and error correction" type maintenance activities, partly because software can be more closely matched to user needs, and partly because it will be more structured and transparent, appreciably simplifying the maintenance task.

Secondly, the current process of changeover to distributed and integrated data processing will call for the conversion and integration of a vast stock of older programs, involving "software evolution" type maintenance activities. These conversion and integration tasks, requiring different and higher engineering qualifications than for traditional maintenance tasks, will be one of the main challenges of the 1980s for data processing departments (see below).

42

f) Software Packages

Whatever advances may be achieved in software tools, and however rapidly they may spread, software production remains a difficult and costly process. This applies both to applications software and systems software, but still more to the latter which is usually far more complex. According to certain estimations, whereas an average management application may cost up to $1 million to develop, developing systems software can cost from 10 to 100 times the cost of the hardware on which it runs, i.e. many million dollars. Observers estimate that Adabas, the highly sucessful data-base management system of Software AG, cost some $10 million and that MVS, the most recent IBM operating system, cost billions of dollars.

These enormous costs for developing software, contrasting with the very low cost of reproducing it (which involves no more than copying out a set of instructions on to some kind of medium), account for the central importance now accorded to software packages.

In contrast to custom software, packaged software is purchased as such by the user, together with documentation and sometimes appropriate training. The cost of software packages can thus be spread over several users. An application software package should cost many times less than the custom equivalent, this being in principle closely proportional (depending on the seller's margins) to the number of users of the same software. In the case of systems software, there is usually a much larger potential stock of users, and consequently a much bigger difference in costs. Moreover, the skills required for developing systems software are usually much greater than for applications software. This is why the packaged software approach has become appreciably more widespread for systems software than for applications software up to now.

As computing has spread to new kinds of users on the demand side, increasingly complex applications are developing and economic restraints are tightening; on the supply side experience of package software is accumulating, and techniques for adapting software packages to particular needs are developing. In this context packages are gaining ground very rapidly, to the detriment of custom software.

The result is that users are increasingly seeking to adapt their problems to the best available software solutions, rather than to tailor software solutions to their own individual problems. This movement implies a more or less sweeping reorganisation in business and government organisations computerising their activities. From this point of view, organisational flexibility clearly becomes an important condition for the successful implementation of software packages.

It should also be borne in mind that software packages are subject to constant technical advances which are consequently passed on to users rapidly. The market lifetime of an applications package is rarely more than five years.

Furthermore, packages can substantially reduce users' maintenance activities. This is because package suppliers themselves generally adapt their products to technical advances in hardware and software environments and to possible institutional changes in applications fields (new legislation on accountancy, tax codes, wage rates, etc.) passing these on cheaply and sometimes at no charge to their customers. On the other hand, this makes the user dependent on an external firm for his maintenance activities, especially in the frequent case when the contract of sale prohibits any internal manipulation of the package by its user.

A recent technological trend in packaged software has been the emergence of "parametered" products. This enables a package to be easily adapted to the user's own organisation, needs and situation, to the extent that the designers have been able to anticipate such features. This combines the advantages of "buying" and "making" and may smooth the

43

way for packaged software into markets hitherto difficult to enter because packages have been too standardized and inflexible. However, parametered software is unlikely to become flexible enough in the near future to oust totally custom software – which will long retain a substantial market share especially for the larger-scale applications.

3. Present Software Stock in the Face of Technological Progress

a) State and Value of the Software Stock

The most significant feature of the software currently in use in Member countries is its relatively high average age. This software has been continuously accumulating over the last 15 years on (or around) the computer systems gradually installed in Member countries, and mostly bears the hallmarks of the state of the art in the 1960s and 1970s.

This is very surprising insofar as continuing technological progress in hardware, the growth and consequent rejuvenation of the stock of computers, and the vigour of the computer services industry might have been expected to ensure a continuing renewal in the software stock. This has not happened, for several reasons.

In the first place, the computer system in many business and government organisations is structured around a core – a central computer and its systems software – dating from the 1960s/1970s. The core will have constituted the basis for an accumulation of subsequent developments, which have had to be adapted to its characteristics and constraints. Once the major original investment had been made, marginal increments of hardware or software capacity later on are too small individually to call for a reappraisal of the original configuration, even though cumulatively they may represent appreciably more in terms both of money and of effort. Another point is that the lack of amortization (due to the fact that software never physically wears out), along with the economic crisis, has prevented many businesses and organizations from reconsidering the central configuration of their systems. The result has been the accumulation into the 1980s of a mass of software written in the languages of the 1950s and 1960s, running on systems software and architecture from the 1960s and 1970s. An estimate suggests that this stock might have approached a value of $500 billion worldwide in 1982.

Another estimate suggests that the worldwide stock of application programs written in COBOL alone totalled $100 billion in 1982. A further estimate assesses the worldwide stock of application programs running on IBM hardware at $200 billion in 1984. Allowing for the certain large margin of error, these estimates indicate the existence of a huge stock[6] of software currently in operation, most of this being in OECD Member countries.

The hardware manufacturers' upward compatibility policy has been a further influence in this direction. The hardware manufacturers, seeking to conserve their clients' stock of software while enabling them to buy or lease the most recent generations of hardware, channelled their market innovations between 1960 and 1980 into additional effectiveness but with constant software structures. This strategy has been reflected (especially after the IBM-360) in the stability of architectures, operating systems and the range of compilers available for successive hardware generations. By making existing software portable, this has reinforced its durability and its weight in subsequent developments. Only in the 1980s have the first serious breaks in the software environment begun to occur.

This brings us to the second major feature of the present stock of software now in service in Member countries – its increasing heterogeneity and fragmentation. The process is very important because it is now conflicting with the movement towards hardware integration, requiring growing software compatibility among computer sites, and the spreading of computers throughout the economy, which requires a growing degree of software portability among different computer locations.

Three recent factors have been tending to make software more heterogeneous and fragmented.

b) Manufacturers' New Architecture Strategies

In the first place, hardware manufacturers' new "architecture" strategies: the opportunities offered by great technological strides on the hardware side (large scale integration, 16 and 32 bit micro-processors, mass memories etc.), the rapid drop in the cost of this hardware and the intensifying competition on computer markets have prompted manufacturers to propose new "distributed" architectural solutions, radically different from the centralised architectures which dominated the 1960s and 1970s[7]. Changing over to distributed computing usually means abandoning the upwards compatibility policy, requiring large scale revision of the existing stock of software. For instance, IBM, through its new 4300 and 38 systems, is now trying to generalise its new SNA distributed architecture, its new MVS operating system (and its top-of-the-range version MVS/XA), and its new data-base management systems IMS and DB2, incompatible with earlier software generations. Similarly, CII-Honeywell Bull and ICL are seeking to establish a new distributed architecture with their DSA and VME systems respectively. To avoid discouraging their customers, the manufacturers are offering methods and even software to help "migrate" from programs operating in accordance with the older architecture (to new systems), but this kind of conversion today appears to be costly and risky, if not practically impossible. The result is that in each manufacturer's stock of computers, and even in one and the same user's installation, generations of totally incompatible software co-exist with all the inevitable problems of data bases, program libaries, transfers, transparency, training and maintenance this entails. According to a 1982 survey by 01 Hebdo, 59 per cent of IBM users in France called for "standardization of systems software" and 44 per cent of CII-Honeywell Bull users called for "harmonization of small and large systems software". In fact, software interfaces are already available permitting a certain degree of portability for different generations of software but, in most cases, at the expense of severe losses in efficiency. Meanwhile the International Organization for Standardization, in closer consultation with the various parties concerned, is trying to promote a common architecture with the aim of gradually gathering the agreement of all manufacturers and users worldwide (see "Network Architectures and Local Area Networks" above). The future for the architecture conversion problem remains, for the moment, decidedly uncertain.

c) New Hardware and New Software

The second new factor making for so much heterogeneity in software is directly associated with the appearance and general introduction of minicomputers and microcomputers, up to now mainly promoted by suppliers independent of the large mainframe manufacturers. The new hardware has its own systems software, making it incompatible with mainframes. For example, DEC software had become almost a standard for minicomputers and the microcomputer world is dominated by two operating systems, CP/M for 8 bit micros and MS-DOS for 16 bit micros, produced by small independent software companies. IBM has had a version of MS-DOS specially produced for its PC. Known as PC-DOS, this is totally unrelated to any other IBM software. This IBM decision is also tending to make this sytem the overriding standard for the new generation of 16 bit microcomputers. Other highly effective operating systems are still seeking to impose themselves on the market, under the auspices of

45

one or other of the hundred or so microcomputer manufacturers competing in world markets: Unix (Bell Labs), UCSD (UCSD), Pick of Pick, DOS and SOS (Apple), Oasis (Phase One). Among these, Unix emerged recently as the strongest candidate for standard operating system of the emerging 32 bit super microcomputers (see Table 4).

Table 4. **Market share of operating systems for business microcomputers 1983, installed base**

CP/M	39 %
CP/M-86	3 %
MS-DOS, PC-DOS	30 %
Apple-DOS	13 %
UCSD	10 %
Unix	2 %
Oasis	2 %
Pick	1 %

Source: Trade Press.

The problem of heterogenous operating systems is accompanied, for minicomputers and microcomputers, by problems in communication and in interfacing the various types of hardware within local networks (linking different computer media to one user). Here there are fewer competing systems, with one suggested standard at the forefront (Ethernet), but new possibilities are still expected to emerge.

The last factor making microcomputer software heterogeneous is more conventional: the diversity of source program languages – Assembler, BASIC, Pascal, C, etc. This diversity, aggravated by the different "dialects" of a given language, and therefore of the compiler, on different hardware, restricts software portability among microcomputers and a fortiori among micro and minicomputers and mainframes.

It must be emphasized that this software heterogeneity and fragmentation, characterising the stock of mainframes, minicomputers and microcomputers, must be seen as a sign of technological vigour but at the same time as a problem, one which is now tending to become rigid (less and less reversible as applications software and data bases are accumulated around different systems software and different hardware). The problem is crucial because tomorrow's distributed computing will require applications software to be portable and data bases to be transparent not only within local networks but also national and even international networks, within a given firm or government organisation, and also between different firms and departments. At the same time, compatability problems have already begun to undermine full exploitation of economies of scale in software reproduction. Not surprisingly then, users are anxious not to face the same problems a few years hence as the big users are now having in conversion, but being too strongly motivated to postpone their entry into microcomputing, are taking refuge with the manufacturer least likely to lead them into the dead end of incompatibility, i.e. with IBM. This probably accounts for the "tidal wave" IBM's microcomputer has provoked on the professional microcomputer market since 1981. But is it healthy that uncertainty and risk aversion should be dominating the market to this extent?

In this connection, two important recent initiatives in microcomputer standardization, aimed at improved machine compatibility and better software portability should be noted.

The first concerns programming languages for home computers, the second the integration of applications software for professional microcomputers.

A standard microcomputer programming language was adopted in Japan in July 1983. Called MSX-BASIC, it is a new version of BASIC specified by the United States MicroSoft Corporation. Marketing terms were negotiated between MicroSoft and Japan Soft Bank, the largest microcomputer distributor in Japan, which itself had earlier begun to specify a standard language. Fourteen microcomputer manufacturers (including Matsushita, Sony, Toshiba, Sanyo and Hitachi) have already adopted the standard . In 1984, it was estimated that 400 000 MSX machines in Japan and 100 000 in Europe had reached the market, and in the few months following their introduction over 600 MSX software packages in Japan and more than 200 in Europe were launched onto the market. The Japanese manufacturers state that they deliberately opted for a standard of foreign origin for easier international acceptance and adoption. That, however, is taking time and to date, only two US firms (Atari and Spectra), one European (Philips) and one Korean (Daewoo) have agreed to align with the standard. Even in Japan, some of the big microcomputer manufacturers (NEC, Sharp, Sord) are not committing themselves, some of them arguing that MSX is already an obsolete technology.

In the integration of applications software for professional microcomputers, another MicroSoft product called "Windows" is being promoted as a standard. Designed as an intelligent interface between different applications software, this is an extension of the MicroSoft MS/DOS operating system, which divides up a microcomputer screen into several sections, enabling the user to work simultaneously with several programs and to interchange data among them. Announced in November 1983, it has already been adopted by 23 microcomputer manufacturers and software houses, undertaking to produce machines and programs in accordance with it. Even so, it has not become a real standard. Other software houses have announced competing interfaces (DRI, Visicorp, Quarterdeck) and claim they have the support of other firms. Meanwhile and more recently, IBM, which up to 1984 had reserved its position , came up with its own windowing product, Topview. This software, compatible with any IBM-PC applications program, is expected to be available on IBM machines in 1985 and at once would appear to be a natural and strong candidate for becoming a de facto standard.

d) New Users

The third and final important factor in making the stock of software so heterogeneous results from the proliferation and diversification of computer users. Computing is spreading into small and medium-sized firms and local government; also into those departments of the larger firms and government organisations which had previously used computers only marginally. This process leads to heterogeneity in several ways: the emergence of new types of applications software intended for new purposes: SME management, municipal management, documentation systems, small word-processing systems etc.; by the use of new software/hardware integration techniques, especially to develop turnkey systems intended for non-specialist users; by the rise of source programs written and maintainable in "popular" languages, especially BASIC and RPG; by the proliferation of data bases and "individual" program libraries within large organisations. This process of user proliferation and diversification sharply differentiates the new forms of software from the features of the conventional software environment of the larger computer department (Assembler, FORTRAN, COBOL source programs; IBM 360/370 or equivalent architectures; Codasyl centralised data bases, specialised computer personnel etc.).

47

e) The Fascinated Confusion of Users

The two major features of the existing stock of software just mentioned – the preponderant influence of the architecture of the 1960s and 1970s, and the growing process of heterogeneity and fragmentation – generate its third main characteristic: the hazy and problematical way in which the increasingly numerous non-specialist users perceive it.

In large firms and government organisations, the predominance of centralised systems, with limited software flexibility and capacity, controlled by data processing departments and poorly understood by most of the end users has made the latter somewhat frustrated. The final usefulness of computer applications, sometimes disproportionate to the amount of work entailed, the slowness of computer departments in designing new applications, frequent delays and bottlenecks in current applications, endless problems of incompatibility, and mushrooming of data bases have led to exasperation in an appreciable proportion of users in many computer locations. This is a situation many observers have described as the "end-user revolt" of the late 1970s. Nor have most users seen the impact of the recent development of "user-friendly" software aids whose availability they have learnt of from press articles and advertisements, either because their own computer departments have been unable to introduce such aids into the existing systems, or because the new aids have not performed as spectacularly as claimed. In this context, the development of microcomputers appeared to hold out a hope of "reconciliation" with computing for many users, so many of which soon discovered the hardware and software limitations and the lonely impositions these involved. However, all this has not impeded the growing use of computers in large firms, and government organisations, with remarkable benefits.

For the smaller and medium-sized firm and the smaller government organisation, the main software problem is not of adapting an older system or organisation, since it will not have had one, but a problem of strategy and of how to choose from the numerous alternatives on offer today. Confronted with a very wide range of hardware, software, turnkey computer systems, integrated office automation systems (which are constantly diversifying and renewing), many lack the skill and information needed to assess them and to define a strategy. Smaller users are therefore in a difficult position: they must obtain the maximum yield on their investment without locking themselves into a hardware or software solution that will lead nowhere or soon become obsolete. Many small users are nevertheless taking the plunge, choosing a variety of configurations, and thus maintaining the vigorous, and very heterogeneous character of the small systems market.

B. TRENDS IN ECONOMIC ORGANISATION: EMERGENCE OF A SOFTWARE INDUSTRY

How are software producers (supply) and users (demand) structured economically in Member countries? What are the relationships between the economic structures and technological trends? How does technological progress affect the development of the structures and to what extent are they succeeding in making the most of it?

To answer these questions, it is necessary to describe the general trends in the economic organisation of software development. First, those on the supply side (channels for technological advances) are examined and then those on the demand side (channels for their integration into the economy).

Two main constituents have to be distinguished on the supply side: the internal supply of software by user installations (business and government organisations), as opposed to external supply via the market. The latter has sub-constituents differing appreciably according to the nature and origin of the suppliers (hardware manufacturers or specialist service firms).

1. In-House Software Production by User Firms and Organisations

a) Data Processing Departments

Business and government organisations using computers have established specialist departments responsible for the design, maintenance and operation of their systems. The highly specific character of the qualifications necessary to use computers, and the centralised nature of the hardware infrastructure imposed this pattern of organisation of in-house skills during the 1960s and 1970s. These departments purchased almost all their equipment from specialist suppliers and concerned themselves mainly with software design and maintenance, running the installation and planning for the computer requirements of the business or government organisation.

Over the last two decades, data-processing (DP) departments have grown regularly in size and importance in proportion to the penetration of computing into the most diverse activities. By the early 1980s, the computer department occupied a key place in the infrastructure of many organisations (somewhat like the electrical system in a traditional industry). A new feature of this central position was, in most cases, that the DP department was surprisingly independent of the general strategies or constraints of the business or government organisation, defining its own aims, how they were to be achieved and at what cost, with the organisation's hierarchy having rather limited power to control it. The idea soon emerged of hiving the department off altogether as a separate profit centre, the better to subject it to economic constraints and targets. But the diffuse nature of data processing activity within an organisation does not apparently lend itself very well to this. Some firms have opted for this solution, at the risk of moving towards a situation in which final users' decentralised decisions may prevail against firm-wide integrated projects.

Against this background, DP budgets for business and governments grew fairly regularly, enabling data processing departments to develop in-house most of the applications and data-base software their users required. Because systems software was so complex and costly, most of it was still designed and produced outside, in the form of software packages. But up to the 1980s, computer departments were, on the whole, the main source of applications software for large business and government organisations, which were themselves the main consumers of software.

Figure 9 shows DP budget breakdowns for the United States (1984), Germany (1983), and Japan (1982) illustrating this through the preponderence of staff salaries in relation to outlays on purchased software (which, admittedly ought to include the costs of software "bundled" in hardware purchases).

Another sign of this was the distribution of DP personnel throughout the economy: a 1979 survey in France showed that they were concentrated among user firms (73 per cent of senior computer staff) as against hardware manufacturers (15 per cent) and service bureaux/software houses (12 per cent). One of the worlds largest software houses, Informatics, estimates that in 1976, only between 10 and 15 per cent of all instructions executed on United States computers were software purchased from outside suppliers. An IBM source confirms the same picture for the United States at the beginning of the 1980s.

49

Figure 9 DATA PROCESSING EXPENDITURES
A. US INFORMATION PROCESSING EXPENDITURE BY CONSTITUENT ITEMS, 1984

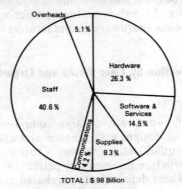

TOTAL : $ 98 Billion

Source: International Data Corporation (forecast)

B. WESTERN EUROPEAN INFORMATION PROCESSING EXPENDITURE BY CONSTITUENT ITEMS, 1983

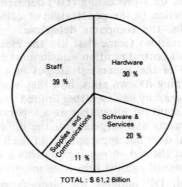

TOTAL : $ 61,2 Billion

Source: International Data Corporation forecast.

C. AVERAGE DATA PROCESSING BUDGET OF 1000 BIG USERS IN JAPAN, 1982

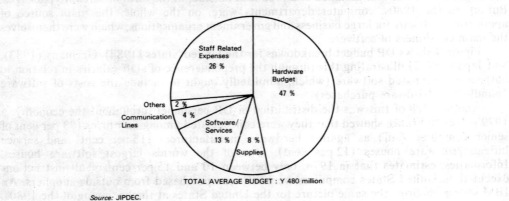

TOTAL AVERAGE BUDGET : Y 480 million

Source: JIPDEC.

However, there is increasing evidence, in most OECD countries, that in-house data-processing departments now tend to focus on the maintenance and enhancement of existing software, an increasing share of which is purchased outside in packaged form (see Section 4 below, "Remarks on Demand Trends").

A serious problem for most such in-house departments is rapid staff turnover. Caused partly by the high salary levels in this sector (see Table 5), but also, in many cases, by insufficient job motivation and career difficulties, staff turnover is costly for data processing departments because, to a large extent, their operating methods are not formalized but exist in the form of individual staff skills. So, whenever any professional leaves there is a problem of organisation, varying in seriousness according to what was the person's actual role in the department.

b) Impact of Microcomputers and New Software Technologies

How are technological trends affecting this pattern of in-house software production? They are doing so mainly in four ways.

In the first place, the introduction of microcomputers and the changeover to distributed computing create a tendency for decision centres and systems development to proliferate within large user units. According to a 1982 survey in the United States, only 55 per cent of decisions to purchase microcomputers were taken by data processing departments, while 45 per cent were taken by user departments. This goes hand in hand with a decentralisation of the in-house production of software: another 1982 survey in the United States showed that only 19 per cent of software being run on microcomputers had been produced by data processing departments, as against 28 per cent by user departments and the remainder by outside suppliers; whereas even for minicomputers, the proportions were exactly opposite with 52 per cent produced by the data processing departments and 12 per cent by user departments.

A major trend associated with the spread of microcomputers is the growing acceptance of the *Infocentre* concept. Introduced in the United States during the late 1970s, adopted by IBM in 1981, Infocentre can be broadly defined as "a service strategy and a way of organising the data processing department to give the final user direct access to the computers, together with the necessary education and assistance". In practice, this means that the user himself learns how to develop some of his own applications and can directly access his organisation's data banks. The Infocentre concept finds an ideal instrument in the microcomputer which serves as an intelligent terminal. Its software includes a transparant data base and a program library, both available on a mainframe and accessible from different microcomputers, thereby combining the aims of integrated fourth generation software and local networks. Little software is yet available on the market to support this concept, but observers expect some more soon. Infocentre is regarded as the main plank in IBM's strategy for the late 1980s, which are working on it, but so too are independent software houses, such as Cullinet, MSA, McCormack & Dodge, Boole & Babbage, Informatics etc. In fact most of these firms made a start early in 1984 by introducing new software – the "micro-mainframe link" – with which to "interface" microcomputers and mainframes. At the end of 1983, 45 of 71 very large US firms reported having begun to set-up Infocenters, and 85 per cent expected to have them by 1985.

Secondly, technological advances are putting pressure on data processing departments themselves to keep more closely abreast of the latest trends in the state of the art and make better use of them. This is because the large DP departments which have been gradually built up into near bureaucracies suddenly face a wave of innovations in hardware and software;

51

many have difficulty in keeping up with the new trends which, nevertheless, pose a challenge to much of their activity; decentralisation, as mentioned above, is only one of these challenges. The resulting uneasiness inside data processing departments has been attested on several occasions. A recent American survey of 71 leading firms showed that 51 per cent of data processing department personnel did not favour the installation of Infocentre systems, whereas 66 per cent of high-level managers and 76 per cent of final users favoured them. Keeping up with and evaluating trends in the state of the art, identifying and recruiting the very few real specialists in it, trying to achieve the organisational flexibility necessary to exploit them constitutes the major challenge for in-house departments during the 1980s.

A third, parallel source of pressure has been the increasing recourse to external products and services on the software side. This is partly because many software packages cost less and perform better than they would if developed in-house, but also because many technological adaptations (changing over to integrated systems at national if not international level, converting systems software etc.) require external specialist services making the trend to outside suppliers highly visible. Datamation has estimated that United States firms spent 10 per cent of their computer budgets on external software in 1982, as against only 2 per cent in 1978. The Tebeka Report anticipates a similar shift in the distribution of computer staff in France: 77 per cent of total computer professionals employed by external software suppliers (hardware manufacturers and bureau/software houses), as against 23 per cent employed by users by 1985, whereas in 1979 the proportions were 27 per cent and 73 per cent respectively.

The fourth direction for the reorganisation of in-house supply stems directly from the other three: some large users, facing increasingly high costs to keep skilled data processing departments, are seeking to amortize a proportion of their investment by marketing the products and services of their departments outside, sometimes though not always by establishing a separate subsidiary. In all instances, the large firm will attack the market where it is itself strongest, i.e. in applications software for its own sector of activity. Particularly noteworthy instances are Boeing, Lockheed and McDonnell Douglas in the United States, Imperial Metal Industries, Pechiney Ugine Kuhlmann, Elf-Aquitaine and Alitalia in Europe. It is interesting to note that these industrial firms have been incurring such heavy computing costs, especially for software development, that they are even prepared to sell their application-specific skills (which may be strategic) to their most direct competitors.

c) *Reorganisation of the Data Processing Function within Firms and Organisations*

Are these organisational shifts of a kind to ensure that software supplied in-house adapts to technological trends?

They evidently are, because several major users have recently been able to introduce new computer strategies, based on simultaneously exploiting in-house and external resources, thus enabling them to embark on an adaptation to the new technologies. Nevertheless, three main kinds of obstacle can arise and, sometimes, pose a serious threat to successful adaptation.

First, organisational inflexibilities. These arise mainly from inadequate capability or will on the part of the teams in place to conceive, plan and implement thorough going changes. Recent assessments show for example that it is harder to retrain a COBOL programmer in the new software technologies than to train a layman from scratch, and that the total real demand for the mainstream specialists is actually lower nowadays than it was ten years ago. Even if individual in-house personnel or outside consultants apply pressure for innovation, they can come up against general, often involuntarily inflexibility in the DP department, perhaps

52

aggravated by the difficulty or impossibility of renewing staff. This problem may more particularly affect large Government organisations.

Next, difficulties in identifying and recruiting personnel who are real specialists in the new technologies. Continuing pressures on this labour market are making these specialists scarce, and the relative imprecision in defining such specialisation makes it difficult to identify them. This sharply limits the scope for many users to internalise such resources. Important factors in how easily the user firm will be able to hire such specialists include how attractive the sector is, what kind of computer activities are involved, and geographical location, with salary level apparently a secondary factor (Figure 10). Public sector agencies seem especially prone to this kind of recruitment difficulty, largely because of their budgetary patterns and salary scales may often be too rigid.

Tables 5 and 6, showing the 1982 trend for various data processing labour markets in the United States, illustrate these pressures. The emphasis on professional experience is in fact the indicator (the only possible one, although unsatisfactory) of the qualitative differences in each of the markets. According to several indicators, the situation is similar for most OECD countries. However, countries are unequally "endowed" with computer skills, though a

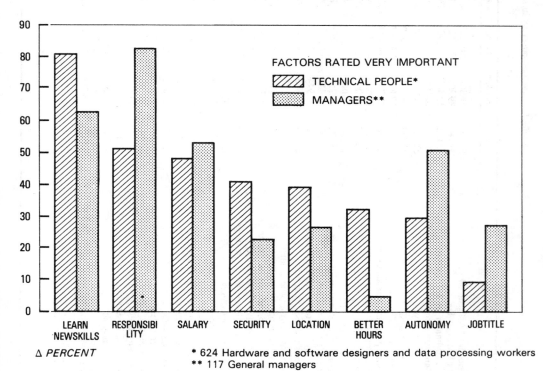

Figure 10 **PRIORITIES IN CHOOSING A JOB FOR TECHNICAL PERSONNEL AND MANAGERS IN DATA PROCESSING IN THE UNITED STATES**

Δ PERCENT

* 624 Hardware and software designers and data processing workers
** 117 General managers

Source: Columbia University, Business Week, February 20, 1984.

53

Table 5. Average salary by industry
Dollars

	All	Manufact.	Finance	Insurance	Government	Medical	Transport	Education	Utilities
Vice-president of MIS or DP	50 469	54 368	50 220	41 456	52 100	60 750	52 167	42 625	80 000*
Director of MIS or DP	39 185	39 203	36 222	39 157	39 280	37 501	39 400	35 061	35 950
Services coordinator or user liaison	35 671	53 440*	33 000	23 000*	38 058	25 100	—	51 700*	—
Systems analysis manager	35 247	38 966	30 833	33 000	33 833	29 167	32 500*	28 915	38 333
Senior systems analysis	32 783	32 015	33 450*	28 302	31 517	29 500*	30 000*	32 287	32 667
Lead systems analysis	29 837	30 591	27 000*	—	28 425	31 140*	—	25 000	—
System analysis	27 556	27 835	25 000*	30 500*	29 254	26 500*	—	22 243	28 800
Applications programming manager	33 551	35 733	37 920*	25 250	37 212	35 000	33 667	29 282	35 000*
Lead applications programmer	28 952	29 500	25 667	16 000*	29 880	27 019	19 000*	22 500*	37 500*
Senior applications programmer	26 427	27 069	25 750	25 047	27 013	26 455	21 710*	21 816	32 500*
Applications programmer	21 288	21 088	20 261	19 655	22 542	22 900	21 167	17 427	25 000*
Intermediate applications programmer	19 628	20 259	16 060*	19 066	21 701	21 375	14 500*	15 841	17 000*
Junior applications programmer	16 789	17 353	16 240	16 024	16 708	17 245	15 500*	12 913	20 000*
Systems analysis programming manager	35 562	33 944	39 710	38 603	34 574	38 758	34 633	33 962	38 500*
Lead systems analyst programmer	30 531	30 833	33 266	30 120	29 747	32 600	35 000*	26 547	—
Senior systems analyst programmer	28 726	27 843	30 331	27 915	28 019	28 814	—	26 035	19 000*
Systems analyst programmer	24 302	24 338	24 170	25 020	23 193	23 167	26 800	21 450	28 000*
Intermediate systems analyst programmer	22 788	22 090	23 494	23 976	22 025	23 840	27 266*	18 183	39 000*
Junior systems analyst programmer	18 719	18 915	18 977	17 100	18 693	19 833	—	17 048	32 000*
Operating systems programming manager	36 172	38 464	39 000*	39 180	36 957	30 000	36 550	28 750	42 000*
Senior systems programmer	32 156	32 883	36 376	32 289	31 945	30 178	28 000*	26 083	42 000*
Intermediate systems programmer	27 120	27 519	30 500*	26 773	26 908	27 674	27 000*	22 000	35 000*
Database administrator	29 379	30 917	30 000*	35 030	32 117	22 000*	32 800*	32 000*	28 000*
Data or telecommunications analyst	26 666	30 262	32 000*	26 244	25 930	—	16 500*	19 667	27 000*
Computer operations manager	27 495	26 808	28 940	30 956	29 245	26 288	28 850	32 472	30 800
Shift supervisor	22 072	21 105	22 245	22 024	23 962	20 219	21 000*	24 250	24 500*
Lead computer operator	17 363	17 149	17 489	17 331	18 108	20 378	13 400	15 659	19 605
Computer operator	14 848	15 168	13 659	14 581	16 322	14 476	12 714	14 019	15 933
Production and IO supervisor	22 149	24 706	19 486	23 657	22 686	22 179	—	19 226	26 000*
Production and IO clerk	13 722	13 540	11 298	12 757	14 621	14 144	21 575	13 857	—
Data entry superviser	17 318	17 696	19 597	17 194	17 121	15 828	22 675	16 887	—
Data entry clerk	12 605	12 573	12 324	12 038	12 899	12 832	13 944	11 931	16 267
Word processing operator	14 959	15 756	14 500*	12 389	13 600	15 000	13 000*	18 500*	18 500*

* Fewer than three sites reported.
Source: Datamation, 1983.

54

Table 6. **Pressures on data processing job markets,**
United States, 1982

"Top Ten" demand ranking mid-1982	Job title (and average most sought-after years of experience)	Rise in demand from mid-1981
1	Systems/software programmers (4.2 years)	+ 10.1
2	Applications programmers (3.6 years)	+ 9.6
3	Telecommunications specialists (2.6 years)	+ 8.9
4	DP auditors (3.3 years)	+ 8.3
5	Systems analysts (4.3 years)	+ 7.8
6	Data base managers (9.0 years)	+ 7.4
7	Software engineers (4.8 years)	+ 7.1
8	Systems managers (6.5 years)	+ 6.7
9	Software programming managers (5.9 years)	+ 6.2
10	DP operations managers (8.1 years)	+ 5.8

Source: Fox-Morris.

greater endowment does not necessarily relieve these pressures. If so, this would mean that forces of national supply and demand are interacting positively, which could ultimately lead to international differences in the spread of the new technologies.

One last possible difficulty for DP departments relates to the availability and to the costs of external software products and services, which are becoming more and more useful and necessary to their activities. For DP departments in different countries, and even different regions, the packaged software available will differ in quality and cost (costs are inversely proportional to market size) and the design and consultancy services available will differ in technological level. In spite of rapid progress in internationalisation in several areas, the supply remains very unevenly available in countries, especially for applications software, and even for different regions, especially as regards high-level consultancy services. Thus, even on the optimistic assumption that these software packages and services have already matured sufficiently to perform their role in spreading the new technologies throughout the market, they are less than fully available, and at unequal costs, for data processing departments in different geographical environments.

2. Supply of Software by Hardware Manufacturers

a) *Traditional Presence of Manufacturers in the Software Market*

From the early 1960s, computer manufacturers had to provide software with their hardware. Some of this was systems software, necessary for the general running of the machinery, some was applications software designed for the specific requirements of large customers installing computer systems. The systems software was included in the price of the hardware and not invoiced separately ("bundled"), while applications software was usually the subject of a turnkey contract. Some manufacturers also designed customs software as part of their time-sharing services.

But this ancillary status of software as a sales support for the hardware evolved appreciably over the 1960s and 1970s. The key date here was 1969, when the United States Department of Justice required IBM to invoice its hardware and software separately (to "unbundle" it). In later years, other Member country manufacturers adopted this marketing approach which, moreover, had now come to seem imperative. Systems software had become too costly and diversified to be considered as an accessory to be provided free, while manufacturers wished to sell specialised applications packages which by definition could not be of interest to all their customers. This arrangement by which hardware manufacturers supplied software separately, through unbundling is today regarded as having founded the software market and thereby the software industry.

Having introduced this market, the hardware manufacturers took a large share of it, while soon meeting competition from independent software suppliers. The manufacturers' strength lies mainly in systems software, closest to the hardware, and secondly in the universal kinds of applications software (accountancy, management, payroll, etc.) where they can make use of their close relations with computer users and the strength of their sales network. They offer only software packages, and practically no customs software except for very large orders. They themselves design most of their systems packages, often in conjunction with their hardware projects; but for applications software they often rely on products developed by software houses (or even by their own customers) with which they enter into exclusive distribution agreements. Although different manufacturers do have appreciable differences in strategy, the above broadly describes their stance in the software market (except for the IBM compatible manufacturers, who concentrate on hardware production).

In spite of their leading position in the software market, it is at present impossible to say that the computer manufacturers have become software houses. In fact, software production is still a limited part of their general business, even if many intend to increase this share significantly in the future. IBM, for example, aims to increase it at the level of its mainframe sales by 1988 and up to a third of its total business by 1990s (through price as well as volume increases).

The two tables below illustrate the share of hardware manufacturers in the software markets and the share of software and services in manufacturers' total sales in the United States for 1983. Tables for other Member countries would probably show a similar pattern (Tables 7 and 8).

b) Hardware Manufacturers' New Software Strategies

Recently, certain new forces have begun to affect the hardware manufacturers' position in regard to the supply of software:

   i) The shift to distributed, integrated computing;
   ii) The slowdown in the overall growth of computer hardware markets;
   iii) Increasing national and international competition in those markets and pursuit of competitive strategies by creating "captive" hardware markets through exclusive software availability;
   iv) The large growth prospects for software markets;
   v) Increasing competition in those markets, especially by independent software houses now beginning to compete with the hardware manufacturers even in their own special reserve of systems software.

With new competition both in hardware and software, the manufacturers are developing their software strategies on four fronts:

In the first place, they are working on systems software incorporating principles of distributed and integrated processing. By doing this they hope both to make their hardware more competitive, supplying software exclusively for it, and to extend their share of the

Table 7. **Hardware vendors' shares of software markets, United States, 1981-1983**

$ million

	1981		1983		% growth
	Revenue	% of total	Revenue	% of total	
Systems software					
Hardware manufacturers	2 025	49.3	3 660	45.6	80.7
Independents	820	20.0	1 854	23.1	126.1
Subtotal	2 845	69.3	5 514	68.7	93.8
Application software					
Hardware manufacturers	295	7.2	455	5.7	54.2
Independents	965	23.5	2 060	25.6	113.5
Subtotal	1 260	30.7	2 515	31.3	100
Total	4 105	100	8 029	100	95.6

Source: IDC/US Department of Commerce, 1984.

Table 8. **The share of software and services in the revenues of major US hardware vendors, 1983**

$ million

	Company	Total corporate revenue	Total SP&S revenue
1.	International Business Machines Corporation	40 180	2 813
2.	Digital Equipment Corporation	4 272	1 404
3.	Control Data Corporation	4 500	1 260
4.	Burroughs Corporation	4 390	830
5.	NCR Corporation	3 731	805
6.	TRW Inc.	5 493	790
7.	Hewlett-Packard Company	4 710	461
8.	Harris Corporation	1 423	250
9.	Honeywell Inc.	5 753	229
10.	The Perkin-Elmer Corporation	1 015	214
11.	General Instrument Corporation	974	213
12.	Sperry Corporation	2 810	146
13.	Data General Corporation	829	133
14.	Tandy Corporation	2 475	76
15.	Apple Computer Inc.	983	69
16.	Prime Computer Inc.	517	65
17.	Commodore International Limited	681	62
18.	Four-Phase Systems	541	60
19.	MDS Qantel	170	9
20.	Altos Computer Systems Inc.	75	6

Note: These ratios are influenced by the various manufacturers' hardware and software pricing strategies.
Source: ICP, 1984.

because of the benefits the supplier can derive from selling other associated software. This is because an operating system is somewhat like a user base which can accommodate a range of other software, especially with the current trend towards integrated software systems. The software supplier may thus find it increasingly difficult to hold on to his market share if he has no part in the development of systems software, or no user base over whose software "environment" he has full control. This is what accounts for the many standards battles being currently fought out in the various systems software, in which almost all hardware manufacturers – mainframe, mini and microcomputer – are involved.

It should be noted that manufacturers are not acting purely offensively here. Independent firms have gained remarkable positions in several systems software segments and the manufacturers have to try to re-establish their control over these strategic environments. For example, the IBM share of the market for data-base management systems for IBM and compatible installations was 48 per cent in 1981 and 45 per cent in 1984 (through its three systems IMS, DL/1 and DB2) the remainder of the market being occupied by independent suppliers such as Cullinet, Cincom, Software AG and ADR. Similarly, the highest rated systems software in Datamation's Systems Software Survey 1983 is almost all from independent firms, apart from IBM's HASP telecommunications package. Similarly, the most extensively used microcomputer operating systems have been produced by independent houses such as Digital Research, Microsoft and Microfocus. However, IBM's recent attempts to regain control of the market for systems software are perhaps beginning to bear fruit and IBM may now be recovering market share lost in recent years to the "independents" (Between 1980 and 1984 IBM's software revenue has grown at a 49.8 per cent compound rate in the United States).

It should be pointed out here that the phenomenon of independent software suppliers competing with hardware manufacturers in systems software is almost exclusively a North American one. Elsewhere, hardware manufacturers retain much firmer control over the software environment for their machines.

The second component in the manufacturers' new software strategy is "firmware". This refers to software designed to be embedded once and for all in the hardware (e.g. through read-only memories, see above).

There is obviously a good deal at stake here. At one extreme, the coming of firmware into general use would purely and simply mean the end of any separation between the two industries of hardware and software. Hardware suppliers could then survive only by becoming software suppliers, and vice versa.

Up to now, the state of the art limits the field for efficient applications of firmware. It is mainly used in compilers, and to a certain extent in universal machines, and machines designed to utilise a specific language (Lisp, Ada). However, with advances in very large scale integration (VLSI) and in the design of specific circuits, the opportunities for applying firmware will extend in the future.

The manufacturers are conducting research in this area, which may enable them to position themselves in growing segments not only of software markets but also of hardware markets, especially at the expense of the "compatible" manufacturers who can no longer compete on hardware alone. Some recent operating systems from leading manufacturers are already using firmware (observers regard IBM's 4321 computer with its inbuilt SSX operating system as a first step backwards towards "rebundling"). It is still too soon for applications software to be embedded in firmware but applications are already appearing in microcomputing (Apple's Lisa, Tandy's Model 100, Convergent Technologies' Workslate, for example). Several observers consider that firmware is bound to increase in importance over the next few years, some even anticipate that machines entirely dedicated to specific applications will become widespread. Clearly, the hardware manufacturers still have some cards to play here.

However, the hardware manufacturers will not be the only ones to exploit firmware, even though they may at present be in the best position to do so. Component manufacturers and software houses could also introduce products based on this technology over the next few years (as Intel is already doing with its System 2000 distributed processing system).

Hardware manufacturers have another advantage at the outset in software markets: their close relations with computer users and the size of their sales networks. They have recently been using this advantage to increase their share of the applications software markets.

But competitive applications software can be developed only from a very full understanding of the applications concerned. Since the hardware manufacturers are not particularly well placed in this respect, except in those applications in which they are themselves heavily committed such as sales management or production management, they approach specialist software houses and even users for suggestions for software packages, in order to perfect them, include them in their catalogues and market them. At the same time they encourage the independent software houses to design software to run on their hardware and market it directly. Almost all the manufacturers have adopted this strategy recently, both for the mainframe and for minicomputer and microcomputer software. The supply of applications software plays an increasingly important role in the competitive strategies of the hardware manufacturers, especially in microcomputing (see Table 9 and Figure 11).

Several manufacturers can be seen to be engaging in this applications software offensive. The most telling instance is probably that of IBM, which set up a large independent group in 1982 from scratch, wholly specialising in software sales – the Information and Programming Services Business Unit (IPS). (It is noteworthy that the unit is designed as an independent profit centre, not as another IBM marketing instrument. One of its executives recently said "IPS is first and foremost in business to make a profit by selling software, rather than by

Table 9. **Importance of software as a selection factor for large US firms buying microcomputers**

Selection factor	Percentage rating factor as very important	Average score (1-5)
Available software packages for current applications	65	4.57
Ease of use	56	4.48
Compatibility with existing mainframe, mini or micro computers	56	4.37
Availability of large number of software packages	53	4.35
Vendor reliability/reputation	48	4.30
Quality of service available	44	4.24
Expansion/upgrade capability	34	4.07
Quality of training available from vendor/seller	25	3.72
Compatibility with existing PC peripherals	23	3.66
Current use of same model by others in company	21	3.62
Cost of system	17	3.54
Ability to get service from another vendor already on site	13	3.14
Amount of processor memory	12	3.55
Mass storage available	12	3.43

Source: Datamation, 1983.

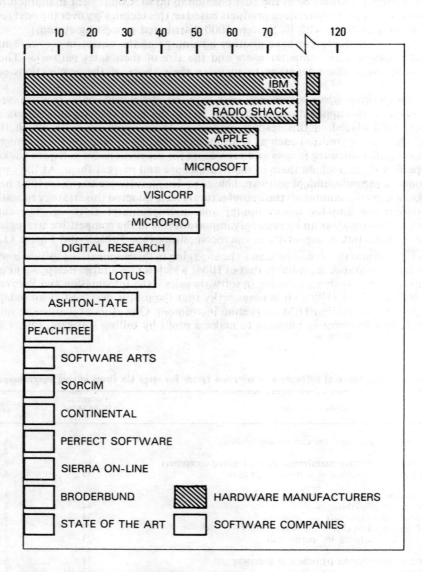

Figure 11 **LEADING US SOFTWARE PUBLISHERS FOR OFFICE PERSONAL COMPUTERS**

(estimated 1983 revenues in $ million)

| | 10 | 20 | 30 | 40 | 50 | 60 | 70 | 120 |

IBM
RADIO SHACK
APPLE
MICROSOFT
VISICORP
MICROPRO
DIGITAL RESEARCH
LOTUS
ASHTON-TATE
PEACHTREE
SOFTWARE ARTS
SORCIM
CONTINENTAL
PERFECT SOFTWARE
SIERRA ON-LINE
BRODERBUND   HARDWARE MANUFACTURERS
STATE OF THE ART   SOFTWARE COMPANIES

Source: Future Computing/Mini-Micro Systems, March 1984.

60

encouraging hardware sales. Only secondarily is IPS a "good corporate citizen" ... it will not offer any products that interface to non-IBM data-base management systems".) In the meantime, with an emphasis that has become an industry talking point, IBM has been encouraging software firms specialised in specific industrial applications to design programs to run exclusively on IBM machines (the Value Added Remarketer program, VAR). Apple is another advanced example of this trend. Having brought out its most recent models, Lisa and MacIntosh, whose development investment was mainly in sophisticated software, it strongly encouraged outside service firms to design exclusive applications software by offering heavy OEM (Original Equipment Manufacturer) discounts. (Apple has announced that it intends to have 90 per cent of MacIntosh applications packages written by third parties, and that 110 software firms are already engaged in this, including Microsoft, Lotus, Ashton-Tate, Software Publishing, etc.) In another market segment, scientific and industrial applications, Hewlett-Packard has been combining an intensive in-house effort with heavy reliance on outside sources: its R & D outlays for applications software are thought to have increased from 3 per cent of its total R & D budget in 1980 to 15 per cent in 1983, while continuing to work with over 500 service firms specialising in different applications.

In more general terms, a 1984 survey by Pain-Weber Inc. of four of the largest mainframe computer manufacturers and three of the largest minicomputer companies in the United States, showed that although 35 per cent of their average R & D budget was devoted to software research and 65 per cent to hardware in 1981, these shares were set to alter to 55 per cent and 45 per cent respectively in 1985.

The policy of supplying turnkey systems is an extension of the policy of supplying applications software. Here the manufacturer supplies a complete hardware/software system for a specific purpose. These systems are not necessarily integrated technologically (integrated software systems, firmware etc.) but are marketed and maintained as a single package. They are aimed mainly at the very large market represented by small and medium-sized firms, wishing to avoid becoming involved in engineering and to have just one computer supplier to deal with.

The hardware manufacturer can provide a turnkey system in one of two different ways.

The first is the standard turnkey system. This is designed for a wide public and marketed directly by the manufacturer. There are many of these in the small business systems segment. Some manufacturers also specialise in more specific segments (Burroughs and Nixdorf in banking applications, Olivetti in insurance, Hewlett-Packard in production management).

Secondly, there are custom systems. In fact, these are usually designed not by the manufacturer but by a system house they have endorsed. Special relationships between manufacturers and software houses designing turnkey systems on the basis of the manufacturer's hardware have been mushrooming recently (programmes such as IBM's Value-Added Remarketer, ICL's Trader Point, Hewlett-Packard's HP Plus). This pattern of organisation somewhat resembles the selling of hardware on an OEM basis, but differs in that the manufacturer's brand name is retained on the finished system; and also the manufacturer involves and briefs the approved system houses more closely about its technology strategy, with the result that these system houses are now tending in a rather special way to form part of the manufacturer's consultancy and sales network.

At the international level, the hardware manufacturers are the leading channels in making software available to a greater extent than the DP departments of multinationals or of the software firms operating internationally. What the hardware manufacturers are disseminating consists mainly of systems-software, which are universal and closely follow exports of hardware; to a secondary extent they also export those kinds of applications software which are not subject to marked national peculiarities (statistical, modelling applications, etc.).

These software flows however are not necessarily in only one direction, from the firm's headquarters country to the countries where their subsidiaries are. Many manufacturers, especially IBM, have development centres in several countries contributing considerably to their stock of software. (Two very important recent software developments "abroad" have been Burroughs' fourth generation LINC software development system, produced by a New Zealand software house; and IBM's key AS telecommunications monitor produced by IBM United Kingdom).

When applications software requires a more "national" flavour, the manufacturer either develops it in the country concerned or contracts it out to a local software house.

c) Impacts of the New Software Strategies

To what extent are these recent attitudes on the part of hardware manufacturers towards software contributing to the dissemination of new software technologies in Member countries? This raises several points.

In the first place, hardware manufacturers have developed very high levels of skill in software technologies, especially systems software, and they are playing an essential role in establishing the software infrastructures for tomorrow's distributed/integrated computing. One particularly important aspect of this role is that manufacturers who encourage their users to convert to new software are emerging and they are developing and offering conversion aids to facilitate the "migration" from earlier generations of software.

The manufacturers' software contribution has three advantages, which give it a character of its own:

i) A much closer connection than anywhere else with the most advanced trends and opportunities on the hardware side;

ii) A big market to aim for, justifying very high development investment, and

iii) An international market, enabling innovations to spread quickly to other countries.

At the same time, the growing commitment of manufacturers to software makes for greater differentiation in the hardware available on the market. The differences are increasingly tending to be less in physical performance than in the performance of their systems software, which in turn affects the collection of applications software and services available. This process is liable to become a serious difficulty for the computer user (business or government organisations) with a restricted hardware choice horizon, because he may find himself with access to only a limited range of hardware and therefore software, because of earlier investment in a particular family of equipment, or for national policy reasons. This problem will surface more and more acutely in the 1980s, especially in Member countries with national hardware policies.

It must be observed finally that manufacturers' recent software strategies seem likely to restore, in the not too distant future, de facto tied sales situations in several segments of the software market. More than through firmware, which will influence markets in a remoter future, it is through policies of not disseminating technological information about new hardware generations that the manufacturers are striving to re-establish control over those software markets they regard as strategically important (mainly systems software), because in this way they can be the only source of software when introducing new hardware models. In view of the very long lead times for software development, especially for systems software, independent suppliers may find it impossible to compete at the critical moment when such markets are launched. The problem becomes particularly acute with the relinquishment of "upward compatibility" policies for software eliminating the "automatic" portability of existing independent software on new hardware. According to some observers IBM's first adoption of this policy – since 1969, that is – dates from the introduction of its new 38 series[8]. This has also been Apple's policy for its III (no longer on the market) and Lisa models. It is also possible that this has always been the case for manufacturers in Member countries other than the United States, partly accounting for the underdevelopment of independent systems software suppliers. In all events, though no value judgement can be made about it, widespread introduction of such policies would mean a de facto return to the practice of tying, via temporary monopoly situations in certain software markets.

3. Supply of Software by the Computer Services Industry

a) The Place of the Computer Services Industry in Software Production

Software houses have grown very rapidly since the early 1970s, in almost all Member countries. They have developed by providing a wide range of services including:

i) Time-sharing services;
ii) Consultancy and engineering services;
iii) Turnkey systems;
iv) Custom-software design and writing, and
v) Software packages.

These services combined constitute what is today called the computer services industry.

The computer services industry accounts for a minority share of total software production in Member countries, in relation to users' in-house production and software supplied separately by the hardware manufacturers. But it constitutes the most vigorous component technologically and economically (Tables 10, 11 and 12).

The following figures show the size, composition and growth of the industry in the United States, Europe and Japan (Figures 12, 13 and 14).

Computer services are an emerging industry with a low degree of concentration. In 1982 the United States had nearly 6 500 computer service firms with a total turnover of $26.5 billion (Table 13). According to the US Census for Service Industries, concentration ratios in the computer services industry lowered even further between 1972 and 1977 (Table 14). This has also been the *most rapidly growing industry* in the United States in recent times (Table 15). The United Kingdom has some 3 000 firms in the industry, most with under 20 employees. In Japan, 70 per cent of software houses are under ten years old[9].

Governments are very interested in the job creation potential of this sector. In 1982, the US computer services industry was employing some 450 000, the French industry 34 800, the UK industry 33 900 and the German industry 23 600. This gives an average annual turnover per employee of $60 000 in the United States, $49 000 in France, $44 000 in the United Kingdom and $52 000 in Germany (at the exchange rates of 1982, and according to ECSA/Quantum Science calculations). This relatively low labour productivity can be linked to the low capital intensity of the sector, which also increases its propensity to create employment for a given level of investment. But it should also be noted that the sector is appreciably improving its productivity, and bearing in mind that its internal structure is changing to the advantage of high productivity segments, its propensity to create jobs must be expected to decline in the future (Figure 15 and Tables 16, 17 and 18).

Table 10. **Independant computer service companies in the US packaged software market, 1983-1989**

$ million

	1983				1989			
	System/ utility	Application tools	Application software	Total packages	System/ utility	Application tools	Application software	Total packages
Independents								
Large-scale system	195	420	740	1 355	1 055	2 555	3 265	6 875
Medium-scale system	255	580	980	1 815	1 510	5 520	7 295	14 325
Micro-system	115	295	330	740	985	4 475	4 700	10 160
Total	565	1 295	2 050	3 910	3 550	12 550	15 260	31 360
Hardware manufacturers								
Large-scale system	815	340	115	1 270	3 975	1 700	290	5 965
Medium-scale system	1 335	735	295	2 365	6 760	3 940	1 090	11 790
Micro-system	230	235	105	570	2 515	2 090	675	5 280
Total	2 380	1 310	515	4 205	13 250	7 730	2 055	23 035

Note: These figures are not entirely comparable with the previous figure because of the differences in sources.
Source: IDC, 1984.

Figure 12 THE COMPUTER SERVICES INDUSTRY IN THE UNITED STATES

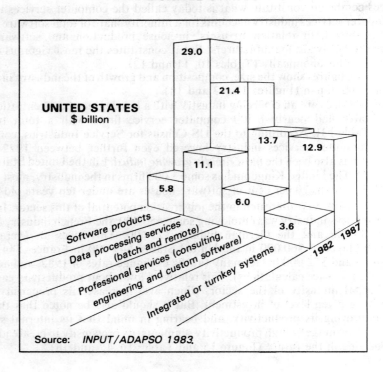

UNITED STATES
$ billion

29.0

21.4

13.7

12.9

11.1

5.8

6.0

3.6

Software products

Data processing services
(batch and remote)

Professional services (consulting,
engineering and custom software)

Integrated or turnkey systems

1982   1987

Source: INPUT/ADAPSO 1983.

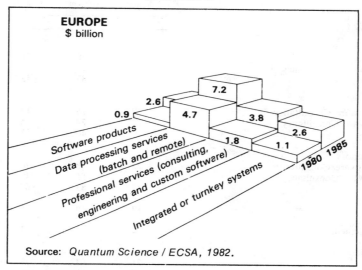

Figure 13 **THE COMPUTER SERVICES INDUSTRY IN EUROPE**

EUROPE
$ billion

Software products
Data processing services (batch and remote)
Professional services (consulting, engineering and custom software)
Integrated or turnkey systems

1980 1985

Source: *Quantum Science / ECSA, 1982.*

Figure 14 **THE COMPUTER SERVICES INDUSTRY IN JAPAN**

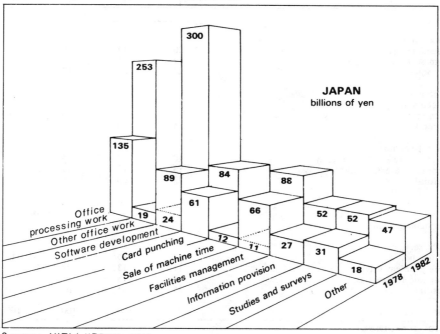

JAPAN
billions of yen

Office processing work
Other office work
Software development
Card punching
Sale of machine time
Facilities management
Information provision
Studies and surveys
Other

1978 1982

Source : *MITI / JIPDEC, 1983.*

65

Table 11.   **Software and services**

	Austria	Belgium	Denmark	Finland	France
Hardware manufacturers					
Packaged software	46	60	38	26	317
Custom software/Consultancy	17	22	15	11	89
Subtotal	63	82	53	37	406
System houses					
Packaged software/Consultancy	7	16	12	14	90
Custom software/Consultancy	12	24	15	18	169
Subtotal	19	40	27	32	259
Independent vendors					
Packaged software/Consultancy	22	28	20	11	184
Custom software/Consultancy	31	55	47	50	753
Subtotal	53	83	67	61	937
Training	12	18	15	13	95
Facilities management	2	3	3	4	16
Processing services					
Local batch	31	63	77	45	315
Remote problem solving	26	52	89	52	366
Remote autotransaction	25	74	81	51	395
Subtotal	82	189	247	148	1 076
Total	231	415	412	295	2 789
Hardware manufacturers					
Packaged software	20	14	9	9	11
Custom software/Consultancy	7	5	4	4	3
Subtotal	27	20	13	13	15
System houses					
Packaged software/Consultancy	3	4	3	5	3
Custom software/Consultancy	5	6	4	6	6
Subtotal	8	10	7	11	9
Independent vendors					
Packaged software/Consultancy	10	7	5	4	7
Custom software/Consultancy	13	13	11	17	27
Subtotal	23	20	16	21	34
Training	5	4	4	4	3
Facilities management	1	1	1	1	1
Processing services					
Local batch	13	15	19	15	11
Remote problem solving	11	13	22	18	13
Remote autotransaction	11	18	20	17	14
Subtotal	35	46	60	50	39
Total	100	100	100	100	100

Source: IDC/ECSA, 1984.

Germany	Ireland	Italy	Netherlands	Norway	Portugal	Spain	Sweden	Switzerland	United Kingdom
		A. In dollars millions							
459	11	233	83	34	8	74	68	67	361
129	3	61	30	13	2	26	22	24	85
588	14	294	113	47	10	100	90	91	446
94	9	51	40	10	1	12	18	16	107
120	8	65	43	14	2	18	27	23	124
214	17	116	83	24	3	30	45	39	231
257	8	85	58	18	4	30	30	37	191
343	9	270	152	42	5	44	65	69	326
600	17	355	210	60	9	74	95	106	517
112	5	50	37	12	4	18	21	20	96
9	1	10	14	3	1	2	4	3	12
289	9	242	94	67	9	73	81	72	203
184	4	63	94	79	3	14	100	75	188
255	9	159	115	74	5	23	81	80	242
728	22	464	303	220	17	110	262	227	633
2 251	76	1 289	760	366	44	334	517	486	1 935
		B. Percentage share							
20	14	18	11	9	18	22	13	14	19
6	4	5	4	4	5	8	4	5	4
26	18	23	15	13	23	30	17	19	23
4	12	4	5	3	2	4	3	3	6
5	11	5	6	4	5	5	5	5	6
10	22	9	11	7	7	9	9	8	12
11	11	7	8	5	9	9	6	8	10
15	12	21	20	11	11	13	13	14	17
27	22	28	28	16	20	22	18	22	27
5	7	4	5	3	9	5	4	4	5
—	1	1	2	1	2	1	1	1	1
13	12	19	12	18	20	22	16	15	10
8	5	5	12	22	7	4	19	15	10
11	12	12	15	20	11	7	16	16	13
32	29	36	40	60	39	33	51	48	33
100	100	100	100	100	100	100	100	100	100

Table 12. **Western Europe: software and services market, 1983**

	$ million	% share
Hardware manufacturers		
Packaged software	1 885	15
Custom software/Consultancy	549	5
Subtotal	2 434	20
System houses		
Packaged software/Consultancy	497	4
Custom software/Consultancy	682	6
Subtotal	1 179	10
Independent vendors		
Packaged software/Consultancy	983	8
Custom software/Consultancy	2 261	19
Subtotal	3 244	27
Training	528	4
Facilities management	87	1
Processing services		
Local batch	1 670	14
Remote problem solving	1 389	11
Remote autotransaction	1 669	14
Subtotal	4 728	39
Total	12 200	100

Source: IDC/ECSA, 1984.

Table 13. **Revenue and number of firms in the US computer services industry**
$ million

Year	Total		Processing services		Software products		Professional services		Integrated systems	
	Number of firms	Revenues	Number of firms	Revenues	Number of firms	Revenues	Number of firms	Revenues	Number of firms	Revenues
1970	1 400	1 900								
1971	1 500	2 350								
1972	1 600	2 760								
1973	1 700	3 230								
1974	1 900	4 410								
1975	2 550	4 580	1 557	3 290	993	1 290				
1976	2 584	5 325	1 556	3 605	1 028	1 720				
1977	2 977	6 300	1 942	4 700	618	600	417	1 000		
1978	3 391	7 750	2 089	5 580	752	940	550	1 230		
1979	4 055	9 446	2 140	6 706	1 095	1 210	820	1 550		
1980	4 336	14 903	2 132	8 800	1 225	2 631	978	3 472		
1981	6 178	22 311	2 259	11 220	1 605	3 765	1 284	4 570	1 030	2 756
1982	6 470	26 430	2 130	12 484	1 879	5 295	1 348	5 329	1 113	3 322

Source: ADAPSO/US Department of Commerce, 1984.

Table 14. **Low level of concentration
in the US computer services industry, 1972-1977**

Sales as a percentage of total sales of the industry

	1972	1977
4 largest firms	18.4	13.0
8 largest firms	26.9	19.7
20 largest firms	39.4	29.9
50 largest firms	51.0	41.3

Note: The 1982 edition of the US Census of Service Industries was not yet available
in 1984 for updating these figures.
Source: US Bureau of the Census/Price Waterhouse, 1984.

Figure 15 **SALES PER EMPLOYEE IN
THE US COMPUTER SERVICES INDUSTRY**

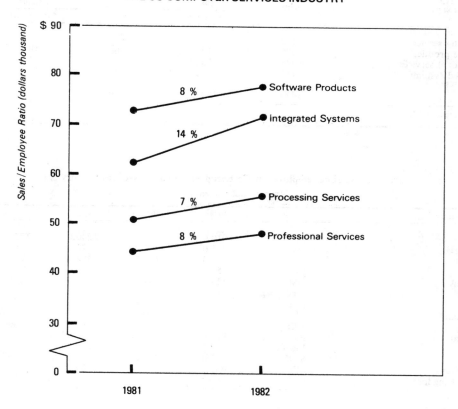

Source: INPUT 1983.

69

Table 15. **Growth of computer services market in US in comparison to other industrial sectors, 1976 to 1981**

Industry	Average annual percentage growth rate
Computer services	20
Securities	18
Banking	17
Electrical and electronics	12
Total manufacturing	11

Source: Input/ADAPSO, 1983.

Table 16. **Employment in the US computer services industry**

Type of company	Number of companies	Non-captive US revenue 1982	Employees	Public companies pretax profit margins
		$ million	Thousands	Percentage
Processing services	2 130	12 484	226	13.2
Software products	1 879	5 295	68	18.3
Professional services	1 348	5 329	110	5.7
Integrated systems	1 113	3 322	46	12.9
Total	6 470	26 430	450	11.8

Source: Input/ADAPSO, 1983.

Table 17. **Sales per employee in the European computer services industry**
In national currency

Country	Currency	1979	1980	1981	1982
Belgium	BFr	1 910.0	2 080.0	2 240.0	2 730.0
Denmark	DKr	225.0	300.0	328.0	366.0
Finland	FM	146.0	167.0	184.0	226.0
France	FFr	258.0	243.0	312.0	320.0
Germany	DM	125.0	109.0	122.0	126.0
Ireland	£Ir	11.7	19.5	b	24.5
Italy	Lire[a]	38.4	39.1	49.2	72.1
Netherlands	FL	117.0	120.0	133.0	149.0
Norway	NKr	b	351.0	b	380.0
Portugal	Esc	994.0	752.0	896.0	b
Spain	Peseta	3 150.0	3 160.0	3 020.0	3 800.0
Sweden	SwKr	342.0	318.0	320.0	390.0
Switzerland	SFr	n.a.	n.a.	136.0	122.0
United Kingdom	£	17.3	19.3	22.8	25.0

a) Millions.
b) Small sample.
Source: Quantum Science/ECSA, 1983.

Table 18. **Employment in the French computer services industry**[a]

	1978	1979	1980	1981	1982	1983	Average annual growth rate 1978/1983
Total employment	28 500	32 200	34 400	36 200	40 000	43 000	+ 8.6
Managers	13 300	15 100	17 070	18 850	21 200	24 000	+ 12.5
Non-managers	15 200	17 100	17 330	17 350	18 800	19 000	+ 4.6
Sales per employee (FF 1 000)	189	214	247	292	325	367	+ 14.2

a) These figures are not fully comparable to ECSA figures used in Table 17, because of the differences in sources.
Source: DIELI/ministère de l'Industrie, 1984.

Professional services (design, engineering and customs software), software packages and, partly, turnkey systems together make up the contribution of computer service firms to the production of software. They accounted for 53 per cent of total computer services industries (CSI) production in the United States in 1982, 46 per cent in Europe in 1983, and 34 per cent in Japan in 1981.

In fact, time-sharing services, the largest segment of the CSI also involves supplying software. Time-sharing houses write most of the necessary processing software on a custom basis and are increasingly tending to offer catalogues of packages accessible as part of their services. The breakdown of time-sharing services in the United Kingdom illustrates this trend (Table 19).

Table 19. **Distribution of time-sharing services in the United Kingdom**
Million pounds sterling and percentage share

	1980		1981	
Machine time + custom software	105.7	(43 %)	128.0	(46 %)
Machine time + software packages	63.8	(26 %)	87.6	(31 %)
Machine time only	74.4	(31 %)	65.9	(23 %)
Total	243.9	(100 %)	281.5	(100 %)

Source: CSA.

Over the last ten years or so, software houses have therefore played an important and growing role in the development and dissemination of software in Member countries. Their contribution is growing in three directions, all of which are becoming particularly important in the present context of technological changes.

In the first place, software houses represent a high level of skills at the disposal of business and government organisations who cannot or do not themselves wish to build up the full range of resources necessary to design and implement computer systems. Through their various services software houses are helping them to evaluate and exploit the opportunities of the new technology. They are especially useful to smaller businesses and government organisations

71

which would be too marginal individually to call on the specialist services of the hardware manufacturers who, in any case, do not possess all the skills of software houses.

This aspect of their contribution is becoming more important nowadays since almost all in-house data processing departments, even of large users, are finding it impossible to evaluate and apply developments in the state of the art by themselves. Thus the presence of software houses and the level of their skills can be seen as a decisive channel for the diffusion of software technologies throughout society, i.e. for easing the software bottleneck.

Secondly, software houses are themselves playing a part in advancing the state of the art. Several important software innovations of recent years have been produced by software houses (fourth generation data-base management systems, software engineering aids, microcomputer software). In several sectors, software house packages are more highly regarded than those of the manufacturers. Software houses, being independent of the marketing constraints and strategies of the hardware manufacturers and by definition close to the concerns of the users, act therefore as a main channel for the marketing of software innovations.

Thirdly, since they operate internationally, software houses encourage the international dissemination of the new technologies. In spite of the proximity constraints between buyer and seller in software transactions (because of training, documentation, maintenance, etc.), many software houses have been fairly vigorous in offering services and products in foreign countries, sometimes in association with local software houses, sometimes by establishing direct subsidiaries. In view of the constraints mentioned above, such subsidiaries cannot be just marketing units: they have to possess the necessary technological know-how and resources to carry out design, maintenance and conversion work. Many subsidiaries have been set up after a preliminary phase of co-operation with a local service company, enabling the parent company to see whether the local market is worth entering and to gain some experience of it.

Few statistics are available for the internationalisation of the computer services industry, partly because it is still emerging and non-institutional, but also, more systematically, because of the many different official forms internationalisation can take, e.g. exporting, establishing subsidiaries, granting licences, etc.

The software houses with the most foreign business are American, mainly in time-sharing services (ADP, GEISCO) and systems software (ADR, Cincom, Cullinet, Pansophic, Computer Associates). In 1979, five of the nine largest vendors of software packages in Europe were American, including the three leaders. According to a 1981 CXP survey, packaged software of American origin has a preponderent share of the total systems packages available on the French market: over 80 per cent in operating systems, 45 per cent in the data-base management systems, and 60 per cent in software aids. This share falls sharply in applications packages more dependent on national characteristics, but rises again in universal applications packages: 65 per cent in project management, and nearly 50 per cent in technical applications. CXP has also noticed, more recently, that 45 of the 80 best-selling software packages in France (over 100 sold in 1983) were of foreign origin. A 1982 Syntec survey confirms the same, mainly American, presence in this market (Figure 16).

A recent study showed the same type of foreign – mainly American – competition in the Japanese software market (Figure 17).

US software houses are not the only ones operating internationally. Since other national markets are so narrow, it is even probable that the most outward-looking firms are not from the United States. In fact, whereas 12 per cent of US computer service firms' sales were realised abroad in 1982 (Table 20), 20 per cent of total French software house sales in 1980, 24 per cent in 1982 and 20 per cent in 1983 (Table 21), are known to have been abroad, with a

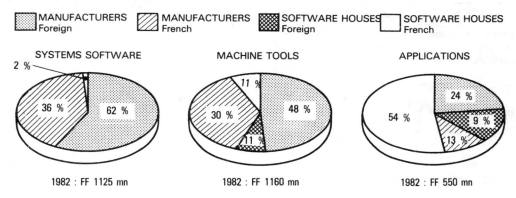

Figure 16   **INTERNATIONAL COMPETITION IN THE FRENCH MARKET FOR SOFTWARE PACKAGES**

MANUFACTURERS Foreign   MANUFACTURERS French   SOFTWARE HOUSES Foreign   SOFTWARE HOUSES French

SYSTEMS SOFTWARE
2 %
36 %   62 %
1982 : FF 1125 mn

MACHINE TOOLS
11 %
30 %   48 %
11 %
1982 : FF 1160 mn

APPLICATIONS
24 %
54 %   9 %
13 %
1982 : FF 550 mn

Source: Syntec.

Figure 17   **INTERNATIONAL COMPETITION IN THE JAPANESE MARKET FOR SOFTWARE PACKAGES**
(estimated 1983 revenues in $ million)

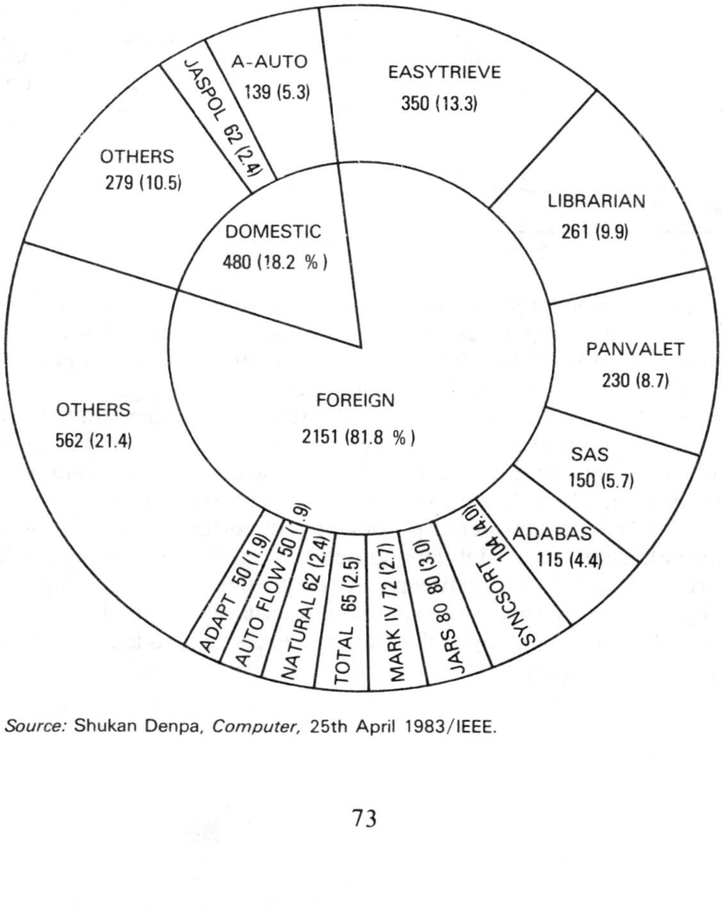

A-AUTO
139 (5.3)

JASPOL 62 (2.4)

EASYTRIEVE
350 (13.3)

OTHERS
279 (10.5)

LIBRARIAN
261 (9.9)

DOMESTIC
480 (18.2 %)

PANVALET
230 (8.7)

OTHERS
562 (21.4)

FOREIGN
2151 (81.8 %)

SAS
150 (5.7)

ADAPT 50 (1.9)

AUTO FLOW 50 (1.9)

NATURAL 62 (2.4)

TOTAL 65 (2.5)

MARK IV 72 (2.7)

JARS 80 (3.0)

SYNCSORT 104 (4.0)

ADABAS
115 (4.4)

Source: Shukan Denpa, *Computer,* 25th April 1983/IEEE.

73

Table 20. Foreign sales of US computer services firms
In per cent

Market sector	Year	Foreign sales	US sales	Captive sales
Processing services	1981	7	85	8
	1982	7	83	10
Software products	1981	31	69	0
	1982	28	72	0
Professional services	1981	7	93	0
	1982	12	88	0
Integrated systems	1981	12	88	0
	1982	12	88	0
Total	1981	13	83	4
	1982	12	83	5

Source: Price Waterhouse, 1984.

Table 21. Foreign sales of French computer services firms, 1982

Countries	Direct exports		Subsidiaries sales abroad		Total	
	FF million	%	FF million	%	FF million	%
Western Europe	220	24	1 130	67	1 350	52
Eastern Bloc	100	11	—	—	100	4
Middle-East	75	8	10	—	85	3
Africa	190	20	110	7	300	12
North America	230	25	390	23	620	24
South America	70	8	25	2	95	3
Others	35	4	15	1	50	2
Total	920	100	1 680	100	2 600	100

Source: Syntec, estimates 1982.

particularly high proportion for some firms: 50 per cent for Sema, 40 per cent for Cap Gemini Sogeti (820 of whose 4 000 employees are in the United States). British software houses made 7 per cent of their sales abroad in 1981, 13 per cent in 1982/83 and 14 per cent in 1983/84 (July-June periods), as against only 3 per cent in 1971.

Also to be noted here is the key influence of national language affinities and differences on the trends towards internationalisation. For software packages in particular, which best lend themselves to international marketing, documentation and the "long distance communication" accompanying the product are very important and, at the same time, language intensive. Documentation is considered particularly important for applications packages in specific, non-formalized areas of skill as opposed to systems packages intended mainly for computer experts (who will most likely have adopted English as a working language in any case). Accordingly, software suppliers expanding internationally look first at those parts of the world market that have language affinities, and users look to the same type of areas for supplies. Conversely, translating software documentation is a highly skilled and expensive task. The influence of language areas in the international software package market is therefore especially strong and, in practice, regardless of cultural considerations, this puts producers and users in the non-English speaking countries at a disadvantage. That, too, is why some of the non-English speaking software houses, with products requiring heavy investment and aimed at the international market, may work them up directly in English. One example is Adabas, produced by Software AG in Germany, whose documentation was originally written in English and which has enjoyed great international success.

The language problem works in the same way on the international market for custom software, though here other factors, geographical and cultural, make long-distance dealing and international investment more costly in any case.

b)   *Growth and Competitive Conditions in the Computer Services Industry*

The growing role of software houses in designing and disseminating new software generations implies substantial changes in their operating and competitive climates. Adapting to the new conditions will probably be difficult for a great many of the constellation of software houses at present constituting the CSI.

These new conditions have been brought about by a combination of new elements largely associated with technological changes. Although significant differences are to be found in this respect between the different segments of the industry, especially between the mainframe and microcomputer software markets, concerning product life cycles, R & D expenditures, marketing techniques and cost, these new conditions may be summarised under the following headings.

- *Greater technological resources:* The increasing complexity of hardware and operating systems, the availability of increasingly sophisticated development aids, and the growing requirements and constraints of users impose more demanding conditions on software creation. Whether developping software packages, customs software or turnkey systems, the software house now need more sophisticated technological resources (both in terms of equipment and people) than in the 1970s.

- *More difficulty in obtaining information:* The first condition for adapting productive resources to the state of the art is satisfactory information about it. But the highly fragmented character of research and innovation in software and, to a lesser extent, hardware, make it very difficult to obtain such information. Acceleration of progress, both in hardware and in software, the fragmentation of standards and the rapid turnover in "software environments" are tending to exacerbate this information problem for most software houses.

- *Scarcer qualifications:* The human resources capable of assessing and applying state of the art opportunities are scarce in this context. Since current innovations do not allow for the rapid recycling of existing employees, software houses are looking to the labour market where the qualifications they seek are becoming scarce and costly. The exceptionally high rate of job rotation in the industry (from 10 to more than 50 per cent according to firms in France and the United Kingdom) is a special feature of the problem. On the one hand, it does speed up the spread of knowledge through the industry and invigorates the labour market, but on the other hand makes it very difficult for software houses to earn any return on their in-house training investment, which can at present be substantial (about 6 per cent of turnover in France, according to an industry association estimate).

- *Unevenly available, costly aids:* The new development aids are to a large extent offered by highly specialised software houses, with a restricted geographical range at the regional and national level. At the same time these aids are becoming more and

75

more costly. This creates noteworthy differences between software houses in their access to and use of these important tools.

- *The packaged software challenge:* The risks of technological discrepancies would not loom so large if the market situation was the same as in the 1970s, when software houses offering custom and strongly demanded services could prosper with a moderate degree of competition, and were not obliged to keep up too closely with the state of the art. But in the 1980s, the packaged software phenomenon has suddenly raised the level of competition to the national if not the international level for several segments of the market. It was estimated, for example, in mid-1984 that around 20 000 software packages were available on the US market for the 5 million or so personal computers in use. Of these 200 or more were word processors, 150 spread sheets, 200 data-base programs and 95 integrated packages that offered at least the three functions. Software packages are thus compelling the software houses to become much more competitive, nationally and internationally.

- *The development of software packages:* For many software houses, the most immediate response strategy to the package challenge is to develop packages themselves. But apart from the technological pre-requisites, this strategy implies substantial development investment for an uncertain return. (Figure 18 represents this specific pattern of investment in the case of large and medium-sized packages.) Packages therefore have very different financial implications from custom development services (the difference here being somewhat like the difference between industrial production and sub-contracting in manufacturing activities). This leads to a type of economic activity which many software houses find unfamiliar and far more costly and risky.

- *Marketing software packages:* Packages also imply a marketing activity out of all proportion to that required for conventional activities. Launching a software package always requires a promotional campaign over the whole potential market, in order to reduce the costs over the long run (like the large-scale and successful launch campaign in 1983 for the Lotus 1-2-3 integrated microcomputer software, which cost about $3 million). Most software houses, incapable of conducting such an operation, have to go through several intermediaries (manufacturers, publishers, distributers, dealers etc.), which is difficult and increases pressures on their costs (the designer's share of a software package is estimated to be less than 20 per cent of the final price. The share is even lower (about 10 per cent) for microcomputer packages, where there are more intermediaries; but that is often largely offset by sales volume[10].

- *... generating a severe financial constraint:* All these factors considerably increase the financial prerequisite for competition in the growing sectors of the CSI. This is a new constraint for most of the software houses active in these segments, prompting them to seek new financial and organisational arrangements. In the United States, where these trends have been taken furthest, a very marked increase in mergers and acquisitions has been taking place in the CSI: 87 transactions with a total value of $688 million took place in 1980 and 118, with a total value of $766 million in 1981 (including the acquisition of Peachtree by MSA, System Development Corp. by Burroughs, Lamda Technology by GEISCO, DASD by Cap Gemini Sogeti), 146 acquisitions with a total value of more than $1 billion in 1983, and 143 acquisitions with a total value of more than $3.5 billion in 1984 (including the acquisition of Tymshare by Mc.Donnell Douglas, and of ESD by General Motors) (Figures 19 and 20). Meanwhile a great many competitive software houses which have grown rapidly and wish to remain independent have been going public (MSA, Pansophic, Lotus,

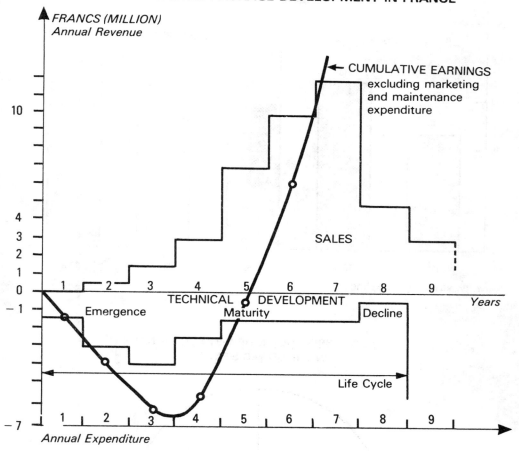

Figure 18 **LIFE CYCLE AND PROFITABILITY OF BIG AND MIDDLE SIZE APPLICATION PACKAGE DEVELOPMENT IN FRANCE**

Source: Syntec.

MicroFocus and others): ten software houses went public in 1982 in the United States, and 20 in 1983.

But only an existing firm with an established market position can raise finance via a merger or an equity issue. Would-be new companies cannot, and neither can they hope to borrow from the banks, with their very cautious attitude towards new companies in this 'intangible' sector. The only remaining source of funds for the entrepreneur, very unevenly available in the different OECD countries, remains venture capitalists[11].

The fact is that in view of the rising costs of developing and, especially, marketing software, a new company now needs substantial long-term funding at the outset,

77

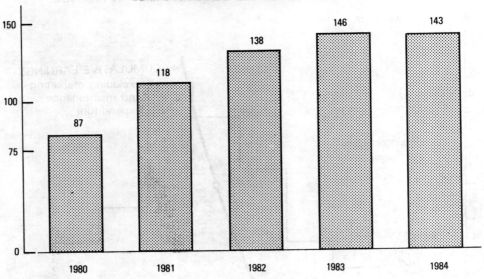

Figure19 **NUMBER OF ACQUISITIONS IN US COMPUTER SERVICES INDUSTRY, 1980 TO 1984**

Source: Broadview Associates/IDC.

Figure 20 **BREAKDOWN OF 1983 ACQUISITIONS IN THE UNITED STATES**

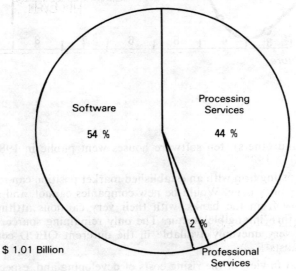

Software 54 %

Processing Services 44 %

Professional Services 2 %

$ 1.01 Billion

Source: Broadview Associates/IDC.

Table 22. **Software houses financed by venture capitalists**

Company (main product)	Investors	Amount ($ 000)	Date formed
Personal Software (Visicalc)	A Rock and Venrock Associates, Venrock, Lemoreaux Glynn, Newmarket	500 2 100	1980
Digital Research (CP/M)	T A Ass, Hambrecht & Quist, Rage Mill Partn, Venrock	n.a.	1981
Microsoft (MS/Basic, MS/DOS)	Technology Venture Investors	1 000-2 000	1981
Telesoft (Ada compiler)	CCH Computax	3 000	1981
MicroPro International (Wordstar)	Adler Group	1 000	1981
Software Publishing (PFS)	Melchor Venture Management	250	1981
Lotus (1-2-3)	n.a.	5 000	1982

Source: *Business Week, Datamation.*

together with management support for the non-technical aspects of the venture. This need is especially important for a firm with its eyes on the packaged software market, which has to finance all the development investment itself, taking all the risks, and requires a strong marketing arm. Since the packaged software markets are the liveliest in software demand, they provide the most opportunities for the creation of new firms. The presence and support of venture capitalists, as the most appropriate source of funding and "piloting" for this type of initiative, therefore becomes crucial. In fact, many newly created firms in the sector are now being funded and sponsored by venture capitalists. According to the Venture Capital Journal, 18 software houses were formed in the United States in 1980 with support from venture capitalists, and 90 in 1983, with a total funding of $180 million. Table 22 shows the best known of these.

According to certain observers, the lack of a fully developed venture capital market in countries outside the United States may be a major factor in their comparative backwardness in the packaged software sector. Some analysts go so far as to say that the lack of venture capital is the main reason for European weakness in this field. A Canadian Government report makes a similar assessment for Canada.

- *Challenge of integrated software:* Fourth generation software, involving close interconnection between systems software, applications software and data bases, raises a tricky problem for the software houses: how can they remain competitive without becoming software "superproducers" i.e. without having to offer full software systems? Some software houses (Cincom, ADR, Cullinet) have indeed chosen the superproducer strategy, but this is obviously not open to the whole industry. Most software houses find themselves in a technological dilemma here which will become sharper over the 1980s, involving difficult choices of market slot, reference standards and "environment" for the design and marketing of their products and services.

One innovative response to this challenge, seen more particularly in the United States, is for software houses with complementary specialisations to enter into technological and marketing co-operation agreements. The firms concerned can thus offer integrated software and exploit the synergy of their technical skills and marketing resources, while sharing heavy investments and still maintaining a degree of flexibility in their technical and environmental options. Such co-operative agreements have brought together, in particular, conventional software houses and microcomputer software specialists for the purpose of developing integrated, distributed software systems (ADR and Visicorp, Visicorp and Informatics, Cullinet and Information Science, Computer Associates and Information Unlimited, Martin Marietta and Mathematica).

— *The disadvantages of the uncertain legal and economic status of software:* Software houses are also experiencing a range of difficulties stemming from the uncertain legal and economic status of software. The most important of those relates to the protection, especially at international level, of the intellectual property in "computer programs". There is a general recognition of the pressing need for adequate protection of computer programs both nationally and internationally. Such protection is needed to encourage the creation of new software products as well as international trade. The increase of piracy makes software houses' R&D investment all the riskier, especially on packaged software markets. In a study made by Future Computing, a United States market research firm, the micro software piracy costs are estimated in United States as having created $1.3 billion lost revenues between 1981 and 1984.

An increasing trend exists in OECD countries to consider computer programs as works protected by copyright provided that they were original productions, constituting individual, creative expression of the set of instructions developed in them. In the countries where computer programs were protected by copyright it is stated that copyright provides an effective means of protection. However, the protection under existing international copyright conventions would promote the production and international circulation of programs *without delay,* by means of extending the protection granted to national creators of computer programs to nationals of other contracting states of international copyright conventions.

Another consideration is that the still uncertain economic status of software (is it a service or a product?) and of software expenditure (current expenditure or investment?) creates certain difficulties, especially for accountancy, tax and bank practices (should sales taxes or similar levies apply to sales of software; should investments in software qualify for tax incentives to investment; how can a bank assess heavy investment in software; how should software firms' assets and profits be evaluated, etc?). It is interesting to note that even inside the United States, practices vary from state to state, and the position is still more complicated internationally. More precision at the national level and, later on, some degree of harmonization internationally in the economic assessment and accountancy treatment of software would certainly be desirable, especially as the industry is at present in a phase of rapid internationalisation. These issues are discussed in more detail in the "Role of Action of Governments".

– *The challenge of the manufacturers:* At the same time, software houses are having to re-position themselves in relation to the new hardware and software strategies of the manufacturers. This involves following up or even anticipating the introduction of new hardware and software, and adapting to these innovations. Since manufacturers aim to dominate certain software segments, and to co-operate more closely with software houses in others, and since they organise their information and pricing policies and marketing accordingly, software houses will have to rethink their strategies and their specialist market slots in the light of those challenges.

In response to this combination of new competitive conditions, an increasing proportion of software houses will have to adopt more active technological and commercial policies, which will certainly be beneficial to users in the 1980s. These policies will probably be developed in the three more or less alternative directions of:

i) Greater economies of scale in production and marketing;
ii) Greater specialisation by type of equipment, environment and application (vertical marketing) or;
iii) Developing very high-level skills for consultancy and custom engineering purposes.

It is hoped that the fruits of this effort, in terms of information, services and products, will be available and put to optimum use throughout Member countries.

4. Evolution of Demand

a) Data Processing Budgets

How are users reacting to the trend in the software supply pattern which has been outlined above? It is too soon to be able to sketch an answer to that question. Major recent trends in the development of demand can however briefly be reviewed as a guide to which user sectors are being most immediately affected by the new forces on the supply side.

Data processing budgets are growing surprisingly quickly in Member countries, in view of the constraints of the economic conjoncture. This is already a beneficial sign from the standpoint of the dissemination of new software technologies. Tables 23 and 24 suggest how these budgets have grown in the United States, and show their structure in the United States, Europe, Japan and Australia. (See also Figure 9 above).

Budget structures show considerable differences from one area to another. More than differences in the costs of constituent factors, these differences are accounted for by unequal levels of demand externalisation. Australia resorts considerably to outside services, while Japanese users make very little use of outside services for their software requirements (the situation seems not to have changed to any great extent since 1978). Europe in fact masks some rather different situations: France makes quite extensive use of outside services, in contrast to Germany where users endeavour to satisfy as much of their requirement as possible in-house (see Annex IV, Figure 4).

Some information is available about how demand breaks down as between customs software and software packages, through the supply structure of the computer services industry in the various countries. In the United States, packaged software accounts for a substantial share (19 per cent of computer services firms sales and 53 per cent of software sales), in France it is underdeveloped (11 per cent of computer services firms sales and 27 per cent of software sales) and in Japan its share is negligible. Other European countries show an unequal dissemination of software packages (Tables 25 and 26).

81

Table 23. Growth of data processing expenditures in the United States, 1979-1985

Estimates

	1979		1985	
	$ million	%	$ million	%
Software and services	7 850	15	21 050	19
Personnel	23 820	46	52 300	46
Hardware	16 510	32	31 700	28
Other	3 740	7	8 200	7
Total	51 920	100	113 250	100

Source: IDC.

Table 24. Distribution of data processing expenditures in various OECD areas

Percentages

	United States 1982	Europe 1981	Japan 1978	Australia 1982
Personnel	45	35	30	37
Hardware	31	30	42	29
External services - Software	7	16	5	16
Communications	8	} 19	} 22	4
Supplies	4			7
Other	5			7
Total	100	100	100	100

Sources: IDC, ECSA, MITI.

Table 25. Software packages as percentage of revenue of computer services firms, Europe, 1980 and 1983

Percentages

	1980	1983
Belgium	7.7	13.2
Denmark	4.1	8.9
Finland	2.9	9.7
France	9.0	11.5
Germany	21.7	21.1
Ireland	21.9	27.4
Italy	9.0	13.5
Netherlands	7.2	15.1
Norway	5.0	8.8
Portugal	11.6	14.7
Spain	10.3	17.9
Sweden	5.0	11.2
Switzerland	10.4	13.4
United Kingdom	9.0	20.0

Source: Quantum Science/ECSA, 1983.

Table 26. **Share of software packages in total software sales in selected areas**
In $ 100 million

	United States 1981	Germany 1980	Australia 1980	United Kingdom 1980	France 1980	Japan 1981
Total software sales	90.6	8.7	2.12	7.5	15.8	10.3
Software package sales	47.8	3.3	0.98	2.3	4.3	0.36
Software package/Total sales	52.8%	37.9%	37.7%	37.3%	27.2%	3.5%

Notes: 1. US and European data is based on a survey by Input.
2. Australian data is based on a IDC survey.
Source: JIPDEC, 1984.

Externalisation of demand is a barometer of sensitivity to technological innovations, which are disseminated in the first place by products and services from the specialist suppliers. Some in-house potential always remains essential however to assess and make the most of what the external suppliers have to offer.

Recourse to packaged software is a more advanced form of this external orientation. It enables several data processing requirements to be satisfied at low cost, provided the organisational flexibility needed to make optimum use of packages can be developed. Offering the user an appreciably wider procurement horizon than do custom services, software packages also enable him to be surer of benefiting from advances in the state of the art. They must however be used skillfully: packages "parachuted in" for different applications can cause disruption, incompatibilities and opaque areas inside computer systems.

b) *According to Size of Firms*

Taking Member countries together, large firms make distinctly greater use of computer technology than small and medium-sized firms. The following table shows the discrepancies for firms of different sizes and of different sectors in Germany (Table 27).

Small firms, however, have benefited considerably from the recent development of microcomputers, software packages and small turnkey business systems, all of which bring computing within their grasp. Smaller and medium-sized firms have been increasingly numerous in reacting and investing in this equipment: the market for small business systems is one of the most rapidly growing in the OECD area, and a recent CXP survey in France shows that packages for small and medium-sized firms were the most vigourously growing segment of the packaged software market.

The small or medium-sized firm does not have the major current problem of large firms, obsolescent software stock and inflexible data processing organisation, and can therefore enter computing with the new generation of hardware, software and organisational configurations. But it is also heavily dependent upon its environment to solve the difficult problems this raises of information, assessment, and access to skills, products and services. Where the environment is unfavourable, smaller firms may be liable to commit themselves to sub-optimal arrangements, which could affect their subsequent development in computing.

Another problem for small and medium-sized firms is that they cannot easily commit heavy, long-range investments in the present economic climate (significantly, in the United States from 1981 to 1982, the smaller users i.e. those with annual data processing budgets of under $500 000, had to reduce their data processing outlays by 8 per cent whereas outlays were rising for all users).

83

Table 27. DP installations and density in Germany by sector and size of firm, 1983

Branch		Total	Number of employees								
			1-4	5-9	10-19	20-49	50-99	100-199	200-499	500-999	1000 and over
Industry and crafts	N	43 357	4 711	2 716	5 094	9 706	7 980	5 893	4 511	1 508	1 238
	D	10	2	3	12	32	61	76	85	87	97
Construction	N	10 416	—	1 642	1 425	3 020	1 947	1 510	704	168	—
	D	7	—	4	6	22	43	74	81	100	—
Wholesale trade	N	19 860	1 654	9 668	4 468	2 991	1 649	795	251	38	—
	D	11	1	30	32	38	70	90	75	100	—
Retail trade	N	12 310	1 654	2 057	3 500	2 760	1 309	686	155	189	—
	D	3	1	2	13	26	57	75	40	100	—
Transport and communications[a]	N	1 919	317	535	283	246	259	96	105	56	22
	D	5	1	10	10	12	32	24	38	66	78
Credit institutions and insurance	N	4 640	1 388	22	1 024	786	510	397	221	79	13
	D	7	3	3	21	25	40	81	86	91	30
Services and liberal professions	N	23 472	12 299	5 788	2 555	1 566	419	415	345	70	15
	D	4	2	7	13	22	22	53	81	100	79
Total	N	115 974	20 369	22 628	18 349	21 075	14 043	9 792	6 292	2 108	1 288
	D	6	2	7	14	28	54	74	80	89	94

N = Number of firms with computer installations.
D = Computer density, i.e. percentage of firms in each category with computer installations.
a) Excluding railways and PTT.
Source: GMID, 1983.

Chapter II

THE PARTICULAR CASE
OF EMBEDDED MICRO-ELECTRONICS SOFTWARE

Since the 1970s, when microprocessors were first developed, they have come to be applied in an ever-increasing number and variety of industrial products. Microprocessors were first used for simple computing purposes (pocket calculators, computer peripherals, process control) but then moved into applications that were considerably more sophisticated (microcomputers, telephone switchboards, radar systems etc.) and more diversified (toys, washing machines, machine tools etc.). Today it can be asserted that microprocessors are the main medium through which electronics and computers – the information technologies – are penetrating into household and industrial equipment.

Since microprocessors are programmable micro-electronic circuits, every microprocessor system must by definition incorporate its own control program. Therefore as microprocessor applications diversify and spread, a program must be written for each one and reproduced on a large scale; these programs, considered together, constitute the field of "embedded micro-electronics software"[12].

This section examines technological and industrial trends currently to be found in the production of this type of software.

A. TRENDS IN TECHNOLOGY: INDUSTRIAL APPLICATIONS
AND SOFTWARE REQUIREMENTS OF "MICROCOMPUTERS ON A CHIP"

Since micro-electronics systems are extremely diversified in scale, complexity and physical configuration, it is practically impossible to describe a "typical" application from the standpoint of production conditions and cost components (no application could possibly typify both a washing machine with a 2K byte system and a radar unit with a 50K byte system). A recent United Kingdom survey of 1 200 microprocessor-using companies discovered that development costs could range very widely, from under £50 000 to over £1 million per application.

However, a general table can be drawn up for the principal phases in building a microprocessor system, the critical human and material resources required and the relative costs that these imply.

1. Definition, Specification and Analysis of a Microelectronics Application

The initial concept for a new micro-electronics system nearly always comes from inside the user industry (i.e. the industry making the product in which the micro-electronics technology is to be used). It may come from the R & D department in an existing firm, or from a firm or even an individual originally outside the industry but gaining access by means of the new application.

The concept often originates when somebody realises that micro-electronics technology could be used to perform some function or other in the product. This leads on to a feasibility study to test the conceptual validity of the idea and its overall technological and economic practicability. If the findings of the study are positive, a structured representation of the proposed system is worked out. This constitutes the specifications for subsequent phases of the project.

Responsibility for this phase, or at least for initiating it, is nearly always assigned to applications engineers who are not usually micro-electronics specialists. The latter will step in only after the idea has been launched and pursued in some detail, for a cursory assessment of its validity and viability.

The first phase of the "initial concept" for an application therefore involves very little in the way of direct costs (the emergence of an idea is not really an economic production activity to which any cost can be assigned). But it can only be generated by individuals or teams who are experts both in the structure of an industrial application or product and in the general scope offered by micro-electronics technology. Competence in both fields is rather rare within the stock of skills available in Member countries, and has not yet been disseminated on a large scale by vocational training. Another consideration is that since this skill is not identified precisely with any one occupation, its scarcity does not seem to have the direct effect of increasing the remuneration it can claim on the labour market. In these circumstances, scarcity would seem to cause a bottleneck.

Detailed analysis of the proposed system is carried out by a micro-electronics specialist. The end result is a detailed, complete flow chart for the application (system architecture).

On the basis of this "architecture", the most effective possible hardware configuration is designed for it. Here one of two alternative approaches can be taken according to the complexity of the software structure.

One is to support the system on micro-electronic components (microprocessors, memory) available "off-the-shelf". This involves deciding which microprocessor has the most suitable range of instructions, word-length and speed for the control system proposed and which memories have the most suitable structure and capacity to carry out the program. This solution holds hardware costs down to a very low level, but makes it necessary to adapt the software to the performance of hardware already available on the market.

The alternative is to design and order a custom hardware configuration, usually a single circuit comprising microprocessors and memories. This is done when the control system requires very special speed, reliability, memory-size and/or has to cope with special environmental conditions – temperature, magnetic field, vibration, etc. Custom hardware optimises the configuration in state-of-the-art terms, but raises the project's hardware costs. Recent progress in semiconductor technology: flexible automation in their production (chip foundries), custom circuits produced from open standard circuits (gate arrays), the use of ready-made software modules to design custom circuits (cell libraries), and the building of microprocessor systems on the basis of prefabricated micro-electronics modules (bit-slice microprocessors), has cut these costs considerably. These, however, remain high in relation to the continually declining costs of standard circuits (the unit cost of a gate array was about $150 in 1984, as against $30 for a standard 16-bit microprocessor and $5 for a 64K RAM memory chip).

As stated, the phases of analysing and specifying the hardware configuration require the intervention of micro-electronics specialists. In fact, many of these have no formal qualification in the field (there being practically no such qualification as microprocessor technician or engineer in Member countries until very recently). The microprocessor specialist may come from a very wide range of background – computer science, electronics, mathematics, even philosophy or law, and nearly all have "on-the-job" experience of design rather than formal training. Some offer their services as consultants, in software houses, or by seeking a salaried position. They are in fairly short supply in Member countries and usually congregate, especially the consultants and software houses which need a continuous market, in those regions which are vigorously introducing micro-electronic technologies.

Feasibility study, hardware specification and system analysis do not constitute a very onerous task. Between a few weeks and a few months of one specialist's time is usually enough (and in view of the "own-initiative", non-formalized nature of the work, only a major project in, say, aerospace, air traffic control, weapons etc. will require work by a team or in a "workshop"). The work is almost wholly intellectual, requiring no particular facilities at this stage.

In these circumstances, the costs are mainly for microelectronics engineering manpower, for a limited period of work; but since the manpower is very scarce it can command a fairly high cost for a brief specialist assignment. (In the United States, an experienced micro-electronics specialist will expect to net $3 000 to $4 000 monthly.) Another point is that since these skills are so patchily distributed over regions and countries, the direct costs can be swollen by the costs of working at a distance (iteration, transport, telecommunications, translation, etc.).

It is often suggested that this phase in the development of the software will eventually be computerised or automated. It is foreseen that expert (artificial intelligence) systems will, in the not too distant future, analyse an application and directly work out the optimum architecture and software structure. Since even the intellectual formalization of this operation remains to be achieved, the prediction seems unlikely to materialise during the 1980s.

Once the system structure and the hardware configuration have been defined, programs have to be written and tested. Although this phase is often organically linked to the preceding phase, it requires special skills and facilities.

There are two types of programming and testing, requiring different resources and entailing different costs; the programming of standard circuits, and "programming" custom circuits.

2. Programming of Standard-Circuit Based Systems

Whilst the qualifications used in earlier phases rely on the own-initiative analytical skills and knowledge of specialists in the various fields of application and in micro-electronics, programming involves a relatively systematised and formalized technique: the use of high-level programming languages.

Microprocessor programming languages use symbolic instructions to generate a set of operational instructions corresponding to given functions (as do computer languages), this appreciably facilitates and accelerates the writing of micro-electronics system control programs.

Most microprocessor programming languages are adaptations of conventional computer languages (BASIC, PL/1, Pascal, etc.). More recently, languages such as C, Fourth and Ada designed specifically for certain types of advanced applications, have proved to be appropriate for general microprocessor programming. Lastly, "high-level assemblers" specific to certain hardware manufacturers are available (PL/M from Intel, MPL from Motorola, Plus from Signetics/Philips). A recent survey has counted about 20 different languages currently used in microprocessor programming.

These languages have features of their own making them suitable for particular purposes (BASIC for simple applications, Pascal for real-time, Ada for large-scale applications). But for many applications languages may be interchangeable, and are therefore in competition. Each has its own supporters in the universities, among the hardware manufacturers and users. But at present there seems to be a lack of any systematic assessment of their respective capabilities and best fields of application (even if such assessments exist they remain unknown to most users). This limits the range of choice and decision-making for firms engaged in micro-electronics applications, particularly in user industries which are not specialists in this technology. The situation here seems to be one of relative inertia, characterised by partial training and incomplete information among users.

Disregarding this problem, the fact that the qualifications required to program in a high-level language are practically the same as for computer programming means there are more human resources available in this field. There are also more opportunities for people to learn high-level language programming, and it does not take long. Insofar as microprocessor programming can be dissociated from the analytical phase, it is in itself a less expensive operation, especially as it benefits from considerable productivity gains attributable to the programming languages (Intel estimates these gains at over 400 per cent between 1975 and 1980).

On the other hand progress is being made in extending the range of instructions available on microprocessors (the Intel 4004 had 45 instructions, the 8086 has 133), raising efficiency in assembly language. This is the equivalent of replacing some high-level language symbolic instructions by machine instructions directly available on the microprocessor. This in turn makes for pronounced sophistication and differentiation in the various brands and types of microprocessors available on the market (future microprocessors are expected to contain up to 2 000 different instructions). This trend shows that technical progress is continuing in microprocessors, but it also raises serious problems of training and information for microprocessor systems analysts and programmers.

For the same reason, microprocessor users, producers and consultancies are tending to look towards a standard reference architecture for microprocessor instruction ranges (Softech's P-code, Intel's universal code, the United States Defense Department's 1750 instruction range architecture, Berkeley University's Minimum Instruction Set Code for example). But there is at present patent uncertainty as to whether, and how, such standardization could be brought about.

When the program has been written, the next stage is to construct and test a prototype. This phase involves testing the viability of the hardware, of the software, and of how they fit together.

The prototype consists of a temporary assembly of the various components (microprocessors, memories, interfaces etc.) of the system as designed. It is tested, in several stages and operations, with the help of "micro-electronic application development systems".

These application systems are not yet, as their name might suggest, software engineering tools. They are essentially test instruments with two functions – to simulate the behaviour of the designed system in response to real environmental signals, and to emulate the signals themselves "in circuit" and check whether the prototype behaves satisfactorily in these artificially created random situations. They therefore play an essential role, especially in the development of mass-market applications (which must be able to function under a very wide range of conditions over their lifetimes and would be difficult to maintain, e.g. in vehicles, measuring instruments, toys etc.), or high-risk applications (air control systems, aircraft, weapons etc.).

Substantial progress has been made with these development systems. Although they were no more than simple emulators a few years ago, they have since developed considerably, incorporating new test functions and covering greater numbers and more complex types of hardware and languages. At first they were dedicated machines, but have now grown into minicomputers or microcomputers with special software. Some system-development software is even offered as a package that can be run on different computers. Meanwhile, certain "software engineering" functions are beginning to be added to these systems, to facilitate the earlier phases of analysis and programming for the application.

Development systems are available from hardware manufacturers (Intel, Motorola, Texas Instruments) who offer equipment exclusively tailored to their product, and also from independent companies offering "universal" systems (Tektronix, Philips, Hewlett-Packard, Enertec, Gould, Aim etc). Users disagree about the value and effectiveness of the two types of hardware. This is another instance of lack of full, systematic information about technological appropriateness and trends in the state of the art. Another difficulty associated with using them is that the lifetime before technical obsolescence can be very short, which is increasingly difficult to reconcile with their mounting cost (up from a few hundred dollars some years ago to as much as $15 000 to $50 000 nowadays).

It must also be pointed out that the availability, (sale, leasing, timesharing), costs and maintenance arrangements for development systems vary with country and region. This introduces appreciable differences in efficiency and the programming/test costs for firms using microprocessors in different geographical locations.

3. Programming of Semi-Custom-Circuit Based Systems

The production conditions and cost structure of the programming phase show special features in the case of the gate array/standard cell hardware options. Figure 21 shows how the two are expected to grow over the 1980s.

It is a feature of both options that their configuration stems directly from the software structure adopted, which makes programming easier. Programming refers here to the last stage of the overall design of the product, which is facilitated thanks to fewer constraints in the way of hardware-imposed detours. And since these technologies are designed for more complex, costly applications, they have justified the development of more sophisticated program-generating tools. This is consequently a more advanced area technologically than standard circuit programming.

At the same time, greater qualifications are needed to write such programs, since programming here includes part of the hardware circuit design. These qualifications are then extremely scarce, concentrated in countries and regions which are in the lead in microprocessor technology.

The equipment required for programming gate arrays and standard cells is also highly specialised. In practice these are computer-aided design systems; evolving very rapidly, they are also very costly (from $100 00 to $150 000 in early 1983). Offered and maintained by a small number of specialised firms, their availability also varies with country and region.

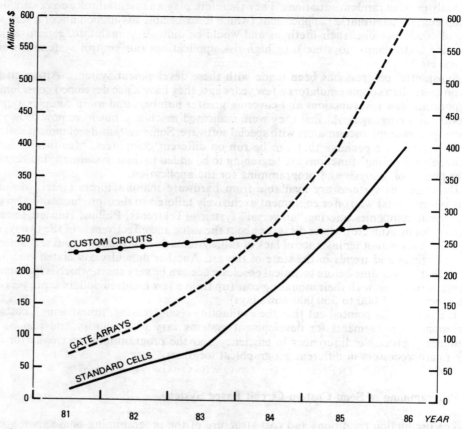

Figure 21   **US MARKET FOR SEMI-CUSTOM CIRCUITS 1981 TO 1986 (projected)**

Millions $

CUSTOM CIRCUITS

GATE ARRAYS

STANDARD CELLS

YEAR

Source: Electronics.

Access to the qualifications and equipment necessary to make optimum use of these technologies, and keep abreast of the state of the art, is therefore difficult and costly. But with them, highly efficient programs can be formulated in a short time (a top-of-the-range gate array now costs $50 000 to develop in the United States, a standard cell $100 000, while it could cost as much as $250 000 and take longer to develop a custom circuit fulfilling the same function).

4.   Industrial Reproduction of a System

Once the prototype circuit has been tested and optimised, putting it into industrial production constitutes a specific phase. Three production methods are current, differing in how the software is incorporated in the circuit.

In the first method, when the circuit has a totally or partially custom hardware configuration (gate arrays and standard cells), it will be mass-produced by a semi-conductor manufacturer. The circuit, generally integrating microprocessor and memory on one chip, will be made and tested in its finished form by the manufacturer. Entirely intended for one predefined application, it will be wholly and completely firmware.

The second alternative is to use standard circuits, microprocessors and read-only memories (ROM). The ROM will incorporate the program and will be mass produced by a memory manufacturer, and combined with bought-in microprocessors either by the same manufacturer or by the system constructor. This is another instance of firmware, since the ROMs incorporate dedicated, inalterable programs. However if they are in the form of interchangeable plug-in cards then software alternatives, on other cards, can be introduced in the circuit (as with second-generation video games).

A third possibility is to use programmable read-only memories (PROMs) and electrically erasable ROMs (EEPROMs) to carry the software. In this case the memory, being programmable, can be loaded by means of a development system or microcomputer. This type of system may, therefore, be reprogrammed several times in the course of its lifetime but remains too costly and is used mainly in the "prototyping" of micro-electronics systems.

Mass production of microprocessor systems implies low reproduction costs. Whether standard circuits, gate arrays or standard cells are used, the reproduction of software in the form of firmware, plug-in cards or PROMs and EEPROMs involves low costs inversely proportional to the scale of production. Provided the user firm has access to the products and services of the manufacturers, who need not necessarily be located nearby, it can get its system's micro-electronic modules produced under satisfactory conditions.

B. TRENDS IN ECONOMIC ORGANISATION: EMERGENCE OF SERVICE FIRMS

In this section trends in the economic organisation of embedded software production are examined. Since trends in this field are at present firstly influenced by user strategies, developments on the demand side are discussed first and then those on the supply side.

1. Demand Trends

In the light of these conditions, and of the costs of designing micro-electronics software, how are the user firms seeking to organise its production? Do approaches vary according to product characteristic, sector of activity or size of these firms?

a) Demand by Sector

The demand for micro-electronics software developed at first in those sectors of industry which had immediate opportunities of applying microelectronic control systems and were technologically equipped to undertake application studies. Next, in the 1970s, it spread to other sectors which gradually familiarised themselves with the technology and began to incorporate it in their products. However, by the early 1980s it would be fair to say that microprocessors have still only penetrated a small part of their potential field of application.

As an advanced branch of electronics technology, their penetration of sectors can be expected to follow the same pattern as that of classical electronics which, although it has reached into a greater number and a wider range of activities, itself remains relatively marginal in industry. Microprocessors, through their very low hardware costs and spectacular performance, may give diffusion a second wind, provided that software design and production capabilities become cheaper and, most important of all, available.

Table 28 shows the growth and distribution by sector of the American microprocessor market, and in particular the rapid penetration of microprocessors into the consumer

Table 28. **US market for microprocessors by user sector**

Sector	1979	1983 (estimated)
Office equipment	28 %	23 %
Computers and peripherals	36 %	37 %
Telecommunications equipment	15 %	15 %
Industrial equipment	12 %	11 %
Consumer durables	9 %	14 %
Total market in value ($ million)	107.5	646.0

Source: IDC, Electronics.

Table 29. **Microprocessor applications in Japan**

Household
  Automobiles
  Home appliances
  Calculators
  Toys
  Self-education

Commerce/Office
  Office calculators
  Sales
  Inventory
  Word processing
  Retail accounting
  Banking/Computer terminal
  Office equipment

Data processing
  General purpose computer
  Peripheral terminal calculators
  Science and technology calculators

Industry
  Production machine equipment
  Machine control
  Process control
  Production management

Traffic/Transportation
  Signal control
  Traffic control
  Station management
  Shipping/Flight

Measurement/Test/Monitor
  Measuring equipment
  Analyser
  Monitor
  Medical electronics
  Testing equipment

Telecommunication
  Wire communication
  Data communication
  Image display communication
  Wireless communication
  Broadcast

Source: T. Sasaki, Technova, 1982.

industries. Nevertheless, the "founder" industries, (computers, office electronics, telecommunications) still account for the lion's share. Table 29 shows the wide range of microprocessor applications in Japan. Figure 22, based on a representative sample, shows how micro-electronics technology has penetrated the various sectors of British industry.

Figure 22 USE OF MICROELECTRONICS TECHNOLOGY BY SECTOR IN THE UNITED KINGDOM

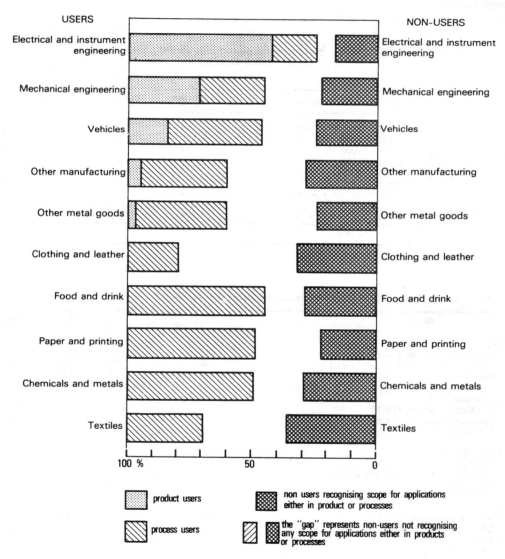

Source: PSI, 1981.

It must be made clear that the sectoral distribution of microprocessor software demand cannot be assessed from that of microprocessor demand. Since micro-electronics system production runs can vary considerably from one sector to another, there is no direct relationship between the two markets. Thus the industrial equipment producers, with a relatively small share of the microprocessor market, are probably heavy demanders of software for their applications, many produced in very short runs. Table 30, taking British industry as an example, shows that most microprocessor development projects (and therefore demand for software) are effectively concentrated in small and medium-run industrial applications.

Table 30.   **Number of microprocessors needed a year
in the United Kingdom**
Percentage

Number of microprocessors	Product users	Process users
1- 100	33	47
101- 1 000	18	5
1 001- 10 000	14	0
10 001-100 000	8	0
100 001-1 million	3	0
More than 1 million	1	0
Don't know/Not answered	24	46
Total	100	100

Source: PSI, 1981.

Table 31.   **Microprocessor application rate in Japanese home appliances**

Appliance	1977	1978	1979	1980	1982
VTR					
Production volume (1 000)	962	1 559	2 245	2 837	4 131
Microcomputer applied unit (1 000)	96	234	920	1 560	3 016
Percentage	10	15	41	55	73
Microwave oven					
Production volume (1 000)	1 724	1 857	1 767	1 577	1 615
Microcomputer applied unit (1 000)	172	464	530	639	888
Percentage	10	25	30	40	55
Air conditioner					
Production volume (1 000)	2 934	3 864	5 478	5 100	5 560
Microcomputer applied unit (1 000)	30	190	820	1 275	1 945
Percentage	1	5	15	25	35
Tuner					
Production volume (1 000)	2 280	2 680	2 820	2 950	3 220
Microcomputer applied unit (1 000)		50	140	200	550
Percentage		2	5	8	17

Source: Japan Electronics Industry Promotion Association, 1980.

The sectoral configuration of microprocessor software demand probably varies from one country to another, reflecting the position and the technological vigour of various industries in different countries. Table 31 shows, for example, how microprocessors have rapidly permeated the household appliance industries in Japan.

Owing to its central role in the design and functioning of micro-electronics systems, software is no "passive" component, whose demand is induced by the exogeneous technological vigour of user industries. On the contrary, its availability and performance with respect to the needs of the various industries, in different countries, are clearly decisive factors in how microprocessor technology permeates those industries, heavily influencing both the level and the pattern of demand. A 1983 survey of 3 800 European factories showed that lack of expertise, development costs and technical difficulties in software are among the major obstacles to the insertion of micro-electronics in products and production processes (see Figure 23).

Figure 23 **THE OBSTACLES TO THE USE OF MICROELECTRONICS IN EUROPEAN COUNTRIES**
% of user factories regarding as very important:

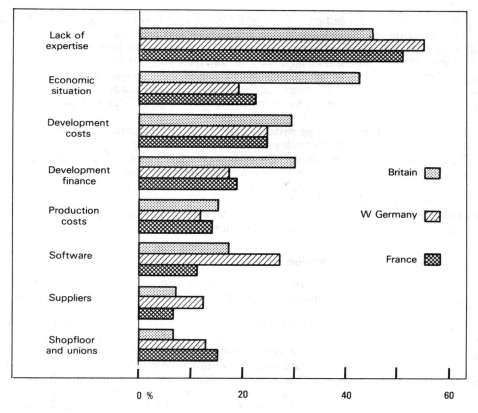

Source: PSI, VDI, BIPE, 1985.

b) Demand by Size of Enterprise

Demand for microprocessor software seems to have developed first within large firms, as part of development projects involving substantial human resources . Large firms seem at first sight better placed than smaller firms to attract and develop these types of advanced,versatile qualifications; and it is on that basis that they have pioneered microprocessor applications in different fields (computing, telecommunications, motor industry, household appliances, etc.). But at the same time, very small firms have proved successful in this field, almost always with the special feature of having been created or run by professionals possessing these scarce qualifications (in microcomputers, measurement instruments, etc.). This situation is easy to explain: in the context of a total qualifications bottleneck, and the poorly developed labour market, the distribution of human resources becomes the determinant of technology diffusion. Size of firm and financial muscle can then be seen as only one important factor. It is powerful enough to influence distribution but not to pull in all the resources.

With the spread of micro-electronics technology and accompanying skills, as small and medium-sized firms become familiar with the new technology and launch projects applying it, a labour market is tending to build up. Larger firms can use their financial capability to acquire critical human resources on this market. Another sign of this process is the acquisition of small specialist software houses by large firms that have not developed the new skills internally.

The trend for the distribution of demand by size of firm is also heavily dependent on the level and structure of software supply, in response to two processes: first, the increasing availability or, alternatively, scarcity of software determines trends both in costs and also in differences in the ease with small and large firms can have access to those resources. Second, how supply is structured in terms of salaried employment versus traded services (by consultants or software houses) circumscribes the scope for development in demand on the part of small firms (which are neither large enough, nor engage in enough new projects to build up their own resources here).

These demand/supply linkage patterns may generate substantial differences from one country to another in how the technology spreads among differing sizes of firm. One sign of such differentiation can be identified as between the United States and Japan. In the United States, several specialist software houses and consultants offer their services as sub-contractors to develop systems defined by user firms of different sizes. In Japan, on the other hand, design capabilities are concentrated within a few large electronic groupings, in some cases as specialist subsidiaries, thus developing and maintaining full and integral mastery of the design process from specification to final completion.

c) Demand by Country and Region

Very little information is available about the comparative growth of microprocessor software demand as between countries and regions. Nevertheless attention can be drawn to a number of differences.

Differences from country to country can be observed in the diffusion of microprocessors, almost invariably highlighting the vigour of American and Japanese firms (in microcomputers, video games, toys, robots, household equipment, even the motor industry).

To a lesser extent, regional differences seem to be identifiable through the growth of regions that are particularly active in the use of microelectronics technology (the West and East Coasts of the United States, Kyushu Island in Japan, the South West and Scotland in the United Kingdom, the Stuttgart area in Germany and the Paris and Grenoble areas in France).

Country and regional differences show how important the environmental factors are in the diffusion of the technology (and therefore in microprocessor software demand). The regional level and pattern of software supply is one such factor, though not the only one. University research, the presence of very large firms specialising in microelectronics technology, regional policy, are all factors influencing these differences, simultaneously invigorating the supply and the demand for specialist skills in this field.

These differences have more influence on the diffusion of microprocessor technology among small and medium-sized firms than among the large or very large firms. The large firm can avail itself of expensive hardware and services from the most reputable firms, and operate on a large enough scale to have access to these critical resources in whatever region or country they may be available. To some extent it can thus more easily "evade" its own environmental constraints than a small firm can. Yet the familiarisation and involvement of smaller firms with the new technology is what will channel it through the industrial fabric of a country or region.

2. Supply Trends

How is micro-electronics software supply organised in Member country economies? Are there different sorts of organisation, exerting different influences on the dissemination of the new technology? Which factors encourage or handicap the different sorts of organisation?

a) In-House Production by User Firms

Included in Project Development

Up to now, most microprocessor software has been developed as part of user firms' project activities, with the firm's R & D department designing the microprocessor based product also being responsible for specifying, writing and testing the control software (whether or not the same firm actually mass produces the micro-electronic module). The R & D departments do this by taking on the necessary skilled personnel and equipment.

The major advantage of this type of organisation is that it ensures full transparency and synergy between the design of the product and that of its control system. The product designer can take direct advantage of the skills of the micro-electronics specialists, while the latter fully understand the architecture of the product and are able to adapt it to the capability and constraints of the technology.

The main disadvantage of this pattern of organisation is its high cost. It means that the R & D department of a firm, or departments of a group, need to acquire and internalise these very special, scarce and costly resources.

So it is mainly large firms with substantial resources which opt for that solution. Smaller firms can also develop internal skills, provided that their R & D activities are sufficiently intensive to amortize them, and provided that their technological objectives are of only average level, not requiring highly sophisticated qualifications or equipment.

Organised as a Specialised Skills Centre

This is an evolved form of the first type of organisation, found in a much smaller number of firms. The firm still internalises the resources needed for developing micro-electronics systems, but instead of including them in its R & D department, brings them together into a specialised skills centre to serve different departments or units.

The main benefit of this solution is that it exploits the various learning curves and economies of scale applying to the development of micro-electronics systems, while at the same time conserving the firm's internal control over them. Such skill centres, sometimes even set up as subsidiaries, gain varied and cumulative experience, and can make repeated use of a software module developed for a special case. They can thus ensure some degree of compatibility and of technological homogeneity within the firm, thereby not only facilitating the circulation of ideas and of information but also the organisation of marketing and after-sales services.

The disadvantage of this approach is that it brings back the separation of product designers from the microprocessor specialists inside the firm. Since the intention is to establish a centre of general, wide-ranging skills, it also requires highly sophisticated and expensive human and physical resources.

This pattern of organisation is the prerogative of the very large firm, and appears to be an effective way of diffusing microprocessor technology within it. At first glance there seems to be no international differences under this heading, but the organisational culture of transparency and of pooling resources within firms that it demands seems to be unequally developed from one country to another. This is probably why this pattern is especially successful in Japan.

b) External Supply by Component Manufacturers

The production of microprocessor software by microprocessor manufacturers for their customers was the first channel by which the technology spread. At the outset, during the 1970s, the microprocessor manufacturers were practically the only people who had mastered this technology, so they had themselves to demonstrate its value and efficiency, which they did by co-operating with their larger customers to develop the first systems incorporating microprocessors (calculators, telecommunications equipment, computer equipment, etc.). As the technology spread, in relative terms, and firms built up their own internal skills, the hardware manufacturer's "consultancy service" role gradually diminished, except for projects on behalf of very large customers implying the development and mass production of custom items (motor car electronics for example). However, with the recent sharpening of competition on the microprocessor market, some manufacturers are trying to revitalise their software services, which they would like to use as a competitive weapon on the hardware market.

Hardware manufacturers may supply software in one of two different ways: custom design and writing, reserved mainly for the largest customers; or by providing standardized software development instruments (development systems and software module libraries).

The advantage of these forms of supply is that the user is guaranteed a software capability which corresponds to advances in hardware. This is because microprocessor manufacturers have invested heavily in exploring the software potential of the successive hardware generations they launch onto the market, and in development systems and software module libraries with which to program them (according to Intel, 75 per cent of the development effort for its 8086 and 8186 models went on system support products. According to Motorola, 50 per cent of recent development costs have been for software. Matra-Harris has announced that this proportion, amounting to some 20 per cent for 4-bit microprocessors, has risen steeply with the launch of 8, 16 and 32-bit circuits).

The main disadvantage of this supply pattern is that it ties the user to a particular hardware manufacturer. This is because the design services manufacturers offer are exclusively associated with the large volume supply of hardware, while their development systems are used to program the same hardware. So the user looking to a hardware manufacturer to satisfy his software requirements is liable to obtain a service that may be biased by the manufacturer's marketing objectives; the user installing such a development system is thereby tied to the hardware supplier for the entire lifetime of the equipment.

The hardware manufacturers' software services are usually available in all countries or regions in which they have a commercial presence (notably via computer networks and CAD systems remotely accessible by all agents and representatives). But their services are mainly concentrated and tailored to the customers they regard as the most commercially worthwhile and long-term.

This type of supply consequently encourages the diffusion of microprocessor technology among heavy users, and in countries and regions where the hardware manufacturers are located or represented.

c) *External Supply by Service Firms*

Firms specialising in microelectronics software began to form in the second half of the 1970s. They were set up by the few specialists in the new technology, to take on the task of designing and writing software for user firms who could not or did not wish to internalise all the necessary resources.

Tables 32 and 33 indicate the present activities of these firms in different regions of France.

The micro-electronics software houses, depending on their level of skill and the needs of their customers, produce software for standard circuits, gate arrays or standard cells. But

Table 32. **Microelectronics service firms in France, 1981**

| | Turnover (FF million) | | | | | |
	−1	1-5	5-10	10-50	50+	Total
Number of firms	14	15	8	2	1	40
Total turnover	6	31.6	55.74	23.70	57	174
Percentage turnover	3	18	32	14	33	100

Source: DIELI.

Table 33. **Location of microelectronics service firms in France, 1981**

Region	% by region
Paris Region	23
Champagne-Ardennes-Picardie	5
Nord	13
Lorraine-Alsace-Franche-Comté	8
Normandie-Bretagne-Pays de Loire	9
Limousin-Auvergne	2
Poitou-Aquitaine-Midi-Pyrénées	5
Bourgogne-Rhône-Alpes	11
Languedoc-Roussillon-Provence	14
Other	10

Source: DIELI.

although quite a large number of software houses are already working on standard circuits, far fewer (about 100 in the United States in 1982) have mastered gate arrays and even fewer (under 10 in the United States in 1982) standard cells.

The great advantage of working with a software house is to have direct access to scarce, continuously advancing skills, for a limited time which minimises the cost of the operation. By putting its software design out to the software houses, the user firm thus benefits both from the learning curve economies and to a lesser extent, from economies of scale through software modules.

No major disadvantage is involved in working with a software house. The separation which this type of organisation implies between product designer and the designer of its micro-electronic module can however sometimes cause problems, repetition, various delays, but most of the time the fault lies with poor specification at the outset. Another problem mentioned relates to confidentiality and commercial secrecy, the software house being familiar with the customer's development projects from their earliest inception. Although no specific instances are known of this type of information being leaked, it is possible that the risk makes division of labour between firms more difficult here.

External supply from software houses is thus the main channel whereby microprocessor technology spreads among small and medium-sized firms (though even the very large firm will often call them in for an application that may be for the moment beyond its own capabilities).

But unlike supply within firms, or from hardware manufacturers, this type of software supply is subject to considerable differences as between regions and countries.

The typical software house will be a very small firm (usually under 10 employees) and therefore very limited in its geographical reach. Another consideration is that since these firms are created around rare, highly technological skills, they are inclined to concentrate in regions with a dynamic technological environment (universities, hardware manufacturers, etc.) with reliable markets (plenty of firms as potential customers) and financing potential (state aids, venture capital markets, etc.). As a result, these companies have a very uneven geographical distribution, especially those in the lead with regard to technology (concentrated on the West Coast of the United States); as mentioned in the previous section, this leads to uneven awareness and development of demand, and thereby an uneven dissemination of the new microelectronics technology. This differentiation as between regions and countries may eventually make itself felt in the technological competitiveness of small and medium-sized firms (whose activities are affected by microprocessor technology) in the various regions and countries.

d) External Supply by Component Distributors

An interesting recent development is that component distributors, in their turn, have tried to enter the area of the supply of design services, establishing networks of design facilities. This trend is most visible in the United States where the distribution industry made 23 per cent of total semiconductor sales in 1983. Hamilton-Avnet and Wyle are the major distributors to have adopted this course of action. Notably Hamilton-Avnet plans to invest $10 million over 1984/85 to equip and staff 60 such centres nationwide.[13]

Chapter III

THE PARTICULAR CASE OF
INDUSTRIAL AUTOMATION SOFTWARE

A striking technological feature of the 1980s in OECD countries is the stimulus given to industrial automation. Unlike the automation of the 1950s, the technology in this case makes automation increasingly accessible for short or medium production runs, through flexible equipment such as numerically-controlled machine tools, numerically-controlled machining centres, robots, and computer-aided design and manufacturing systems (CAD/CAM). Table 34 shows this process through the recent strong growth of the industrial electronic equipment market (and its forecast continuance) in the United States.

Table 34. **Industrial electronic equipment markets in the United States, 1981 to 1986**
Million dollars

	1981	1982	1983	1986[a]
Numerical control systems	198.5	265	371.7	998
Automated testing equipment	969.3	1 108.6	1 421.1	2 676
Measurement systems	197.7	239.6	269.1	394
Process control equipment	1 288.6	1 481	1 604.1	2 529
Computerised energy management equipment	440.5	571.2	721.3	1 550
Industrial robots	191.2	217.1	290.2	537
Computer aided design systems	312.4	450.9	744.6	1 801

a) Estimates.
Source: Electronics, 1983.

A feature of the flexible automation systems is the key role that information technologies play. In fact it is precisely these technologies which enable these systems to perform more effectively than their predecessors, endowing them not only with unmatched capabilities to memorise, monitor, calculate and feed-back, but also to have all their functions redefined instantaneously. These capabilities are being extended as the new media for these technologies are included in equipment, as a result of technological advances and declining prices. Whereas ten years ago, computerised numerical control was an extremely costly technique, seldom found in numerically-controlled machine tools, it has almost become the norm now. Similarly, microprocessors are quickly coming into general use for robot control, and minicomputers in CAD systems.

As the information technologies make substantial inroads into industrial automation, they create a need for software to exploit all the capabilities of the programmable equipment. Software characteristics, availability and costs tend then to become the most important factors in the technological evolution and economic distribution of this type of equipment[14].

A. TRENDS IN TECHNOLOGY: BIRTH AND POTENTIAL OF INTEGRATED SYSTEMS

1. Main Types of Industrial Automation Software

Automation software means all programs governing the operation of programmable equipment used to perform design, control, inspection and management functions in industrial processes. Three main types of automation software have to be distinguished, according to the level at which they intervene in the operation of such a system.

a) Three Types of Software

Adopting the computer software terminology, the three different types can be described as systems software, applications software and data-base software. However, all these have properties and functions wholly geared to industrial tasks and equipment, so must in no way be confused with ordinary computer software.

i) *Systems software* is part of the "initial" configuration of an automation system and helps, in the same way as the technological capabilities of the hardware, to determine the potential of the equipment concerned. At present, systems software consists mainly of compilers (making it possible to program the equipment in a high-level language), interface software (so that one item can be connected to another) and functional software (necessary for the whole range of applications, such as servo-control software in numerical control, surface definition software in computer-aided design, etc.).

ii) *Applications software* consists of programmes governing the actual functioning of programmable systems in particular applications. This category covers programs controlling robots, numerically-controlled machine tools and flexible manufacturing systems, programs controlling process, and programs describing an object or a system in computer-aided design.

iii) *Data bases* are increasingly being used in industrial applications. Relating to the technical features of parts produced in an undertaking; manufacturing operations; specifications of the stock and performance of equipment in service; the various materials used, tolerances required, etc., a data base provides essential information for optimising the design of new products and establishing their production plans and programs. These data bases can be accessed easily and directly and can be provided on different media (central mainframe, peripheral memories, even the machine's own control system, etc.).

b) Running on Different Kinds of Equipment

Automation software are also distinguished according to the types of equipment on which they run. The equipment can be classified according to six groups:

    i)   Numerically-controlled machine tools;
   ii)   Robots;
  iii)   Measurement and testing equipment;
   iv)   CAD systems;
    v)   Production management systems;
   vi)   Process-control systems.

Numerically-Controlled Machine Tools

Numerically-controlled machine tools first appeared in the 1950s, but the most important developments were made with information technologies during the 1970s. These developments were in three broad directions: adaptive control (monitoring the machinery process via sensors to adjust a machine while operating), computerised control (replacement of opto-magnetic "tape/tape reader" control systems by electronic "processor/memory" systems) and automatic loading of tools and work pieces (by manipulator arms and palettes). Numerical control thus gradually spread to all kinds of machine tools (lathes, drills, milling machines, presses, etc.) and generated machinery designed to perform many of these functions simultaneously (numerically controlled machining centres).

These developments made possible and relied upon increasingly complex software, fulfilling wide and more varied control functions. One of the most effective numerical control systems available on the world market (Yamazaki's Mazatrol system) offers several systems software and possesses a directly-accessible memory capacity equivalent to up to five kilometres of conventional numerical-control tape, and can accommodate a hundred or so different machining programs. A 1982 NMBTA survey in the United States showed that the stock of numerically-controlled machine tools in service with United States machine tool manufacturers required some 60 to 80 hours of programming per month and per machine, and that the amount of time could increase markedly according to the complexity of the machine concerned. Very approximately, taking a lifetime of five years for a numerically-controlled machine tool, this is the equivalent of some 4 000 hours of programming, costing far more than the machine's hardware itself. The software cost would even double over ten years, the conventional amortization lifetime for a machine tool until recently, when obsolescence began to overtake them so rapidly.

Robots

The first robots appeared in the early 1960s, but in this field, too, the most significant developments occurred after the second half of the 1970s. Through the many classifications, technological development can be identified as having taken place over three generations, corresponding to increasing amounts of information technology incorporated in robots:

    i)   Open-loop programmable robots (operating sequentially, with no feed-back);
   ii)   Servo-robots (controlling their own movement via sensors); and
  iii)   "Intelligent" robots (programming their own operations to achieve defined aims).

These successive generations demand complex, diversified software, as represented in Figure 24.

Figure 24   ROBOTICS SOFTWARE

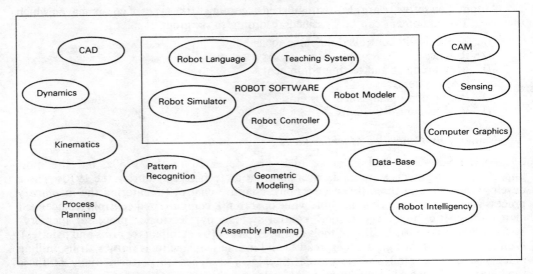

Source: CAM-1.

Not much information is available as to what proportion of hardware costs the software costs represent. According to some estimates, software accounts for over 50 per cent of the cost of developing second generation robots, but this refers only to systems software developed by the robot designers, not to applications software or any data bases required for their use. Another consideration is that systems software costs for third generation robots, still under development, will reach new highs, since they will have to use sophisticated artificial intelligence techniques.

Measurement and Testing Equipment

The importance of measurement and testing equipment is constantly increasing, as automation systems come into wider use. This equipment plays a key role in the reliability and proper functioning of an automation system and in product quality.

At the same time, measurement and testing equipment is itself drawing increasingly upon the information technologies. With evermore sophisticated sensors, especially optical sensors, increasing quantities of information are collected and processed, using microprocessors, microcomputers and special-purpose software. This has lead to a greater role for systems software in the design of measurement and testing equipment, and of applications software in their use.

Computer-Aided Design Systems

CAD systems were first devised by aircraft manufacturers, to cope with the vast amount of calculation involved in aircraft design. Consequently, CAD systems emerged as a particular application of computer technology. They developed rapidly during the second half of the 1970s as they penetrated into new sectors of industry (motors, electronics, building) while computer and memory hardware were constantly growing more powerful and cheaper.

In particular, the arrival of the 32 bit super minicomputers prompted a major development and diffusion of CAD systems, which have become available on a turnkey basis, as special-purpose industrial equipment.

CAD systems are today used in four, complementary design functions:

i) To generate drawings and diagrams;
ii) Engineering calculations;
iii) Kinematic studies;
iv) Manufacturing instructions.

CAD systems use hardware of their own (tables to convert drawings to digital form, video screens etc.) but they mainly consist of a combination of special software. That part of the software which is originally incorporated in the system is large-scale and complicated. It works by interacting with programs and data bases created by the user. So the main costs of developing and using a CAD unit are for software.

Production Management Systems

Production management systems are not strictly speaking automation equipment. They apply computer techniques for the specific purpose of planning, organising and managing

Figure 25 **BROAD FUNCTIONAL CLASSES
OF PRODUCTION MANAGEMENT SOFTWARE**

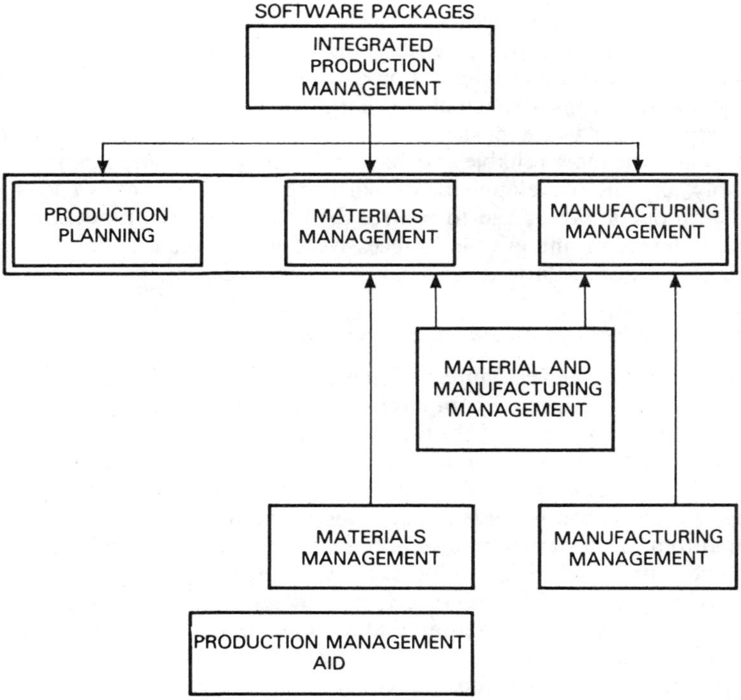

Source: CXP.

105

industrial production processes. Until recently they consisted of special software running on a firm's general purpose computer, but are now beginning to take the form of special-purpose hardware/software combinations, with input and information terminals located on the shop floor and with large real-time software configurations. Figure 25 describes the structure and evolution of this software.

Process Control Systems

Automation of continuous production processes (in the steel, chemicals and petrochemicals industries) had already advanced considerably in the 1950s and 1960s, with computers involved from their earliest appearance. Process control, too, has benefited substantially from recent advances in information technologies, mainly through more sophisticated and varied sensors and microprocessors, which have generated "decentralised control" techniques. The result has been a growing requirement for large-scale, multi-tiered real-time software. But this class of software is designed as a part of the engineering process of the equipment and site concerned (apart from some network software, specification aids and control algorithms), and is not considered in this overview.

2. Integration of Automation Software

Economic pressure for more highly automated and more flexible production systems, together with continuing advances in information technology hardware and media will continue to predominate in Member countries throughout the 1980s. This will prompt even more sustained diffusion of the equipment concerned, generating new automation techniques in the design, machining, handling, assembly and testing of industrial products.

On the software side this movement implies a new technological challenge, and one with considerable potential: the installation of very large, flexible automated production systems. Most of the constituent hardware for such complexes is already available in Member countries and is tending to become more reliable and less costly. Integrating and linking it together now depends notably on the development of software to make the various components communicate with one another, and to control their "co-operative functionning".

Three main levels of integration, successive and complementary but calling upon different kinds of software solutions, have to be considered here.

a) Integration of Design and Engineering: CAD/CAM Systems

The purpose of this first level of integration is to infer the manufacturing procedures for a product directly from its design, via computer processing of a digital model stored in a CAD system. This is in fact an extension of the traditional CAD system function, originally devised and used for "drawing office" tasks but now tending to encroach upon "methods office" tasks. For machining, this integration is reflected in the automatic output of numerical control programmes; in electronic components by the automatic generation of production "masks"; in casting by the automatic design of moulds and; for the future, in assembly by the automatic production of robot programs to assemble complex components.

This aim is simple in principle, but several difficulties are arising at present in connection with the complexity of the software required and the heterogeneity of the target automation systems and their systems software.

In spite of these difficulties, most CAD system producers have already introduced CAD/CAM systems designed to achieve such integration, at least partly. Some major users have also developed such systems for in-house use (IBM in components, Fiat in motorcar parts etc.). But except in micro-electronics, where it is already very advanced, integrating CAD with CAM is still a target to be achieved during the 1980s. Calma-GE, one of the worlds leaders in this market, stated in early 1983 that a very small minority of its non-electronics clients were successfully making effective use of integrated CAD/CAM.

In reaction to these and other difficulties, the *group technology* approach has developed. Here the link between "design" and "methods" is no longer inferred, but simultaneously determined: design takes place in accordance with the capacities and availabilities of existing production equipment, and the attempt is made to design "families" of parts from modular forms dictated by available production methods. This approach has had several applications in electronics (e.g. cell libraries, see Section II on Embedded Microelectronics Software) and in engineering (aerospace, motor industry, machine-tools etc.). The principle is an old one which computer capabilities make it possible to implement, drawing upon complex data-base software. One full group technology software system is at present available on the world market, from the Organisation for Industrial Research (OIR) in the United States.

Large-scale research projects are underway in Member countries into integrated CAD and CAM. Mention can be made first of a main module in the Integrated Computer-Aided Manufacturing Project (ICAM) of the US Air Force, and research by the Charles Draper Laboratory in the United States; also of research at the University of Kobe (CIMS), at the University of Hokkaido (TIPS), at the University of Tokyo (GEOMAP) in Japan; and research into the PRODES/PROMO systems at the Agence pour le Développement de la Production Automatisée (ADEPA) France.

Also worth mentioning is a recent attempt at standardization by the United States Electronics Industry Association (EIA) to facilitate the integration of CAD and CAM. The aim is to make numerical control programs developed out of CAD systems portable, regardless of what system originated the program, or on what numerical control system it is to run. The "EIA Standards Proposal 1546A on a 32 bit binary CL exchange format (BCL)" is expected to improve transparency and interfacing between CAD and CAM in a variety of hardware environments[15]. The proposal was due for publication by late 1983 and its success will depend on how leading equipment manufacturers react to it, especially at international level.

b) *Horizontal Integration of Automation Equipment: Flexible Manufacturing Systems and CAD Networks*

The second kind of integration has a different purpose: to put flexible automation systems, previously interfaced by human operators, into direct communication with one another. (If the automation systems in question were inflexible, i.e. non-programmable, this would amount to the "transfer machines" of the 1950s and 1960s.)

Flexible Manufacturing Systems

This approach is applied in the first place at the machining equipment level, between successive numerically controlled machine tools in a production process, between numerically controlled machine tools and robots despatching or inspecting parts. When direct communication involves only a few systems they are called flexible production units, but when more are involved they are called flexible manufacturing systems (FMS). Such systems are mostly designed by their own users, but turnkey systems are also available, though not very widespread as yet because insufficiently flexible or all-purpose. The largest flexible manufacturing systems in the world are in the Niigita Engineering Plant (Japan), integrating

31 machines and in the Messerschmitt-Bölkow-Blohm facility in Augsburg (Germany) integrating 28 machines.

Flexible manufacturing systems pose enormous software problems. It has up till now been difficult and costly to develop the real-time software required to manage these combinations which are both highly varied (a great many automation units with already complex individual software) and also highly unstable (a great many parts calling for different constantly redefined tools). Furthermore, the software has to be able to solve the problems of software incompatibility inevitably arising among the control systems for various kinds of equipment from different manufacturers.

Some early FMS software systems have appeared on the market recently (GEnet from General Electric for example), together with simulation software for the purpose of designing them (COL and GFMS from Charles Draper Laboratory, SIMSCRIPT from Kearney and Trecker). "Network" software has also been introduced to provide a software infrastructure for FMS (Data Highway software by Allen and Bradley, Modway by Modicon, PC Link/1000AB by Hewlett Packard). Turnkey FMS (Yamazaki's Mazak, Toyoda's Tipros, the Cincinatti-Milacron and Kearney and Trecker systems) and "in-house" FMS also incorporate a mass of software which may possibly become available separately on the market.

Still further progress and better co-ordination of effort, which today is unduly fragmented, can be anticipated during the 1980s. Two large co-operative projects may play an important role, first in *clarifying the problems* and then in finding *general solutions:* the US Airforce ICAM project and the Japanese Ministry of International Trade and Industry FMS project, which both aim to have developed a universal FMS by 1985.

CAD Networks

Opportunities for horizontal integration also appear at the level of CAD networks. These opportunities apply both to CAD systems within a given firm, perhaps distributed among different regions or even countries, and those of two or more firms whose transactions involve exchanging drawings, documentation and technical information, and even between a CAD service supplier and its customers possessing their own CAD facilities. In all these cases data bases need to be made transparent, project drawings and documentation must be made transferable and the graphic and retrieval languages used by the different systems must be made "comprehensible".

This kind of software integration, which will be crucial if extended use is to be made of CAD potential, is today being sought via three different approaches, which are not equally satisfactory:

1. Conversion software;
2. "Computervision compatibility" and
3. Defining standards for interfacing.

Of these approaches the first two seem to have prevailed up to now. They have however the same comparative disadvantages of loss of efficiency and undue dependence on the strategies of the dominant vendor as in the computer world – IBM in computers (see Section I on Data Processing Software), Computervision in CAD. The third approach is more difficult to organise and is therefore the least operational, but looks the most promising for the 1980s. A joint international research effort: CAM-I (Computer-Aided Manufacturing International, based at Texas, United States) is working on this question and has already defined a standard CAD interfacing format: the International Graphics Exchange Specification (IGES).

The same kind of horizontal integration is also being sought for measurement and testing equipment, especially via shared data bases, and manufacturers of this type of equipment already offer software to implement such integration (Genrad's TRACS, Teradyne's TERANET). Figure 26 illustrates this prospect for the future.

Figure 26   **TEST EQUIPMENT NETWORK PATTERN**

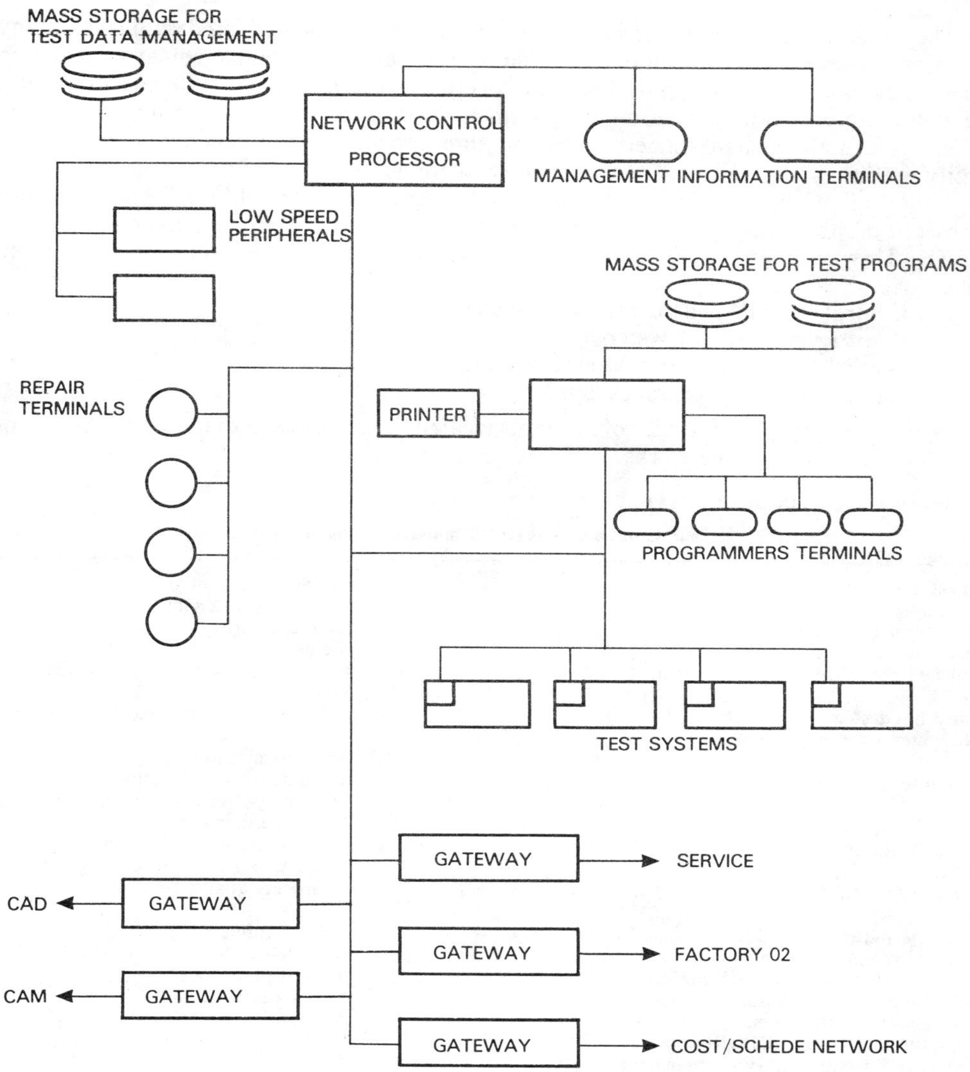

MASS STORAGE FOR
TEST DATA MANAGEMENT

NETWORK CONTROL
PROCESSOR

MANAGEMENT INFORMATION TERMINALS

LOW SPEED
PERIPHERALS

MASS STORAGE FOR TEST PROGRAMS

REPAIR
TERMINALS

PRINTER

PROGRAMMERS TERMINALS

TEST SYSTEMS

GATEWAY ➤ SERVICE

CAD ◄ GATEWAY

GATEWAY ➤ FACTORY 02

CAM ◄ GATEWAY

GATEWAY ➤ COST/SCHEDE NETWORK

Source: Genrad.

109

c)   Integration of Automated Production and Computerised Management: "Computer-Integrated Manufacturing"

The integration of computerised management functions and automated production functions through a single system is the ultimate level for development in automation. But although this prospect, which would ultimately mean the arrival of industrial firms co-ordinated and controlled by an integrated, omni-present computer system, with only marginal human intervention in their functioning, can only be envisaged for the 21st Century, the 1980s are already seeing the emergence of significant first steps in this direction (Table 35).

The integration of computerised management with automated production has many dimensions. They all involve computerised data bases, and bring management information (orders, customers, prices, costs, finance) together with production information (sites, equipment, material, manufacturing programmes, lead times). It is thus becoming conceivable to have management models operating simultaneously with production models, to identify optimum combinations and implement them automatically.

A pioneer venture in this area has been the integration achieved by IBM – for its own purposes – of its production control system EDS and production management system QTATS. This has generated a multi-tiered computer system with four interconnected levels:

1. Central level dedicated computer system;
2. Plant level logistical systems;
3. Workshop level monitoring systems and
4. Equipment level control systems.

IBM is exploiting this system in 27 of its plants located in various parts of the world, by means of a telecommunications network.

Table 35.   **Computer integrated manufacturing functions**

Business and planning support
  Economic simulation
  Long-term forecasting
  Customer ordering service
  Finished goods inventory management
	Manufacturing control
	  Purchasing receiving
	  Shop routing
	  Methods and standards
	  In-process inventory management
	  Short-term scheduling
	  Shop order follow system

Engineering design
  Computer-aided drafting
  Computer-aided tool design
  Group technology
  CAD
	Shop floor monitoring
	  Machine load monitoring
	  Machine performance monitoring
	  Man-time monitoring
	  Material stores monitoring
	  Preventive maintenance
	  In-process quality testing

Manufacturing planning
  Process planning systems
  Parts programming
  NC graphics
  Tool and materials catalog
  Material requirements planning
  Production line planning simulation
  Bill of materials processors
  Machinability data systems
  Computerized cutter, die selection
  Materials/Parts inventory management
	Process automation
	  NC, DNC, CNC
	  Adaptive control
	  Automatic assembly
	  Automatic inspection
	  Computerized testing

Source: CAD/CAM Technology, Spring 1982, Datamation.

110

A system of a similar kind recently announced by Toshiba is said to exploit the transparency and real-time interaction of data bases relating to products and production processes, including quality control, for its electronic components (Manufacturing Automation Revolutionary System, MARS). This system is part of a Toshiba eight-year plan to completely automate its 20 Japanese facilities by the end of the decade, so that only "brain workers" are left.

Another pioneering venture regarded as important is the similar but more localised development by Ingersoll Corporation in the United States.

These have obviously required research and investment on the very largest scale. So it would not be unexpected for these firms, and others having the same type of experience, to try to earn a return on their investment by introducing more universal versions of their internal software onto the market.

In this connection it should be noted that Xerox Corporation has just introduced a software system (Xerox Manufacturing System), aiming to integrate production management with production control, and which Xerox presents as the only wholly integrated real-time production system currently available. Honeywell also claims to be pioneering here with the TDC system announced for 1984, claiming that it will "for the first time allow interaction between plant-level automation and management minicomputers previously functioning independently". Other computer manufacturers are also launching similar products: Communications Oriented Production and Information System (COPICS) by IBM, Interactive Manufacturing Control System (IMCS) by NCR, The Manufacturing System (TMS) by Burroughs. Meanwhile CAD specialists, Computervision and Applicon, have introduced the Solidesign and Bravo systems whose aim is to provide the software infrastructure for such integration. Another software house, Comserv (United States), claims to be "the world's leading independent supplier of mainframe-based manufacturing software" with its AMAPS system.

It is also in terms of merging production management with production control that the "factory level local area network" is receiving attention. This local communications technology has already widened its use for tertiary applications (see Section I, "Data-Processing Software"). It is now perceived as a useful way of avoiding an endless proliferation of specialist communications networks at factory level. A unified local network will, it is hoped, channel all kinds of data relating to automation, management, testing, energy regulation, safety systems, etc., from any origin to any destination. Figure 27 shows a forecast of the market growth for factory level local area networks in the United States. Nevertheless, how extensively this technology does in fact spread will depend on the success of efforts towards standardization in this field, bearing in mind that integrated systems manufacturers will probably have strategies to differentiate their wares. Meanwhile, a committee of the IEEE (United States) is already working on the standardization of "factory LANs". More recently, a very big user, General Motors, gave a strong impetus to these efforts through a joint standard-setting project in this field with other users and the National Bureau of Standards.

3.   Production of Automation Software

Such are the new possibilities being opened up by automation software in the 1980s. But if they are to be exploited on a large scale, and under satisfactory economic conditions, they will require adequate production methods, with high efficiency and productivity.

Trends here differ appreciably as between systems software, applications software and data-bases.

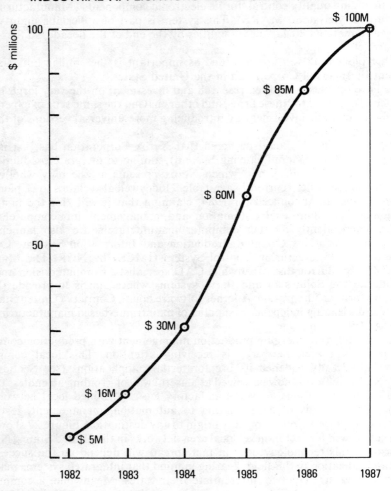

Figure 27 **THE MARKET FOR LANS FOR INDUSTRIAL APPLICATIONS IN THE UNITED STATES**

Source: Yankee Group.

Systems software is at present subject to intensive research in the universities, among the automation equipment manufacturers and in the software houses. Most of the effort is still going into the design and specification problems, and the programs are written by conventional means, mainly in FORTRAN. The fact that this software is incorporated in hardware or sold separately as software packages reduces the pressure on design costs: subject to very large economies of scale, on almost virgin markets, the design costs can be amortized relatively easily. Another point is that being fairly close to data processing software in nature and in the way it is designed, it can more easily benefit from current progress in software engineering techniques. CAP in the United Kingdom has already experimented with using the Ada language to develop a robot-control system.

The question becomes altogether different for applications and data-base software. This kind of software is always personalized, suited only to the place where it is used, and has a limited lifetime, the life of one product or type of product. In this, applications and data-base software in automation contrast markedly with data processing applications software, which has longer lifetimes and lends itself more readily to uniformisation in software package form. Efficiency and cost constraints on production methods for applications and data-base software in automation are therefore becoming crucial for designers and users.

Several approaches have been and are being developed to improve production conditions for these software.

a) Programming Languages for Automation

Numerical-control languages

High-level languages for automation programs emerged just after the earliest numerically controlled machine tools. As in computing, these work on the principle of generating series of machine executable instructions, from synthetic instructions issued by the user describing an application.

The first numerical control language of this kind was APT (Automatically Programmed Tools) developed between 1957 and 1959 as part of the "first major government/university/industry co-operative project in the history of software"[16]. The project was sponsored by the United States Air Force and led by an MIT team, with participation of automatic machining specialists from 14 firms. The outcome was remarkable since APT is still one of the main numerical control languages in use today. It is in the public domain and recognised by the International Organization for Standardization as a standard.

Other languages have been developed since. The most important is Compact II, developed by a small specialist firm in Michigan, Manufacturing Data Systems Inc., which offers it as a software package. Figure 28 shows usage levels for the main numerical control languages in the United States in 1981, by machine tool manufacturers.

In France the most frequently used numerical language is Promo, developed by ADEPA (a public agency). This is followed by MDSI's Compact II. Olivetti's GTL and SCAI are used in Italy, and Fanuc's FAPT in Japan.

These languages are constantly being improved and extended, and seem to meet user requirements well. They have also benefited considerably from advances in computer hardware.

This is because their compilers, which are large sets of software, were until recently available on mainframes. Users could access them only by processing on the large computers, which gave them machine programs in exchange for source programs. For this they had to use their firm's general-purpose computer or, if their firm did not have one, resort to a time-sharing company. (According to the NMBTA survey mentioned above, about 50 per cent of numerical control programming was carried out on in-house computers in 1981, and 50 per cent via time-sharing.) Powerful microcomputers are making many of these languages much easier to handle, since their compilers can now be available on a workshop machine.

It is possible that the present diversity of numerical control languages, especially at international level, will lead to certain incompatibilities in the future in the integration and organisation of automation systems.

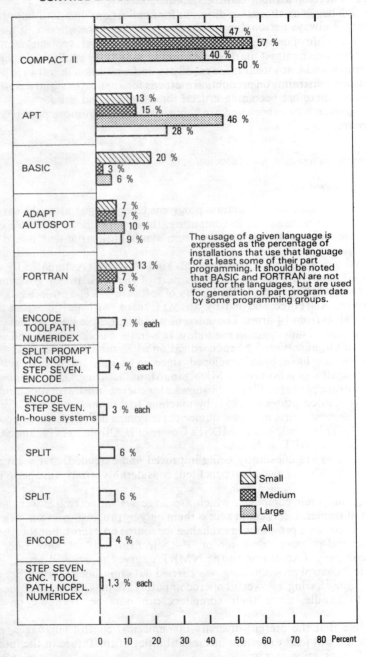

Figure 28 USAGE LEVELS FOR THE MAIN NUMERICAL
CONTROL LANGUAGES IN THE UNITED STATES, 1982

COMPACT II
47 %
57 %
40 %
50 %

APT
13 %
15 %
46 %
28 %

BASIC
20 %
3 %
6 %

ADAPT AUTOSPOT
7 %
7 %
10 %
9 %

The usage of a given language is expressed as the percentage of installations that use that language for at least some of their part programming. It should be noted that BASIC and FORTRAN are not used for the languages, but are used for generation of part program data by some programming groups.

FORTRAN
13 %
7 %
6 %

ENCODE TOOLPATH NUMERIDEX
7 % each

SPLIT PROMPT CNC NOPPL. STEP SEVEN. ENCODE
4 % each

ENCODE STEP SEVEN. In-house systems
3 % each

SPLIT
6 %

SPLIT
6 %

ENCODE
4 %

STEP SEVEN. GNC. TOOL PATH, NCPPL. NUMERIDEX
1,3 % each

Small
Medium
Large
All

0 10 20 30 40 50 60 70 80 Percent

Source : National Machine-Tool Builders Association

114

Robotics Languages

The second main type of language covers the robot control languages. Here there is even greater diversity, because up to now there has been no major national or international project to define any standards. Since there are so many robot producers, from so many different countries, and since control systems vary so much (point by point, continuous, reproduction, etc.) this has made it difficult for reference languages to receive general acceptance. In fact high-level languages are still not much used in programming these systems, as against programming methods based on "learning" (by means of a pointer or remote-control system). But high-level languages will become the norm as second and third generation robots come into widespread use.

The main robot manufacturers and research centres have developed their own control languages, such as Unimation's VAL, Olivetti's SIGLA, IBM's AML (following IBM's earlier language AUTOPASS), Automatix's RAIL, Toyota's TL-10, Hitachi's ARL, Stanford University's ACROYNM, Edinburgh University's RAPT, the University of Tokyo's STROL/STROLIC, and MITI's Electronic Laboratory's RVL/A. In 1984 it was estimated that more than 40 robot programming languages were in use in OECD countries. However, none of these languages seems sufficiently developed to have been taken up by the scientific and industrial community as a standard. Attention must be drawn to three recent developments which may be influential in the future.

The first is an United States Air Force project subcontracted to the McDonnell Douglas Corporation. This is an attempt to adapt the numerical control language APT to robot control, as the University of Edinburgh has tried to do with RAPT. The new language will be designated MCL (Manufacturing Control Language).

The second is a project already completed by the Institute of Applied Mathematics(IMAG) at Grenoble, France: the development of a full language capable of controlling various types of robot action: linear travel, cartesian travel, travel subject to halt conditions, travel subject to sensor data etc. This language, marketed by a small firm specialising in robotics software (Itmi), has been favourably welcomed and may be suggested as a European standard by several French, English and Italian users.

The third is a joint initiative in Germany by major robot manufacturers (KUKA, Siemens, Bosch, GdA, Jugneheinrich etc.) together with robot users and research laboratories. The aim is to standardize the interface for off-line programming of robots. The work began in 1980 and was based on existing German and international standards for numerical-control technology. A draft standard proposal called IRDATA was ready in 1984 and work is now underway towards establishing an integrated "robot programming environment" based on this standard.

b) Group Technology

Group technology, already mentioned in connection with the integration of design and manufacturing is also a method of producing applications software. At present this is the main purpose for which it is used.

Here the group technology principle is identified with the use of software module libraries in data processing applications. Families of existing parts, and their machining instructions are stored in databanks, so that the manufacture of similar parts can be programmed from existing control modules, obviating much of the need to rewrite programs. This results in productivity gains ranging from 50 to 80 per cent in the design and adjustment of new production processes (see Figure 29).

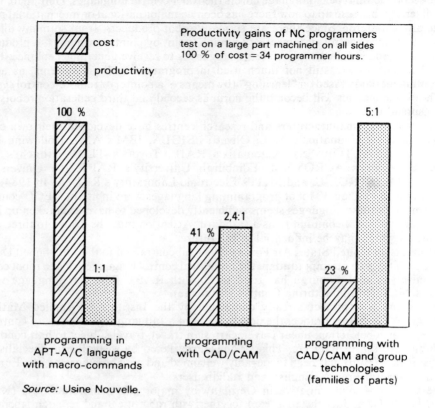

Figure 29 PRODUCTIVITY PROGRESS IN PROGRAMMING WITH GROUP TECHNOLOGIES

cost

productivity

Productivity gains of NC programmers test on a large part machined on all sides 100 % of cost = 34 programmer hours.

100 %

5:1

41 %

2,4:1

1:1

23 %

programming in APT-A/C language with macro-commands

programming with CAD/CAM

programming with CAD/CAM and group technologies (families of parts)

Source: Usine Nouvelle.

This technique is not widespread in Member countries. The main software in which it is used (OIR's Multigroup) received some 80 applications in the United States and fewer than ten in France until 1983 . It is undermined by the attractions of CAD, which favours the proliferation of new plans and new families of parts. The possibilities for including group technology in integrated control software for automated systems, or conversely, excluding it altogether, constitute a technological dilemma for the years ahead.

c) Contributions of Artificial Intelligence

The most recent method in designing applications software is the use of artificial intelligence techniques. For the moment the trend is confined to research laboratories, and has received hardly any applications in industry as yet, but it promises to be a decisive advance in automation during the 1980s.

Artifical intelligence is used here as a technique for decoding synthetic messages and intervenes at two completely different levels: interpreting sensor information, and interpreting program instructions.

In the first instance, it mainly concerns the processing of images collected by vision systems. The complexity of this operation, particularly in the dynamic environment of an industrial process, sometimes rules out conventional "recognition by comparison" algorithms, and relies upon "reasoned" deduction and exploration capabilities. Appropriate expert systems intervene then as systems software for vision applications.

Secondly, artificial intelligence techniques make the automation systems receptive to synthetic functional instructions issued by their operator, which have to be interpreted and implemented. The instructor need not then describe the operations in detail, and can programme the machine very rapidly, with few specific qualifications. This important advance defines third generation robots, still largely hypothetical, but will also probably apply to the programming of other automated systems.

B. TRENDS IN ECONOMIC ORGANISATION: A STILL UNCERTAIN DIVISION OF LABOR

In this section trends in the economic organisation of automation software are briefly examined. Since this field is so new, and trends in it are at present mainly influenced by user strategies, developments on the demand side are taken first and then those on the supply side.

1. Demand Trends

The automation of industrial production systems is mostly carried out inside the firms concerned, especially as regards the software aspects. This is because user firms purchase most of the hardware components for their systems from specialist suppliers, but make their own arrangements to install the components, link them together and program them. Hardware suppliers therefore occupy a relatively marginal position in the installation process, though they offer some consultancy, engineering and systems software support, so far rather limited, to go with the hardware they are supplying.

The demand for software has the same structure as the demand for programmable automation systems. It has grown considerably since the second half of the 1970s in practically all Member countries (though at different rates internationally, with Japan in the lead), in industries that are concentrated and subject to heavy competition (automobiles, electronics) and firms with large investment capacities (mainly the larger firms).

This demand for software benefits from the major technological advances in the field, mentioned in the first section. But a preliminary, overall view suggests that the new opportunities are being exploited on only a limited scale in most of the Member countries. This situation, apart from the earnings shortfall it represents in present uses of automated systems, is clearly an impediment to their further diffusion, especially in complex applications and for small and medium-sized enterprises.

It is therefore important to identify the reasons for the technological standstill at present characterising large segments of stock, and the additional demand for automation software. Six main factors must be taken into consideration.

    i)   In the first place, the usual problem arises of *informing* potential users about the availability and potential of the new software approaches. The problem is more acute here than in the case of computer software, because the users concerned are mainly production managers in industrial design and methods offices, not computer professionals in data processing departments. On the whole, the former are less easily able to evaluate and apply new information technology solutions.

ii) Secondly, there is the problem of the diversity of *decision-makers* inside firms concerned by the integration of automation software and, consequently, involved in projects and applications in this field. The departments responsible for designing products, defining methods, planning and controlling production, running the various factories and workshops are all involved simultaneously in exploiting the new software opportunities. In these circumstances, the traditional sharing of powers and responsibilities within firms may become incompatible with the organisational implications of the new technologies. This is certainly an important curb on their diffusion, and one that probably affects the larger firm, more fragmented and rigid, than the smaller firm which will be more flexible and transparent.

iii) A cognate question concerns flexible automation processes across the board, i.e. not only the software aspects: it relates to the *economic assessment methods* governing investment decisions. Conventional "return on investment" methods have often been shown to be unsatisfactory in assessing the benefits of the new flexible automation technologies, whose most important advantages (possibility of rapid renovation of products, redefinition of ranges offered, tangible reduction in stocks and delivery periods) those methods tend to ignore. The problem obviously has a considerable bearing on investment in the new software approaches.

iv) Evaluation and decision-making difficulties do not stem solely from user organisations or information shortcomings. These difficulties are also made appreciably harder by *incompatibilities in the equipment* available on the market, and uncertainties about future trends. How should the integration of production systems be tackled? Should a firm begin with CAD equipment, numerically controlled machine tools or robots, in order to adapt the other components of the system to this original configuration? What control systems and standards will leave the most room for manoeuvre in the future? Is it right to invest now, or should the firm wait until prices decline further and, even more important, the technological outlook becomes clearer? What are the risks and the lead times for technological obsolesence in the equipment currently on offer? Such questions reflect a generalised uncertainty on the part of users, but in no way could they be said to arise because users are underinformed. They stem from the fragmentation and the technological vigour of the market and, paradoxically, generate a certain amount of justifiable hesitation.

v) The next unfavourable influence is the *weight of past investment*. Almost every industrial firm except one that has just been created possesses a varied stock of production equipment, gradually and independently designed and installed, with differing amortization cycles. It is very difficult to integrate software into such heterogeneous combinations, not designed with a view to integration. So unless the user firm is prepared for massive write-offs, it has to wait until earlier investments have been properly amortized before it can redefine its production systems more closely in accordance with the state of the art.

vi) But here the *macro-economic conjoncture* makes itself all too clearly felt. The slowdown in the general growth of industrial firms slows down the amortization of earlier investment and also reduces their capability, and, to some extent, their motivation for proceeding with further investments. It is true that in this climate such firms are prompted to increase competitiveness by modernizing their production facilities, but few have the resources (notably financial) to tackle the process on a large enough scale to make full use of the synergy from new automation technologies.

2. Supply Trends

Automation software is produced both in-house and outside user firms. But unlike data processing software, the division depends very largely on the function and the kind of software concerned. Systems software, which is highly complex and costly, is almost entirely produced outside and amortized over longer or shorter runs, whereas applications and data-base software, being closely bound up with the specific products and industrial processes of the user, are very largely produced in-house. The division of labour does however seem to have been under pressure recently towards greater external production of applications software at the expense of in-house production.

a) In-House Production by User Firms

Applications software for programmable automated systems has until recent years been somewhat secondary and not particularly complex, except for such very special applications as in aerospace. This has meant that although user firms have themselves been producing almost all such software, they have not developed specialist units for the purpose. Applications software have been devised in a decentralised way, with the various design or methods offices and different factories and workshops undertaking to program their own stock of limited, comparatively unsophisticated, numerically controlled devices, programmable automation systems, test equipment and manipulators.

Recent trends in automation, i.e. more rapid diffusion, greater sophistication and the opportunities for integration, seem to be prompting several firms to reorganise their in-house production methods to an appreciable extent. At first sight, reorganisation is taking place in two directions.

In the first place, advances in integrated CAD/CAM, making it possible to generate manufacturing programs automatically from drawings, eliminate the necessity for several programming tasks. At the same time, this tendency has a powerful influence towards centralisation and homogeneity in software within firms concerned.

The next development is that the large industrial firms are starting to build up specialist automation centres. The purpose of these units is to remedy the organisational shortcomings described above. They start by taking the form of research, assessment, coordination and training units, but also play a part in solving particular engineering and software problems. (Known examples of this type of the organisation are the General Motors Technical Center, Toyota's Joint Research Institute in Robotics, Renault's recently established Direction des Systèmes et Automatismes, the General Electric Manufacturing Engineering Consulting Center, the Westinghouse Industry Automation Division, the Hitachi Robotics Software Centre, the St Gobain Robotics and CAD Centre.)

These units may gradually expand, accomodating high degrees of skill, and begin to offer services and solutions to outside users (as the engineering departments of large industrial firms traditionally have). In fact, this trend is already emerging with the appearance of external departments such as General Electric Computer Aided Engineering-International, Westinghouse Industrial Automation, PSA-Automatique Industrielle etc.

119

The development of in-house capabilities for automation software, especially in the present context of technological change and uncertainties, may be difficult for small and medium sized enterprises beginning to enter this field and even for larger firms. Such users turn to the external suppliers which specialise in design, engineering and software for automation systems.

The external supply of automation software has three constituents; equipment manufacturers, specialist firms and research laboratories.

b) External Supply by Equipment Manufacturers

To extend the scope and thereby increase the competitiveness of their hardware, programmable automation system manufacturers are offering increasing amounts of systems software. This consists of CAD software for CAD systems (of which software is the main component), programming languages for numerically controlled machine tools and robots, monitoring software and languages for turnkey flexible systems. Computer manufacturers also offer those portions of the software which can run on their hardware, i.e. CAD and production management software. Advertising trends in the specialist press suggest that systems software efficiency is becoming a main selling point for increasing numbers of hardware vendors (the importance attached to the programming possibilities for GE's most recent numerical control system – Mark Century 2000 –, Fanuc's System 7, Yamazaki's Mazatrol, Num's Num 760, to the VAL language for Unimation robots, the AML language for IBM robots, the "teaching box" for Hitachi robots etc.).

But the increasing importance of systems software has not so far prompted hardware manufacturers to sell such software separately (in the way software for ordinary computers could be "unbundled"). Vendors still regard this software as back-up for hardware and not as a distinct trade activity. Yet it is not the technical constraint which accounts for this, since some firms are already succeeding in offering automation software independently of hardware manufacturers. It should be noted, however, that the development of firmware may reinforce the practice of selling hardware and software together in the future.

Manufacturers are also offering custom engineering services, which imply the design and writing of applications and data base software for customers. This activity is conspicuous in the field of robotics, (where it adds considerably to marketing costs) and can be expected to gradually become a separate business activity for the manufacturers (as it is already for Cincinatti-Milacron with its Automated Systems Group).

For all hardware manufacturers, their position with respect to software has now become of major importance. The tendency to build up integrated automation systems extends the stakes, since those manufacturers who are capable of offering hardware and software that are compatible and can be integrated within systems will have an almost absolute competitive advantage over those whose products do not have those features. The problem of establishing reference "software infrastructures" becomes highly important here. The "big" manufacturers are trying to impose their systems as *de facto* standards (GE with Calmanet, Computervision with Solidesign) while specialist manufacturers are trying to achieve *organised and concerted* standardization through standards agencies, ad hoc groups (such as CAM-1) and national projects (such as FMS and ICAM).

c) External Supply by Service Firms

Two types of firm specialising in automation software have to be distinguished: those specialising in systems software, and those specialising in applications software.

The first are usually small firms with very high levels of technological skill. They work on a limited number of software products, sufficiently successful to ensure their competitiveness against the big hardware manufacturers. They offer software direct, or on a turnkey basis for hardware that they purchase as OEM. Most of these firms were formed in the early 1980s, and possess very rare skills, so there are at present rather few in Member countries. They inevitably look for a large national if not international market. (Examples are Manufacturing Data Systems Inc. recently acquired by Schlumberger, Structural Dynamics Research Corp. recently acquired by GE, also Automatix Inc. in the United States; CECN-Industries and Itmi in France, Dynax in Japan.)

The second type of firm targets end application markets. These firms provide consultancy, design and engineering services, which may involve devising custom software for specific applications. Most are growing by supplying the requirements of SMEs for outside skills, so for the moment there are not very many firms of this second type in Member countries. Since they provide services on a custom basis, many also have a restricted geographical purview. There are however firms looking to vertical or top-of-the-range applications markets and these inevitably look to national and international markets (Sciaky in robot welding engineering, Automatique Industrielle for large automation projects in France for example). The presence and the development of the service companies will certainly play an important role in spreading programmable automation systems during the 1980s, especially for the SMEs and in sophisticated industrial applications.

d) External Supply by Research Laboratories

A special feature of the automation software market is the important place occupied by public and private (non-profit) research laboratories. This is due in the first place to the fact that this field is precarious both scientifically and technologically, and secondly that there are at present no predominant industrial poles, so that research laboratories play a leading role here as they do not in micro-electronics nor computers. As a result, research by these laboratories is extensively used by software suppliers (both manufacturers and independent)

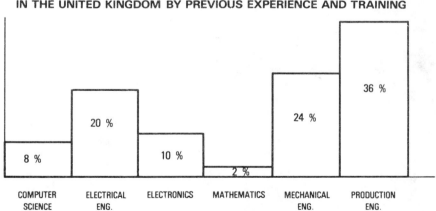

Figure 30 **DISTRIBUTION OF ROBOTICS SPECIALISTS IN THE UNITED KINGDOM BY PREVIOUS EXPERIENCE AND TRAINING**

Source: Granfield Institute of Technology, 1982

and even directly by final users. The Universities of Wisconsin, Standford, Purdue, Rhode Island, Carnegie-Mellon, Florida, MIT, Stanford Research Institute, Charles Draper Laboratories and the Defense Department laboratories in the United States; the Universities of Tokyo, Hokkaido, Kobe, Yamanachi, Nagoya, Waseda, the Tokyo Institute of Technology, and the MITI laboratories in Japan; the Frauenhofer Institutes in Germany; the Universities of Grenoble, Toulouse, Bordeaux and the laboratories of the Centre National de la Recherche Scientifique and of ADEPA in France; the universities of Oxford, Hull, Warwick and Manchester in the United Kingdom; the Milan Polytechnic in Italy; the Swedish Institute of Research and Production Engineering supply software and systems under a variety of arrangements.

One major constraint on the software supply side as a whole, affecting both production in-house and production by the hardware manufacturers, software houses and research laboratories is the scarcity of skilled specialists, aggravated by the pace of change in the state of the art and the increasingly multi-disciplinary character of the qualifications required[17] (Figure 30).

Part II

ROLE AND ACTION OF GOVERNMENTS

INTRODUCTION

The review of technological and industrial trends in software for the three major applications areas of information technology brings out three aspects of the so-called "software bottleneck":

i) The fact that the science and technology of software are still in a formative stage, relative to the spectacular advances in hardware technologies;

ii) The markets for factors embodying this technology (human resources, software engineering tools, etc.) are also in a formative stage and characterised by imperfect information;

iii) Prevailing patterns in the use of software consists on many sites of technological experimentation, which means that not enough account is being taken of economic criteria, the irreversibility of investment, and medium-term forecasting of technology and needs.

At the same time, this review shows how vigorously the software industry is now growing, reflected in the proliferation of specialist firms, the marketing of wholly new products and services, and a visible tendency in user organisations and firms to reorganise their software services. Thus, in spite of macro-economic difficulties in most Member countries, information technology expenditures have continued to grow throughout the OECD area, and software services stand out as one of the industries growing most vigorously and steadily at present.

This industrial dynamism encourages optimism that the software bottleneck will be overcome. It promises a broader, more economic and better balanced exploitation of information technologies. The maturing of software as an industry is becoming apparent, as research activities are diversified and pursued in greater depth, markets grow up for products and factors embodying technology, information channels open up and appropriate methods of economic organisation emerge.

This process is not dictated solely by decentralised market mechanisms. Scientific advances, large-scale training of skilled human resources, standardization of products and interfaces, the development of legal frameworks, and of a culture of economic practices rely upon mechanisms for coordination, funding and organisation at the social level, which are not provided by the market alone. This requires a vast process of social organisation and production of public goods[18], in which governments play an important role.

Most of this role is not explicit; it is the outcome of independent activities on the part of a variety of public sector institutions, spontaneously discharging their responsibilities in their own fields and exerting various kinds of influence on technological and industrial trends in software. In combination, these activities structure the presence and role of governments in the software field.

Chapter IV

RESEARCH POLICIES

Software is nowadays being based on a scientific discipline of its own, distinct both from research into electronic or computer hardware and from pure mathematical research, and is referred to as computer science or information science. As in any scientific field, the organisation, orientation and funding of basic research in software falls mainly within the competence of governmental/quasi-governmental agencies.

A.   ORGANISATION OF SOFTWARE RESEARCH

Furthermore, unlike most other technologies, software research is distinctive in the conspicuous "public good"[18] character of its advances. This is because the subject matter (abstract algorithmic information systems) of scienctific achievements in software can be circulated and used at extremely low cost, and is afforded practically no "legal" protection. This makes basic software research of relatively little interest for private investors (except when an immediate industrial application can be envisaged for a research project, when the fundamental research becomes practically indistinguishable from the development activity). This accordingly widens the responsibility of government for the organisation, funding and orientation of software research.

In OECD countries today, software research can take four principal forms:

- *University research* in the traditional university setting, mainly within computer science departments. Funding and management are decentralised. This is the predominant research pattern in most Member countries.

- *Specialist laboratories* are also important, representing a main component of software research in some Member countries: Rand Corporation and Information Sciences Institute in the United States, National Physical Laboratory and Royal Signals and Radar Establishment in the United Kingdom, Centre for Electronic Calculation in Spain, Institut National de la Recherche en Informatique et Automatisme (INRIA) in France, Gessellschaft für Mathematik und Datenverarbeitung (GMD) in Germany, the Institute for Computer Technology (ICOT) in Japan, and the Software Research Centre in Ireland[19]. Many of these centres have independent status and can undertake large-scale research programmes.

– *Software Research for National Defence:*   The special importance of information technology in national defence systems has warranted a build-up of substantial software research capacities under defence auspices in many Member countries. In certain countries, a substantial proportion of those capacities is in universities and specialist laboratories working on defence research contracts. Particularly in the United States, and under the guidance of various agencies defence-oriented software research has originated many advances in the field.

The COBOL programming language was developed under such guidance and standardized by the Navy in the 1950s. Most of the initial software engineering research was sponsored by the Air Force and NASA in the 1960s. The Ada language and support environment (see above) were developed in the late 1970s and early 1980s as a project of the Office of the Under-Secretary of Defense for Research and Engineering. The Defense Advanced Research Projects Agency (DARPA) has been a major contributor to computer research, most notably in timesharing (MIT's MAC project which led to the MULTICS system – one of the key researchers of this project having developed the Unix system in AT&T's Bell Labs; the University of California, Berkeley's Unix 4.2 project; the University of California, Los Angeles' Locus project; Carnegie-Mellon University's Hydra project); in networking (ARPANET, CHAOSNET, ETHERNET, SATNET); in distributed computing, parallel processing and special purpose architectures (Lisp machines, Dataflow machines, Sun workstations); and primarily in artificial intelligence. DARPA built, or strongly influenced, the Artificial Intelligence Centers of Excellence at MIT, Carnegie-Mellon, Stanford Research Institute, Information Sciences Institute, Rand Corporation, Yale and Fairchild; and recently undertook a $500 million programme in Strategic Computing designed to transfer artificial intelligence and machine architecture technology to military users through joint industrial/academic consortia.

In parallel, in response to technical difficulties in the software of its existing defence systems, as well as the exponential growth of their software expenditures – estimated at $5.6 billion in 1982 and expected to exceed $30 billion by 1990 – the Department of Defense has undertaken a "Software Initiative", which entails another large scale research programme. Spread over the period 1984 through 1990, with a provisional budget of approximately $230 million, this programme aims to develop a set of tools, techniques and new professional skills to be known as STARS (Software Technology for Adaptable Reliable Systems), which is expected to multiply by several factors the productivity and reliability of the software production process within the "DoD community". The STARS programme has won initial funding from Congress and the DoD has selected Carnegie-Mellon University as the contractor for a $105 million software engineering institute to be established as a centre for research and advanced development in software engineering techniques for defence applications.

– *Leading Hardware Manufacturers' Research Centres:*   A few of the leading hardware manufacturers also maintain fundamental research capabilities in the information sciences. Xerox's Palo Alto Research Laboratory, IBM's Yorktown Heights, San Jose and Zurich (Switzerland) laboratories, AT&T's Murray Hill Laboratories, Digital Equipment's Scientific Research Center in Palo Alto and Western Research Laboratory in Los Altos, Tektronix's Applied Research Center in Beaverton, Hewlett-Packard's Computing Research Laboratory in Santa Clara

MAJOR CIVILIAN SOFTWARE RESEARCH PROGRAMMES IN OECD COUNTRIES

* The European Strategic Programme for Research and Development in Information Technologies (ESPRIT), which is a programme for precompetitive co-operative industrial R & D in the European Community, has established software technology as one out of five areas of priority for the Community from 1984 to 1989. Projects in software technology will concentrate on the scientific understanding, engineering practices, methods, tools and management techniques needed for the development, production and maintenance of information technology systems. Projects under the programme will, in general, be financed at a level of 50 per cent from the Community budget.

* The Alvey Project is a combination of joint public/private research programmes on information technology in domains considered most strategic for the United Kingdom. The software engineering programme is considered the most vital part. With a budget of £65 million for 1983 to 1988, of which £38.3 million are to be publicly-funded, the aim is to develop a very high-level, "language-independent" software development environment, IPSE (Integrated Project Support Environment).

* In France, the national software engineering project is one of six priority research projects launched as part of the Plan d'Action Filière Electronique (PAFE). The aim is to develop a universal software engineering system called EPICEA (Environnement de Programmation Industriel pour la Conception et l'Étude des Applications), by co-operation on the part of the main French companies active in this field. The public support to this project amounted to FF 30 millions in the fiscal year 1984 and the same amount is budgeted for 1985.

* In Germany, the Federal Government has charged the Federal Ministry for Research and Technology with the priority of promoting computer-assisted design methods for computer hardware and software which, through future oriented joint projects, is intended to produce modern design methods for the second half of the 1980s. The Federal Government plans to provide funds amounting to DM 160 million for the period 1984 to 1988.

* The Japanese Sigma project aims to develop a set of advanced software engineering tools for promoting a high level of automation in software production in Japan by 1990. The project will be carried out by the co-operation of IPA (Information Technology Promotion Agency) and private research laboratories and it includes measures to support the effective use of the tools developed. Necessary amendment to the IPA Law was submitted to the Diet early 1985. The 1985 budget for the project is 3 billion yens ($12 million), and total amount of 30 billion yens ($120 millions) is envisaged by 1990.

Note: Concerning the software projects of the Department of Defense in the United States, and the fifth generation computer project of MITI in Japan, see above pages 126 and 28.

occupy a commanding position in the scientific community, contributing at least as much to the advance of the science as to their own firm's development activities. It is precisely because of the very low commercial return on its research centre that Burroughs Corporation is now thought to be contemplating pruning it back. Another response to the difference between costs and direct commercial benefits of fundamental research has been to set up co-operative, "pre-competitive" research centres. Examples are the Micro-electronics and Computer Technology Corporation in the United States, the Joint System Development Corporation in Japan, and the JCR (artificial intelligence research centre associated with the Esprit programme) in Europe. In some instances governments are also directly or indirectly helping to fund private laboratories.

There are currently three major issues in the organisation of software research in Member countries.

B.   RESOURCE PROBLEM

The main aspect of this problem is a shortage of human resources available for research. This applies especially to young researchers at the PhD level, fewer and fewer of whom are going into university careers, as most prefer positions in industry. An NSF survey in the United States has shown that these young professionals are more motivated by the interest and working environment they are offered (type of project, facilities available, etc.) than by their renumeration. These priorities (observed in other Member countries too) which used to encourage the bright students to seek university careers are now beginning to work against the universities.

Financial resources are a relatively secondary problem for researchers and research managers in this area. They are nevertheless aware of the discrepancy between the perceived prestige of computer science departments in the universities and the resources actually allocated to them in comparison with older, more influential departments. This is starting to pose problems, since computer science research now tends to require increasingly sophisticated, specialist and expensive hardware and software.

C.   DIFFICULTIES IN CO-ORDINATION BETWEEN RESEARCH CENTRES

In most countries, computer science research is not the subject of any co-ordinated science policy orientation. In fact, this is often not regarded as a problem, diversity of aims and objectives among individual scientists or teams being regarded as an important element for scientific fertility. On the other hand, certain research managers feel that too much dispersal in research potential might be disadvantageous in hindering the formation of the "critical mass" of research necessary to generate scientific advances. Many are also aware of the value of interdisciplinary research in this field, especially involving the science of organisations in application-oriented research projects. Accordingly, a number of co-ordinated research programmes have been instituted:

i) In specialist laboratories, such as the Kayak (office automation) and the Sol (operating systems) projects of INRIA in France;

ii) In ad hoc laboratories, such as the Institute for Computer Technology in Japan as part of the Fifth Generation project, the JCR Laboratory in Munich, and the Software Engineering Institute established as part of the United States Defense Department's software initiative;

iii) In various research centres co-operating horizontally, such as in the Esprit Software Technology Sub-Programme in the European Community; the teleinformatics project COST-11 bis of the Community within the COST framework; the Alvey programme software project in the United Kingdom; the national software engineering project in France; the computer-assisted design methods for computer hardware and software project in Germany; the finalised computer project in Italy[20]; the action programme on microelectronics technologies in Belgium[21], the Finland Centre for the Development of Technology's co-operative IT programme; the Swedish Board for Technical Development's research programme in information processing and computer science; and the planned SIGMA (software development tools) project in Japan, etc. (See box: Major civilian software research programmes in OECD countries.)

One problem with this kind of major research projects, co-ordinated and supported by government, is to avoid administrative red-tape. There have been several instances, especially in Europe, of science projects with administrative costs swallowing as much as half their resources. In several countries, science policy authorities are now seeking ways of slimming down the feasibility and monitoring procedures for projects they are funding, without going to the opposite extreme of losing all control over them.

D. TECHNOLOGY TRANSFERS FROM RESEARCH TO INDUSTRY

This classic science policy problem takes a special form in the software field. As regards research, the inertia typical of software environments and systems (see Part I) impedes any rapid industrial application of software research findings. According to one estimate, up to ten years can elapse between the first publication of software research in the literature and its first commercial application. On the development side, conversely, it is often the scientists who cannot meet industry's requirements. This is due to the fact that since many software development programmes are relatively unstructured and highly labour-intensive, the ordinary university consultation machinery proves inefficient here and raises a need for closer participation by research teams in applied industrial projects.

Different countries and different research systems react in different ways to this constraint. In some countries, the view is that too close an involvement of research centres in industry would interfere with their research mission, and is avoided. Elsewhere, the trend is welcomed and supported by institutional arrangements, with some countries going so far as to authorise their researchers to combine their scientific and university status with responsibilities in private enterprises. It can be inferred that these international differences in the procedures for research/industry transfer might in come cases encourage the tendency for scientists to emigrate.

One point to notice here is that the computer science community is highly internationalised. University exchanges are frequent and the international "learned societies", especially the various committees of the International Federation for Information Processing (IFIP) operate remarkably well. It is to be hoped that this internationalisation will become even more pronounced in the future, permitting decentralised pursuit of high-level research in the various Member countries, counteracting any trend towards undue international polarisation in research potential.

In this respect, the development of telecommunications systems for research centres as special data transmission networks and teleconferencing should contribute to better communications among research centres and between them and industry in the future. Several such networks are already in use in OECD countries. Besides ARPANET – which is the biggest network – in the United States and its connection to JANET in the United Kingdom; CSNET (United States) now reaches Canada, Sweden and Israel; BITNET (United States) is connected to EARN (Europe); and the informal Unix-based USENET is worldwide and available to anyone with access to a machine running Unix. In the United States, the National Science Foundation has embarked on a major project with the Office of Advanced Scientific Computing to develop a network for all scientists (SCIENCENET).

For some countries, however, an emerging source of concern is in the growth of "transfrontier" technology transfers from research to industry (the profitable use of research in one country by industry in one or more other countries). In these instances, the return of the "exporting country's" investment in research seems unduly low, undermining the justification for public funding and raising the issue of "protecting" it. Any movement in that direction would obviously be seriously damaging to international scientific co-operation.

Chapter V

TRAINING POLICIES

A. THE GAP BETWEEN THE SUPPLY OF AND THE DEMAND FOR SOFTWARE SPECIALISTS

The gap between the present stock and the effective need for skilled human resources in information technology is perceived in most Member countries as the main policy problem in this field. In view of the present trends in these technologies, this gap mainly, and increasingly, concerns the various types of software specialists. This point, among others, emerges from an American Electronics Association study (Figure 31) attempting a quantitative measurement of the gap for the United States during the 1980s, which found that the most serious skills shortfall would be for software engineers. According to another American estimate, the shortfall is between 50 000 and 100 000 "software professionals" at present, rising to between 850 000 and 1 million by 1990 failing vigorous action. In France, the Nivat Report, recently prepared for the Government, paints a similar picture, as does that of the Institute of Manpower Studies in the United Kingdom. In Finland, a shortfall of 20 000 in "university trained software professionals" has been forecast by 1995 for a total labour force of 2 million. In Japan, according to 1984 MITI estimates, the demand for software engineers will grow at a rate of 26 per cent per annum, while the growth rate of supply will by 17 per cent per annum, the resulting lack of software engineers amounting to 600 000 in 1990, failing a vigorous automation of software production.

Software professionals are trained at three levels: "technicians", "software engineers", and "in-service trained specialists". A *technician,* mainly covering micro-electronic technicians, analyst programmers and application programmers, qualifies with an average of one or two years training after the baccalauréat or equivalent. Training is provided in public and private sector institutions and comprises a wide range of professional qualifications, varying in level and quality, with very little standardization. *Software engineer* is a more precise qualification, because it is awarded upon graduation from a university computer science department. However, many other kinds of engineer are laying claim to the qualification on grounds of experience in the profession. More recently, some countries have established schools that are independent of the computer science faculties and specialise exclusively in software engineering (CERICS in France, the Swiss Software School. *In-service training* is the third type, and most of this is provided by specialist service firms or by the employer firm. This covers a wide range of types and quality of training, and plays a particularly important role in the industry. In France, for example, computer service companies allocate an average of 6 per cent of their total wage bill to in-service training for

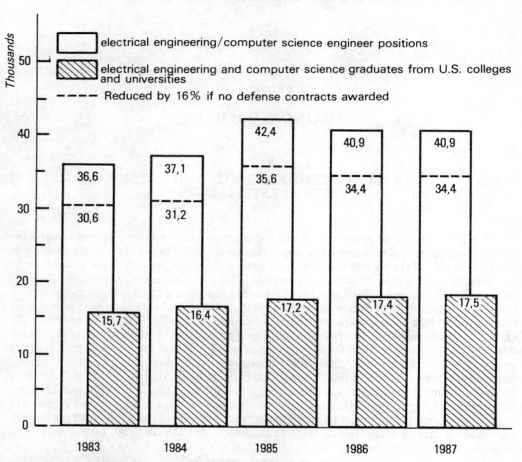

Figure 31 **ENGINEER SUPPLY AND DEMAND IN THE UNITED STATES**

electrical engineering/computer science engineer positions

electrical engineering and computer science graduates from U.S. colleges and universities

– – – – Reduced by 16% if no defense contracts awarded

Source: The American Electronics Association, 1983

staff. Here Japan stands out as the country with the most elaborate in-service training systems, most firmly established as part of a professional's career.

In most OECD countries, governments have announced that they are now preparing active policies to make good the shortfall in software specialists. Few now believe, as some did for a while, that the shortfall would be made good "naturally", with the automation of software design and the decentralised growth of private training services. Chief among those concerned are naturally the governments of those countries where education is entirely a public service. Countries with mixed systems are also concerned, needing to determine to what extent their present system is managing to adapt to the challenges of new technologies. In both cases, authorities are concerned with the following major questions.

132

B. RESOURCE PROBLEM

1. Training Personnel

On the human resources side, teaching personnel are very scarce at higher as well as secondary levels in all Member countries, in public sector and private sector education alike. This shortage is aggravated by various constraints which make it difficult to adjust their salaries to salaries on alternative labour markets.

Accordingly, different educational establishments are trying to devise special arrangements to palliate, at least in part, their instructor shortfall (engaging professionals part-time, retraining teaching staff from other disciplines, etc.). The Secretariat has no information about national teacher-training policies in this field, except for one Belgian experiment, in which a programme over several years has been designed to achieve a manifold increase in the stock of micro-electronics engineering instructors by immediately recruiting them as instructors in the very same system which trained them.

2. Equipment of Training Establishments

As regards material resources, the problem is how to finance the purchase and maintenance of computer equipment by teaching establishments. Falling hardware prices and the emergence of microcomputers have partly alleviated this, though it is still a formidable challenge since there is so much ground to make up.

Several manufacturers are allowing considerable discounts – even giving the equipment away – to educational establishments, who are not failing to take advantage of it, especially in the United States. But this may have the disadvantage of introducing commercial bias into the teaching decisions of establishments receiving free or discounted hardware, since manufacturers are mainly motivated by the prospects of training future customers to use their own equipment. Moreover, especially in the United States, the academic beneficiaries of corporate largesse in terms of equipment are now facing the major difficulty of maintaining, housing and staffing their facilities when there are few resources for such support. The same kind of problem arises in another form in other countries, as part of national school equipment policies, limiting the schools' procurement choices to nationally produced hardware from particular manufacturers.

In training, governments therefore face a variety of resource problems. Numerous studies and observations in many of the Member countries assess the present situation in fairly unfavourable terms and call for sweeping policy intervention.

C. DIFFICULTIES IN FORECASTING QUALITATIVE NEEDS

Another fundamental difficulty in training policy relates not to the quantitative gap between the supply of and demand for specialists, but to a *qualitative gap*. With the arrival of entirely new hardware generations, new software techniques, new programming languages, packaged software, etc., targets here can no longer be set only in quantitative terms (training so many analysts, so many programmers, etc.) but must be given specific qualitative references, up-to-date in relation to the state of the art. It has to be realised that there are no longer any standard environments such as FORTRAN/COBOL/IBM 360-370 or equivalents in the computer world to serve as a universal reference for training programmes. This means that those responsible in the public or private sectors for education policy must be able to reassess the manpower requirements of their economy, as well as the evolution of technology so that training institutions and programmes can be continuously adapted accordingly. But this is proving to be a difficult and expensive task. Several Member countries have set up government or quasi-government commissions to monitor developments and make recommendations on these issues. The Secretariat is not aware of any actual results from these initiatives.

One particular aspect of this question is the need for refresher training for working professionals, who need to update their knowledge and methods as the technology evolves. In almost all Member countries this has so far been attempted by employer firms or organisations' in-house efforts, hardware and software suppliers' back-up courses, and the services of training firms. But some recent observations note various shortcomings in these efforts as generally implemented, and urge a more methodical and careful approach to refresher training activities.

D. SOME CONSEQUENCES OF THE DECENTRALISATION OF TRAINING POLICIES

Since so many challenges are involved, governments may be tempted to adopt or maintain completely decentralised training policies, in which public sector and independent training bodies make their own decisions – working within their own economic environment – about training programmes and courses, endeavouring to solve their resource problems by their own initiatives. This approach does have advantages, especially in allowing the necessary institutional flexibility against a background of staff shortages and technological uncertainties. But it raises two issues deserving attention.

1. Certification of Qualifications

The first is the problem of objectively evaluating qualifications on the labour market. With no co-ordination among training institutions, certificates and diplomas attesting qualification in this field are liable to proliferate, while employers cannot tell what they actually represent. Furthermore, programmer/analysts may come to these occupations from extremely diverse non-formal educational backgrounds. This can cause confusion in labour markets, in remuneration and career systems within employer firms and organisations. In fact, this already seems to have happened in certain Member countries, where information technology qualifications are particularly heterogeneous.

In certain countries, where training activitites are mainly a public responsibility, governments have laid down common qualification standards conferred by competent training agencies (the "assistant engineer for data processing", "mathematical-technical assistant", "economic assistant for information science", "technical assistant for information science" and "certified information engineer" in Germany; the "EDP-assistant", "datanom" and "datalogists" in Denmark; the "datanomists" and "systems analysts" in Finland, the "computer experts" and "accountant programmers" in Italy; the "program analysts" and "computer analysts" in Switzerland). In some countries, training establishments take the responsibilty for exchanging information and a degree of co-ordination amongst themselves. Elsewhere again, governments endeavour to exert a degree of quality control over the activities of independent training enterprises. The United Kingdom Computer Services Association (CSA) has taken a fresh approach by introducing a professional code and standards for those of its members engaging (as training enterprises) in this field. Lastly, an approach prominent in Germany, in Japan, and to some extent in the United States, is to apply country-wide examination procedures for qualifications, regardless of what form the initial training may have taken, attested by national certificates – in Germany the Certificate for Economic Information Engineers; in Japan, the MITI's electronic technician and software engineering diplomas; in the United States the Certificates in Data Processing (CDP) awarded by the Institute for Certification of Computer Professionals, a private association.

It is also worth noting that at the international level, IFIP regularly publishes a "suggested computer science curriculum" for higher-level training establishments worldwide.

2.   Impact on National "Computer Culture"

The second issue associated with the decentralisation of training policies is more subtle, but could be very important, especially for the smaller country; the risk of unduly fragmenting the national "computer culture". If professionals trained in various training establishments acquire skills that are too restricted and incompatible (associated with the use of particular kinds of hardware, particular software methods or programming languages) the formation of a national labour market might be adversely affected. A set of parallel labour markets will form, disturbing the co-operation and circulation of professionals and the economies of learning. In this respect, training establishments should be encouraged to teach specific techniques principally as examples and not as exclusive skills, in order to facilitate the assimilation of different technical approaches by software professionals. There are already signs of "parallel computer communities" emerging in several countries, although the balance in terms of fertility through diversity as opposed to under-exploitation of economies of scale and learning remains unknown. This may be worth considering case by case for small countries. A recent Australian nationwide conference on training needs in the new technologies identified the absence of nationally recognised standards as a major problem in computer personnel recruitment and management in Australia.

Another important aspect of computer culture is familiarising the layman, increasingly using information technology at work and at home, with computer techniques and especially software. The most appropriate place and time for that will probably be primary education ("computer literacy") and secondary education. Yet few countries have so far introduced computer studies into their primary or secondary systems. At present, the United Kingdom has the best score, in managing to equip 97 per cent of its secondary schools with at least one microcomputer by February 1984. This was done in the framework of the Microcomputers in Schools scheme, launched in April 1981, where central government covers 50 per cent of the cost of microcomputers bought by local education authorities. Although more than 100 000 micros have been installed on this basis, the government estimates that there is still a long way to go as there is only about one computer per 140 pupils. France aims to have equipped its schools with 100 000 microcomputers by 1986 and to have trained 100 000 teachers in computing by then. The familiarisation of teachers and pupils with computing itself, and the use of computers as a teaching aid in other subjects are here seen as the two sides of the same coin. More recently French government reformulated this plan, announcing the opening of 11 000 "computer initiation workshops" in educational institutions all over the country. Each workshop should be equipped with at least seven microcomputers, the total cost of the plan amounting to FF 2 billion. Australia too is considering this kind of plan now, under which the Commonwealth Schools Commission would aim to offer every primary and secondary pupil a computer course. In Sweden, computer studies, including practical use of computers (hardware and software) and also the societal aspects of information technology, are offered in primary and secondary schools.

An important problem of "computers in schools" schemes in most Member countries is an alleged lack of appropriate high quality educational software and documentation (courseware) to get the best benefit from the stock of hardware being installed[22].

The countries succeeding in introducing information technology into the schools most efficiently and most quickly will be the first to reap the benefit of talent and ambition throughout their society, to prepare tommorrow's working population to think in terms of the opportunities offered by information technology in all occupational fields and to ward off any possibility of future social "suspicion" of the new technology. However, literacy and familiarising the young with computers can be no substitute for education in computer science as a specialist professional discipline, since the two types of training have very distinct technical, economic and social goals.

E. THE INFORMATION QUESTION

One aspect of training policies relates to the collection and dissemination of information within the scientific and industrial circles concerned. This is because the diversity of scientific work, the rapidity of technological progress and the large number of enterprises active in the field make it very difficult to keep abreast of scientific, technical and market-place developments in software, especially at international level. Different governments are approaching the problem differently. Some limit their involvement to collecting and distributing only the information required for public sector computer departments, leaving the specialist private sector to perform the same function on a decentralised, commercial basis (trade press, bibliographical documentation services, technical and marketing information services, briefing seminars, etc., particularly developed in the United States). Other governments, considering that the private provision of information has not grown enough, or in some cases is not accessible to all those concerned, are themselves providing specialist documentation services, launching campaigns to heighten awareness of scientific and technological progress, publishing bulletins and yearbooks on scientific, technological and even marketing information. This kind of activity appears to have been taken furthest by Japan's Information Technology Promotion Agency (IPA). The information service of the US Air Force, "Data Analysis Center for Software", accessible to academia and industry, is also considered an important information source in the United States, even though private information services are well developed. Several governments (Australia, Spain, Finland, Greece, Ireland, the United Kingdom, Turkey) are currently reappraising policies and scope for action on this matter.

Another way of organising the dissemination of information is through professional and learned societies, non-commercial but also non-governmental. Many of these have, either as their main function or as a secondary function the promotion of systematic, regular exchanges of information among members about scientific, technical and marketing innovations. Several OECD countries have many such societies that are especially active in information technology areas.

F. THE "BRAIN DRAIN" QUESTION

This overview of training policy issues cannot be concluded without mentioning a problem of particular importance to certain Member countries, the emigration of their scarce human resources. If, as some tentative indications suggest, there is any substantial international movement of specialists in this field, systematically favourable to certain countries and unfavourable to others, a difficult policy problem faces the "exporting" countries: How should they try to remedy the "loss" of national investment in training, often realised at the price of scarce public resources with high opportunity costs?

Chapter VI

GOVERNMENT SOFTWARE PROCUREMENT

In most Member countries, government organisations are intensive users of information technology and therefore of software, frequently acting as pioneers in their countries in this field during the 1950s and 1960s. In particular, the defence forces have played an essential role in advancing the state of the art and in the practical implementation of its earliest applications.

The present context of the software bottleneck and technological innovations affects governments in two ways: first, as users obliged to optimise their large software expenditures and to rationalise their numerous and complex computer systems; secondly, as the largest customers on national data processing markets and thereby playing key roles in economic and technological trends in the national software field. The externalisation of government requirements is actually of decisive importance for the computer service industry. United States government organisations, for example, have not been contracting out much of their software requirement (48 per cent of the total DP budget of Federal Agencies in 1982 was allocated to personnel expenditures, as against 3 per cent for buying software from outside), yet they account for 25 per cent of total CSI sales[23]. The proportion has been estimated at 12 per cent for France and according to an enquiry by the professional association (SYNTEC), the French software houses consider that the most striking development in their market between 1970 and 1985 is the rise in the number of government contracts.

The influence of the public sector on the market in fact extends to the data processing activities of nationalised undertakings, whose position varies from one Member country to another. Account should also be taken, in several countries, of major software houses in the public sector.

All of these facts bring forward the question of what software policy user government organisations are applying in the various countries? To what extent do they externalise their requirements? How do they deal with the risk of using most of their personnel and budgetary resources for maintenance of their existing – often outdated – software, as against the development of new applications for new needs (especially if and when existing budgetary procedures introduce a bias towards maintenance expenditures as against new software investment)? How to they choose among the many current technological options? Which standards to they adopt in various fields? In short, are they fully benefiting from the emerging technological trends and can they envisage again acting as pioneers as they did during the first breakthrough in computing?

To determine policy on these urgent questions, governments in several Member countries have established review and co-ordinating bodies. Insofar as the latter have functioned effectively, they seem so far to have been concerned mainly with hardware. Yet it is especially in software that they could and should exert their influence.

The Secretariat has not been able to establish a comprehensive table of management methods for public procurement in software for the OECD area as a whole. Known cases, especially through questionnaire answers, seem to reflect a general trend towards better government organisation here.

The *United States,* being a Federal State, has no unified government procurement system. A number of agencies and arrangements have been introduced to promote better transparency and rationalisation of federal government procurement.

The General Services Administration (GSA) makes recommendations on procurement methods for federal departments in regard to computers. The GSA has become especially active more recently, in view of the growth prospects for federal investment in computing over the 1980s (see Figures 32 and 33 and Table 36). In particular, the GSA developed a procurement system for micro-computer hardware, software and maintenance services in 1983, which is thought to have brought a good deal of centralisation into procurement policy. Some observers expect the new system to have a considerable influence on the US computer hardware and software industry over the 1980s.

Another factor thought to influence the procurement trend has been a recent special Office of Management and Budget circular on federal procurement policies generally. This circular emphasises traditional US policy that government should never duplicate services already available in the private sector. On the software side this would mean that most government needs should be subcontracted to private sector firms.

Figure 32 **FEDERAL INFORMATION RESOURCES SPENDING, 1982.**

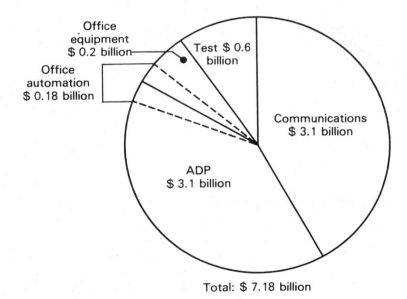

Total: $ 7.18 billion

Source: International Data Corporation.

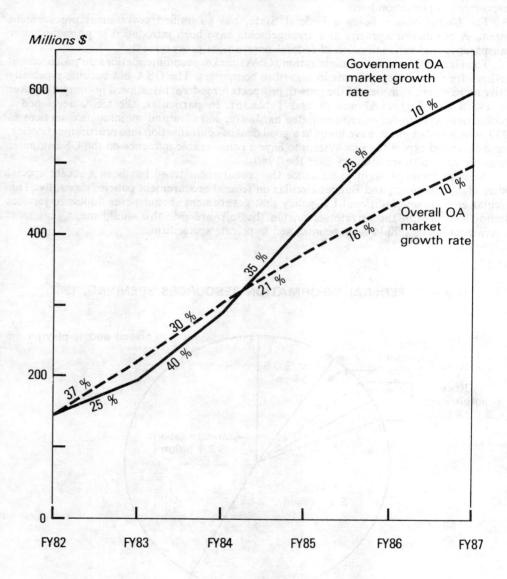

Figure 33 **PREDICTED GROWTH IN FEDERAL OFFICE AUTOMATION SPENDING**

Millions $

600

400

200

0

FY82   FY83   FY84   FY85   FY86   FY87

Government OA market growth rate

10 %

25 %

35 %

40 %

30 %

25 %

37 %

Overall OA market growth rate

10 %

16 %

21 %

Source: International Data Corporation.

140

Table 36. **US government's major data processing contracts**

Federal Agency	Project	Cost $ million
Federal Aviation Administration	Air traffic control and navigation system	9 000
Postal Service	Post office retail sales of stamps, money orders, etc.	500 to 3 000
Postal Service	Payroll record-keeping for postal employees, including a nationwide time clock	1 000
Social Security Administration	Claims processing and other administrative charges	600 to 1 000
Army	Worldwide logistics and planning	415 to 1 000
Patent Office	Storage of text and drawing for patent examinations	325 to 750
Air Force	Administrative and logistic record-keeping	310
Defense Mapping	Map and chart making	240
Justice	Support for investigations (e.g. tracking bogus checks) and administrative chores	150 to 215
Air Force	Intelligence storage and distribution	156

Source: Fortune, 1983.

At the same time, Defense Department procurement has played and is playing an important role in the software sector in the United States, especially as regards those areas and firms on the frontier of the state of the art. The US Army Computer Systems Selection and Acquisition Agency administers procurement in this area for the Defense Department.

In *Japan,* the Government (including local government) and public bodies are considered to be well advanced in the use of information technology. They accounted for more than 10 per cent (in value) of the country's computer stock in 1982 and more significantly, it is they who have Japan's largest computer systems (see Table 37).

Government hardware and software are procured through an "information intensive" consultative system structured around the Administrative Management Agency (AMA), described in Figure 34. But a decision regarded as being particularly important may be taken at Cabinet level, by a Deputy Minister, or by the Council of Directors in charge of Automatic Data Processing. In recent times, the kind of decisions regarded as "important" have been related to:

  i) Government computer procurement rules (requests for proposals);
  ii) "Unbundling" of hardware and software in public procurement (1978);
  iii) Non-discriminatory treatment for foreign manufacturers (1978);
  iv) Publication of Guidelines on EDP Security (computer security code) (1976).

In *France* too, government procurement accounts for a substantial share of the data processing market, both for hardware and software. Government spending on computer equipment amounted to FF 11 million in 1982 (excluding local authorities, the Prefecture of

Table 37. **Japan: general purpose computer utilisation by industry**

As end of June, 1982

	Number of systems	Value (million yen)	Average value per system
Agriculture	100	2 323	23.2
Forestry and hunting	36	370	10.3
Fisheries, etc.	181	3 794	21.0
Mining	151	4 536	30.0
Construction	2 416	61 335	25.4
Foodstuffs	3 590	82 529	23.0
Textiles and textile products	2 205	49 039	22.2
Pulp, paper and paper products	861	17 715	20.6
Publishing and printing	994	41 644	41.9
Chemicals and petroleum refining	3 815	178 459	46.8
Ceramics	903	30 258	33.5
Iron and steel	1 081	132 967	123.0
Non-ferrous metals	1 843	59 752	32.4
Machinery	2 207	86 485	39.2
Electric machinery	4 730	536 842	113.5
Transportation machinery	1 774	201 374	113.5
Precision machinery	919	47 227	51.4
Other manufacturing	3 762	76 737	20.4
Wholesale, retail and trading firms	47 786	728 708	15.2
Finance	6 404	718 159	112.1
Securities	305	68 119	223.3
Insurance	661	151 825	229.7
Real estate	281	5 259	18.7
Transport, telecommunications and new services	3 460	128 359	37.1
Electricity and gas	464	72 086	155.4
Service industries	8 834	406 050	46.0
(Ordinary)	4 779	117 607	24.6
(Data processing)	4 055	288 443	71.1
Hospitals	797	25 177	31.6
Universities	1 168	142 397	121.9
Upper secondary schools	499	10 074	20.2
Other educational institutions	325	10 780	33.2
Municipal bodies	1 607	110 552	68.8
National government	775	147 541	190.4
Government-related organisations	1 120	361 717	323.0
Corporate bodies and farm co-ops	4 185	130 857	31.3
Religious organisations	39	1 130	29.0
Others	110	5 188	47.2
Total	110 388	4 837 364	43.8

Source: MITI.

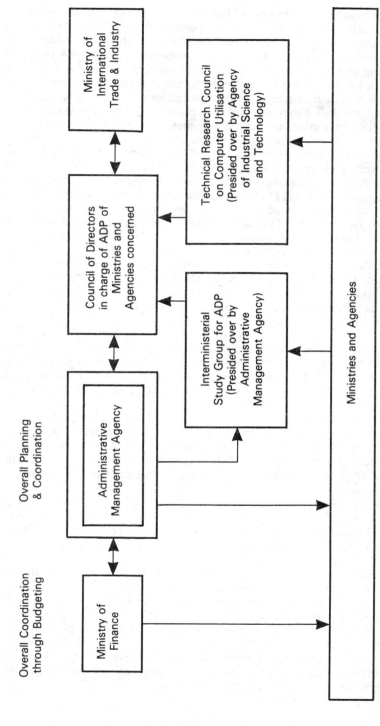

Figure 34 PROMOTION AND ORGANISATION OF INFORMATION
PROCESSING IN NATIONAL GOVERNMENT IN JAPAN

Overall Coordination
through Budgeting

Overall Planning
& Coordination

Ministry of
International
Trade & Industry

Council of Directors
in charge of ADP of
Ministries and
Agencies concerned

Technical Research Council
on Computer Utilisation
(Presided over by Agency
of Industrial Science
and Technology)

Administrative
Management Agency

Interministerial
Study Group for ADP
(Presided over by
Administrative
Management Agency)

Ministry of
Finance

Ministries and Agencies

Source: Administrative Management Agency, *The Status
of Computer Utilisation in the Japanese Government,* February 1979.

143

Police and defence). The "Mission à l'Informatique" attached to the Ministry for Industry was, until recently, responsible for promoting computer applications "within government and its related economy", via the "Computer Commissions" established within each department. Sweeping reforms to this system were however announced in May 1984, to be accompanied by a wide-ranging plan to computerise government agencies. Under the new arrangements, an Interministerial Committee for Government Procurement Policy, reporting to the Prime Minister, will have a mandate to ensure that government "remains in control of its own computer applications". The reform follows a recent combination of studies and consultations in France, which have concluded that government procurement has been used too much as industrial policy instrument, sometimes at the expense of the real needs and interests of the departments. The new plan for "government computerisation" accompanying the reform anticipates, among others, the development and adoption of a family of "all-purpose word processing work stations", compatible and to be usable and maintainable with a standard form of training across the board in government. The target is 1 million work stations and 6 million public sector employees trained to use them, over the next five years.

In *Germany,* each federal ministry is solely responsible for its procurement. Uniformity amongst federal authorities is, however, guaranteed by universal provisions stipulated in the contracting rules for the award of contracts (VOL/A) and in the budget law. In addition, software problems of general interest are dealt with by the Inter-Ministerial Co-ordination Committee for Data Processing (IMKA), which comprises members of all departments.

Furthermore, through its participation in procurement measures on the basis of budget provisions, the Office of Co-ordination and Consultation for Administrative Data Processing (Koordinierungs- und Beratungsstelle – KBSt) can act as the principal agency for the promotion of uniform procurement procedures. KBSt participation consists, above all, of issuing written statements on procurement measures as regards organisation and data-processing techniques. The KBSt also collects and disseminates information on software products and advises federal authorities as part of its market research and advisory role. Public authorities (Federal Government, Länder, local authorities) also co-operate in order to set up common techical standards.

In the *United Kingdom,* the Central Computer and Telecommunications Agency is in charge of government procurement policy. The Agency aims to "optimise departmental computer outlays while supporting the competitiveness of the British computer industry and services". Recent government policy is to contract out a greater proportion of government service and software requirements and to delegate greater responsibility for procurement to user departments.

In *Australia,* public procurement follows procedures adopted by the government in 1981, under the supervision of the purchasing division of the Department of Administrative Services and the Department of Industry and Commerce. Formal procedures for the assessment and procurement of hardware, software and computer services are laid down in the Guidelines for Automatic Data Processing Acquisition and the Guidelines for the Production of Automatic Data Processing Strategic Plans for use in all agencies that come under the Public Services Act. These arrangements are designed to clarify and optimise government computer strategies, and to benefit local industries at the same time. The Australian government has recently decided to reinforce the local industry side of its procurement policy by extending the application of the 20 per cent preference margin for Australian products to software and services. The local content of tender proposals will also, from now on, be reassessed in the light of research and development, engineering and design activities. Australian firms will also be briefed on future government procurement intentions far enough in advance not to put them at a disadvantage relative to their foreign competitors.

Belgium has recently taken its first steps in programming government software procurement. A special fund of BF 1 billion is now set aside every year under the public investment programme for selective government software procurement. The breakdown of government computer spending in Belgium in Table 38 shows the substantial share of software (manpower, services, packaged software).

In *Canada,* a Federal country, the Treasury Board lays down federal government procurement policy for computers and the Department of Supply and Services ensures co-ordination. Tables 39 and 40 give a detailed breakdown of expenditures by major government agency and types of expenditure for 1980-1984. They highlight the predominance of software expenditures, through expenditures on manpower and the limited, but rapidly growing proportion of purchased software.

In *Denmark,* the Department of Administration in the Ministry of Finance evaluates, co-ordinates and authorises government computer projects and outlays, with technical assistance from the state computer services enterprise "Datacentralen". Government

Table 38. **Belgium: 1981 government data processing expenditure**

Departments and quasi-government

	Million BF
Total government	9 696
of which: Departments	3 567
Quasi-government	6 129
The percentage breakdown is as follows:	
Hardware	45 %
Software (packages)	1 %
Services	12 %
Manpower	39 %
Other	3 %

Table 39. **Canada: EDP expenditures by departments/agencies**

Thousands Canadian dollars
Ranked by estimated use in 1981/1982

	1980/1981	1981/1982	1982/1983	1983/1984
National defence	44 874	62 747	67 425	64 068
Employment and immigration Commission	43 918	53 190	60 891	70 765
DSS - Services	43 987	53 026	61 262	66 341
Revenue - Taxation	36 838	49 034	51 665	56 613
Statistics Canada	35 890	45 168	43 636	44 498
Royal Canadian Mounted Police	28 815	33 592	38 499	47 007
Environment	25 140	31 963	35 608	39 352
Health and welfare	17 593	19 549	22 251	23 979
Energy, mines and resources	13 878	18 558	20 357	21 666
National Research Council	15 107	17 897	21 489	23 805
DSS supply	11 866	16 630	21 344	25 613
Revenue - Customs and excise	9 963	16 475	27 613	40 795
Transport	12 269	16 124	20 811	23 193
Fisheries and oceans	10 946	13 463	15 008	15 719
Public works	8 424	12 348	15 568	16 214
Agriculture	10 335	11 593	12 469	13 437
Communications	6 494	9 174	8 937	7 973

Table 40. **Canada: full EDP costs, 1978/1979 to 1983/1984**

Thousand dollars

	1978/1979	1979/1980	1980/1981	1981/1982	1982/1983	1983/1984
Direct EDP costs						
Salaries	135 574	146 575	160 528	197 383	223 524	242 275
Consultants	19 228	19 922	24 882	42 832	51 890	50 080
Equipment rent. actual	47 205	43 993	43 499	53 314	63 497	72 423
Equipment rent. imputed	16 696	21 577	23 935	33 582	38 240	41 115
Equipment maintenance	7 566	9 956	13 051	16 836	19 261	23 239
Data transmission	11 719	13 415	16 462	21 108	26 900	35 029
Service bureaux	33 683	32 375	35 897	44 723	51 141	56 798
Software acquisition	1 944	2 418	3 635	5 832	6 433	7 844
Production supplies	7 868	9 686	10 432	12 917	14 271	15 384
Total direct EDP costs	281 483	299 917	332 321	428 527	495 247	544 168
EDP support costs						
Employee benefits	20 021	21 488	23 651	28 737	33 226	36 164
Accommodation	13 443	16 196	16 418	18 773	19 402	20 243
Office supplies	1 715	1 837	1 246	1 342	1 545	1 404
Travel	2 327	2 311	2 953	4 048	5 328	5 902
Printing, stationery	1 187	1 211	1 691	1 939	2 142	2 295
Telephone, telegraph	1 645	1 773	1 856	2 163	2 387	2 618
Interest, imputed	6 433	8 174	10 443	13 097	14 866	16 404
Other expenses	2 778	2 330	3 057	4 179	4 770	5 452
Department costs	16 667	18 574	21 251	25 748	29 625	32 241
Government costs	2 244	2 479	2 645	3 328	3 744	4 172
Less: Language training	2 120	2 211	1 892	2 189	2 350	1 076
Total EDP support costs	66 340	74 162	83 319	101 165	114 685	125 819
Full EDP costs (net)	347 823	374 079	415 640	529 692	609 932	669 987
Interdepartmental services	15 112	17 415	19 956	27 630	25 741	27 835

spending (excluding local authorities) on software has been estimated at DKr 670 million annually in Denmark. It is also reported that 50 per cent of government computer spending (including local authorities this time) is on buying in computer services from two public sector service enterprises, Kommunedata (local authorities) and Datacentralen. The two firms are, moreover, the largest computer service enterprises in Denmark, with turnovers in 1982 of DKr 529 million and DKr 446 million respectively.

In *Spain* the new National Electronic and Computer Plan comprises a section on public sector procurement of computer goods and services. The plan gives joint responsibility to the General Directorate for Organisation, Procedures and Data Processing of the Presidency of the Government and to the General Directorate of Electronics and Data Processing of the Ministry of Industry and Energy for implementing the new government policy, co-operating with an Interministerial Commission for the Purchase of Data Processing Goods and Services. The main components of the new policy are defined as "greater transparency in the aims and procedures for each procurement project, better assessment of the local industrial impact of tender offers, gradual standardization of the goods and services used, the encouragement of prototype development contracts with participation and support from the Ministry of Industry and Energy, the decentralisation of procurement decisions without fragmenting the market, development of an installment payments system as projects progress, separate tendering for hardware and software so as to treat the latter independently, and better access for SMEs to government contracts".

In *Finland,* the Ministry of Finance defines public procurement policies for computer equipment with a view to "compatibility, efficiency and system decentralisation". There are also less formal co-ordinating arrangements at local authority level. However, these policies have up to now been limited to data-processing equipment and services, and their extension to software is still under review at present.

In *Greece,* the Research and Computer Directorate of the Ministry of the Cabinet Presidency is responsible for government procurement policy.

In *Italy,* a special committee of the Treasury's Governmental Stationery Office (PGS) co-ordinates and supports automation projects in public administration. However, the Government is considering a bill to define standards for promoting and encouraging computer activities in institutional agencies. The bill would create two committees responsible for computer investments, reporting directly to the Prime Minister. Table 41 shows Italian government data processing spending for 1982 (narrowly defined, excluding non-governmental public agencies and services, which represent a computing capacity of the same order of magnitude as the government sector).

In *New Zealand,* the Computer Services Division of the State Services Commission acts simultaneously as central purchasing authority and supplier of computer services through four large data processing centres and four data-entry centres. Estimates for government computer spending in New Zealand are at present available only for hardware purchases, which were $42 million for the fiscal year 1983.

In *Norway* the Ministry of Consumer Affairs and Government Administration (FAD) has co-ordinating responsibilities for software development for governmental needs, with the Governmental Office of Organisation and Management as its adviser and executive body. No

Table 41. Italy: government data processing expenditure, 1982
Million Lira

Government expenditure on computer installations		434 630.6[a]
of which: Current expenditure	375 014	
Investment expenditure	59 616.6	
Current expenditure		
Personnel	215 286.3	
Location		
Hardware	84 745.4	
Software	7 173.7	
Maintenances		
Hardware	18 898.7	
Software	134.9	
Data communications	21 622.1	
Other expenditure	27 152.9	
Total	375 014	

	Number
Electronic data processing centres	149
Computers	
General purpose	225
Mini	5 337
Video-terminals	12 924
Public employees	11 866

a) About 317 million ECU.

147

overall data on public expenditure on data processing is available for Norway, the only data available concerning federal government (not including defence) expenditure in hardware. In 1980 the accumulated installed base was 727 million Norwegian krones.

In *Sweden,* the Swedish Agency for Administrative Development (SAFAD) has the tasks of co-ordinating and centralising government procurement under the Swedish Government Procurement Ordinance. Most software is developed within the user department, but outside purchases are beginning to develop, especially with the spread of microcomputers and word-processing systems. SAFAD provides government agencies with sub-contract agreements for personal computers and related software packages. Table 42 shows the structure of Swedish public data processing expenditures, including National Defence, the PTT and State Power Board.

In *Switzerland* the Office fédéral de l'Organisation is responsible for "optimising the use of computers in federal government". It supports the various departments in project design and, in co-operation with procurement agencies, co-ordinates federal procurement policy in computer markets. Table 43 shows current federal computer outlays for 1982 (including defence and federal polytechnic schools, but not PTT, federal railways and cantonal universities).

In *Turkey,* the Special Experts Committee on Informatics within the State Planning Organisation develops and, to a lesser extent, oversees the implementation of government procurement policy for computer hardware and software. It is however regarded as a temporary body, which may be replaced by a more permanent administrative unit in the near future.

Table 42. **Sweden: government data processing expenditures, 1982**

Million Skr

	Central government	National defence	PTT, railways, power board	Total
Personnel	486	48	198	732
ADP-Equipment[a]	300	33	247	580
Services	79	20	53	152
Other expenditure	225	35	68	328
Total	1 090	136	566	1 792

a) Automatic Data Processing equipment, including software.

Table 43. **Switzerland: federal government current computer spending, 1982**

Million Swiss francs

Depreciation and interest[a]	26
Maintenance	12
Leasing	1
Personnel	50
Other	20
Total	109

a) In 1982, SF 37 million were spent on hardware and software purchases.

Chapter VII

STANDARDIZATION QUESTIONS

Part I of this report highlighted the exceptional importance of standards in software for computers, micro-electronics and industrial automation. Attention was drawn to the extent to which the build-up of integrated information systems (which alone take full advantage of the potential of information technology), the division of labour and effective competition among specialist firms, software portability as between different systems and different sites, the transferability and interchangeability of professional resources, and more broadly, open markets and the numerous potential economies of scale and of learning in this field all depend on the existence of standards.

It was also noted that several software standards exist and are effectively being used, but that there are also applications in which standards are conspicuous by their absence, about which the industries and software houses concerned are vocal in their complaints. It was also observed that most existing standards are "de facto", i.e. associated with dominant suppliers in hardware markets (IBM in data-processing, DEC in minicomputers, Apply, Tandy, Commodore and recently IBM in microcomputers, Intel, Motorola and Zilog in microprocessors etc). In contrast with such "de facto" standards, de jure (i.e. organised, concerted) standardization has proved difficult, in spite of the considerable efforts of various national and international standardization agencies.

The main difficulty about de jure standardization is that the technology in this area moves on so quickly. This means that a standard established after prolonged consultation can soon be made obsolete, perhaps by some new technology, or because users find some new configuration more worthwhile. The "high risk" inherent in investing in standardization acts powerfully to discourage it, whatever the potential benefits, and the risk can never be eliminated without interfering with technological progress or the proper functioning of market mechanisms. As a partial answer to this dilemma, some flexible forms of standardization have recently been developed, like the "guidelines" defining broad reference configurations open to interpretation and evolution, and standardization in terms of "levels" suggesting different levels of detail and precision for each standard.

It is also a fact that de jure standardization is most successful in a monopsonistic or quasi-monopsonistic market where the standard-setter is at the same time the main purchaser, at least at the outset (i.e. the United States Defense Department in relation to the COBOL and then Ada programming languages; public telecommunications monopolies or regulated firms in relation to telecommunications hardware and software).

This situation has up to now worked more or less well, but tends to pose problems through a combination of new factors:

i) The growing *commercial interdependence* between hardware and software, and between the software components themselves;

ii) A distinct tendency towards the formation of *integrated data processing and automation systems* for most users;

iii) *Accelerating technological changes,* the *destabilisation of market structures* and the arrival of *new entrants* on hardware markets;

iv) The growing *internationalisation* of markets, entailing a constant *challenge to dominant positions* in any one country's hardware or software market.

These new circumstances imply, as many of the firms and organisations concerned point out, a greater need for "concerted" standardization in many information technology market segments (see Part I above). This adds still more importance to the activity of the various national and international standards bodies, and especially the various working parties of the CCITT and Committee TC 97 of the International Organization for Standardization (ISO).

However, these bodies lack some of the material and organisational resources for their new tasks (voluntary unpaid work prevails). As a result, they cannot get all the users, small scale producers, or all concerned internationally to take part in their activities. Another difficulty is that neither the scope of their activity nor the ways in which they can step in (react to rapid technological change, or to a leading manufacturer's differentiation strategy, their arrangements for concertation and co-ordination among themselves, their programmes and work schedules, the information and promotional resources available to them) appear commensurate with all the challenges they now face.

An important further aspect of standardization is the implementation of new de jure standards. This is frequently hampered by lack of resources. It is noted that if significant national efforts are not made in this respect, de facto standardization will play a dominant role even if de jure international standards exist.

One particular important aspect of standardization from the point of view of governments, concerns standardization for data processing systems in government departments themselves. As users of very large scale computer systems, governments are among the first potential beneficiaries of better standardization (for terminals, administrative data banks, programming and retrieval languages, and data transmission). This is indeed a major government consideration in several Member countries, as witness the activities of the Institute for Computer Science and Technology of the National Bureau of Standards to lay down Federal Information Processing Standards (FIPS) in the United States; the co-operation of federal and local public authorities within the Committee on Information Processing Systems of the national standardization organisation, DIN (Deutsches Institut für Normung), in Germany; Canada's Government EDP Standards Committee; the Standardization Office of the Swedish Agency for Administrative Development; Denmark's Datacentralen (official supplier of computer services to the government); and Finland's Standards Programme for State Administration.

International reflexion on *policy* aspects of information technology standardization could accordingly be useful to encourage greater precision in defining the aims and instruments of standardization, the relationships between government standardization measures and industrial standardization endeavours and also, the growing international aspects of these problems.

Chapter VIII

TELECOMMUNICATIONS

In conjunction with the introduction of integrated information systems at local, national and international levels, the role of telecommunications is growing. Capacities and speeds, the level of network liability, standards and tariff levels have now a direct impact on the design and management of corresponding software systems and thereby, encourage or discourage systems with a high telecommunications content.

Three types of software are concerned here:

  i) Software for territorially distributed systems (production management systems, sales management systems, videotext systems, various local network applications and their national and international extensions);
  ii) Software totally or partly transferable on-line between different remote facilities, both intrafirm and interfirm (telesoftware/downloading);
  iii) Software accessible and usable from remote terminals both intrafirm and interfirm (telecomputing).

Telecommunications policies, in terms of network performance, services available and tariffs, therefore need from now on to take these new requirements into account for integrated software. Many interested parties, especially users on too small a scale to lease their own lines, along with users in countries with less advanced telecommunications, state that the present limitations in telecommunications services seriously hinder, or make impossible, their access to technically optimum solutions. Most Member countries are currently making a considerable effort to adapt their telecommunications services to the new requirements, notably by introducing reliable and economic high-speed data transmission services.

An additional problem is that the available services and tariff structures at the international level are often less favourable than at national level, which works against intra and interfirm international software connections. This affects the large users to a lesser extent, who can lease and organise their own telecommunications lines.

Various OECD projects are studying and analysing these questions from an economic and international viewpoint, notably in the light of the rapid technical advances on the one hand, and on the other, the current trend in several Member countries to deregulate their telecommunications services[24]. These studies all indicate the benefits which may be expected from greater openness, concertation and international co-operation in this field.

Furthermore, the development and utilisation of advanced telecommunications software should also contribute to a more effective use of telecommunications opportunities in the integrated software systems.

Chapter IX

IMPLICATIONS FOR SOFTWARE OF INDUSTRIAL POLICIES IN HARDWARE

Industrial policies towards hardware in several Member countries are taking on an increasing software content. This is because systems software, applications package catalogues and specialist software houses are constantly reinforcing the differentiation between the "software environment" of hardware supplied by different manufacturers. It is, therefore, clear that industrial policies which support specific manufacturers are nowadays tantamount to public support for the specific software environment of their products, thereby somewhat prejudicing alternative software environments. This aspect of industrial policy is important for local users and computer service industries and will probably require greater consideration during the 1980s.

It has also been noticed in some Member countries that duties on imported hardware (perhaps levied as part of a policy to support the country's own industries) can accordingly increase the costs to and the prices charged by service companies using it, thereby risking discouragement of expansion in demand and the international competitiveness of the local services sector. This question will probably attract more government attention over the years ahead, as the potential of the services sector – particularly software – is more clearly identified and understood[25].

It is worth pointing out that those points do not affect the principle of industrial policies relating to hardware. They emphasize that such policies have important implications for national software industries in terms of costs, performance and standards, so need to be taken into account in assessing the costs and benefits of such policies and in any policy shift. Hardware policy and software policy may also start to compete with one another for funding, when the total public funds available for the science, technology and industrial policy are under pressure.

Conversely, any policy of supporting the software industry raises the question of how far it can develop independently of a local (national) hardware industry. The problem takes different forms for different kinds of software, especially according to how technologically "dependent" it may be on its hardware, and there is no general answer. But given the now widespread trends towards unbundling, together with the growing specialisation of software houses in standard hardware and software environments, geographical nearness to hardware manufacturers is becoming less important as a competitive factor for most software houses.

This is in fact the same kind of question as arose some 15 years ago about the future of software houses independent of the hardware manufacturers. Several commentators then argued that the technological and marketing interdependence between software and hardware would leave the software houses little alternative to becoming points of sale, dominated by the hardware manufacturers, with limited business opportunities in specialist areas. Yet that prediction only proved accurate for certain types of systems software tied particularly closely to the hardware, whereas for almost all applications software and a good deal of systems software, independent software houses ultimately imposed themselves on the market. In a symmetrical development, some manufacturers who integrated vertically (towards software) were handicapped in their software activities by restricting their procurement horizon to the performance and standards of their own hardware. These micro-economic experiences indicate, especially for governments of small countries now transposing the same question to the macro-economic level, that the competitiveness to their country's software industry will depend more on its capacity to keep up with universal technological trends, and to adapt its products to the most competitive hardware available on the world market than on how well it is endowed with (and often limited to) a local, geographically nearby source of hardware.

Chapter X

GROWTH PROBLEMS FOR SOFTWARE FIRMS
AND GOVERNMENT SUPPORT

Part I of this report noted that service firms specialising in software, be it for data processing, micro-electronics, automation or robotics, must overcome certain specific difficulties to enter the market and grow. Apart from the research, training, standardization and telecommunications policy issues reviewed in the preceding chapters, difficulties have also been found to stem from the ill-defined economic and legal status of software. Government endeavours to specify the economic and legal status of software and to introduce appropriate accountancy, tax and legal frameworks are consequently of great importance to the activity and growth of software houses (Chapter XII describes and analyses the state of government thinking and measures on these issues).

Furthermore, it has been found that software houses, especially in data processing, are coming up against financing difficulties, stemming from three sources:

i) The increasingly costly initial investment in development and marketing. This tendency is especially noticeable for software packages, whose development and marketing costs are much higher than for custom software, which is pre-financed.

ii) The high risk nature of such investment, because of accelerating technological progress and obsolescence rates for software, and the internationalisation of markets and competition.

iii) The reluctance of banks and most capital markets to finance such companies, whose assets and output are largely intangible and volatile.

Financial difficulties are unevenly influential in different countries. In particular, the better developed the local "venture-capital" market, the better access a software house will have to high risk development funds and the larger the potential local market, the better the chances that the investment will yield a return, i.e. the risk is reduced. This being so, governments in smaller countries and countries where the venture-capital market is not highly developed, are tempted to remedy those structural shortcomings by taking measures to support their software companies. This special attention to the software industry is spreading at present, with greater awareness of its present and future role in national economies.

Public authorities support the creation, funding and growth of software companies by intervening in three ways.

A. GENERAL POLICIES TO PROMOTE INNOVATIVE FIRMS

This involves extending support measures for investment, R & D and modernization (tax concessions, grants, accelerated depreciation, etc.) to software firms' investments. Measures of this type, today in force in most Member countries, do not automatically apply to software firms whose investments and output are "intangible". So it is often necessary to adapt such policies explicitly to this new field: in the United States software is not eligible for investment tax credits; in Ireland, the authorities have officially stated that software is to be treated on the same footing as manufactured products, so as to make it qualify for government measures; in Greece, recent (1982) investment support legislation contains an ad hoc clause on software companies; in Australia, the government announced in late 1983 that the provisions of the 1976 Australian Industrial Research and Development Incentives Act would now be wholly applicable to investments in software development; in France, the Fonds Industriel de Modernization (FIM), established in September 1983, includes software for the first time within the field of application for participatory loans ("prêts participatifs") designed to support investment in heavy equipment; and in Germany, the government announced that it will take individual measures with regard to software in the framework of its programme on the promotion of the development of micro-electronics, information and communications technology, adopted in March 1984.

In many countries, too, it is noticeable that many software companies locate in technology parks established by governments or local authorities (in Dublin and Limerick in Ireland, in Oulu in Finland, Meylan in France etc.).

B. AD HOC PROGRAMMES

Only a few governments have so far introduced support programmes specifically for the software industry.

The most elaborate programme has been implemented by the *United Kingdom*, the Software Products Scheme (SPS). This subsidises the development of innovative software packages by grants of up to 25 per cent of development costs. The National Computing Centre (NCC) manages the Scheme on behalf of the Department of Trade and Industry (which retains final approval). Projects must be innovative and applicants must demonstrate technical and commercial competence, as well as the need for assistance. The SPS had been running at a fairly low level of activity (average commitments were less than £1 million each year) until it was restructured and re-launched in June 1983. Since then some 215 projects have been assisted and grants of £29 to £39 million have been made, producing investment of £108 million (the maximum grant was 33.3 per cent from the re-launch to June 1984). The direction and operation of the SPS is monitored by an advisory committee including representatives of the industry through the Computer Services Association, the NCC and the Department of Trade and Industry. There are no limits on size of project or grant. The largest grant awarded to date was just over £1 million.

Japan also has a programme to support development investments by software companies. The Information Technology Promotion Agency (IPA) can fund up to 100 per cent of the costs of developing software which it considers to be marketable, and of general interest, sharing the profits from the venture should it be successful. In 1984, 33 projects were supported, with a total budget of Y 3.5 billion. The IPA also guarantees loans from the long-term credit banks to software companies. Between 1970 and 1984, it backed some 1 300 credit arrangements in that way. Every year, the IPA publishes a program registration book for users, giving technical and commercial details of all packaged software offered by Japanese companies.

Another major support measure for software companies in Japan is a special tax arrangement under which 50 per cent of earnings from *packaged software* sales can be paid into a development fund exempt from taxation for four years (of which only a quarter becomes taxable at the end of the fourth year). The IPA records and endorses software packages eligible under this arrangement.

C. EXPORT PROMOTION POLICIES

One way for a software company to overtake what may be an unduly narrow home market is to aim at the international market. But most find this difficult, for financial, organisational and cultural (mostly linguistic) reasons which loom large in this sector. Government export measures, as a result may be supporting software companies.

Support can take different forms, sometimes specifically linked to information technologies (such as the UK Government's IT export scheme). There may be various subsidies to exports, special foreing trade services, support for missions and trade fairs, insurance for export projects. There is a good deal of information showing that many software companies have taken advantage of these measures in the OECD area, except where the fact that their business is "intangible" makes them ineligible (in France, for example, the foreign trade insurance agency Coface will only insure an export project that includes at least 90 per cent French hardware, without any reference to local software-added value).

Chapter XI

FOREIGN TRADE REGULATIONS APPLIED TO SOFTWARE

Even more than through their export support, it is through their import and foreign investment regulations that governments occupy a major role in the development of international trade.

The international environment for such trade has up to now been broadly liberal. Since a software transaction implies proximity between vendor and user, it generally comes about through international investment on the part of service companies, by direct establishment in a foreign country or by association with a local company. The transaction then comes under the (liberal) legislation covering international trade and investment in the services sector, or covering technology sales where a licence fee has been paid. Only the hardware media (tapes, disks, etc.) carrying the software will be subject to a customs duty (like ordinary virgin merchandise, and therefore at a low rate). For software sales by hardware manufactures, the technology sale principle applies when hardware and software are invoiced separately, but when the software is bundled customs duties on the hardware are applied to the whole value of the system traded. Accordingly, it would be fair to say that trade in software has encountered very few tariff or non-tariff barriers in the OECD area, up to now.

During the 1980s however, this may change somewhat. With the growing importance of the service sector, especially software, the very different roles now being attributed to it (advancing technology, creating employment, supporting hardware industries, etc.), government support policies may henceforth generate more restrictive approaches to international trade in software.

In several Member countries, customs authorities have contemplated the issue of customs duty on software. The principle of making it taxable on the same basis as merchandise (not as a service or as technology) has taken hold in official thinking in certain countries. This approach could lead to ad valorem duties on software. However, this would also raise several technical problems (sales of international subsidiaries involving no customs clearance, processing of software transmitted by telecommunications channels, difficulties inherent in any ad valorem levy, etc.) and no country yet seems ready to adopt a final position on the matter. Conversely, foreign trade departments in some other countries are calling for an explicit international consensus on the principle of not taxing information and software contained in carrier media clearing customs. The Customs Co-operation Council is currently reflecting on this question, as is the GATT Committee on Customs Evaluation.

It must be pointed out that issues in software trade are not confined to customs duties, but concern also a range of non-tariff questions relating to international investment in services, technology transfers, industrial property protection, etc.

Certain Member countries are raising the question of voluntary restrictions on exports applied by other Member countries as an important factor in international trade in this field.

The question recently came to the fore again with the US Defense Department's announcement that software should be included in the list of high technology products whose export from the United States has to be reviewed under the Export Administration Act. The question was also considered by the Committee for Multilateral Export Controls (COCOM) in July 1984, and agreement was reached to embargo exports of Ada and Chill language-based software, artificial intelligence systems, disassemblers and decompilers, high-level language developers and switching software for telecommunications, to the Eastern bloc countries.

Chapter XII

LEGAL ASPECTS OF SOFTWARE

The question of the legal status of software and of program protection can have implications for other legal problems raised by the various types of utilisation and production of software and for the law of contracts, as well as tax and accountancy law. This is because the existing uncertainties as to the extent and scope of property rights crop up again for other branches of law in dealing with software.

A. PROBLEMS IN THE LEGAL PROTECTION OF PROGRAMS

A computer software package comprises a number of elements. In its model provisions for the protection of computer software, WIPO identifies that computer software includes:

i) The supporting material (flowcharts, written description of the program);
ii) Documentation on how to use the program;
iii) The program itself.

Further, the program is recognised as comprising two major elements, the underlying process, system of operation or algorithm, and the set of instructions that explain the process in detail. The underlying process, system or algorithm, to the extent that term is equivalent to process or system, may be regarded as processes within the ambit of industrial property (patent) laws, while the written program itself as a set of instructions expressed in a certain form is clearly within the scope of copyright. The combination of all these elements, or indeed, any one of them can be regarded as protectable know-how or trade secrets. Property rights under any of these theories can be owned by either real or legal persons. Under Anglo American copyright principles, a legal person can be regarded as the author of a copyrighted work, but under continental law systems a legal person may only be entitled to certain economic rights of exploitation of work.

The complex nature of computer software has caused some difficulty and confusion among legal scholars who have attempted to analyse it exclusively in terms of either patent, copyright or trade secret law. The keystone to understanding in this area is that, just as with any other complex, technologically sophisticated industry, all modes of intellectual and industrial property law have some relevance.

1. Program Patentability

At first sight, as regards program patentability, positive law is clear: the European Patent Convention (Munich 1973, Article 52), the Patent Cooperation Treaty (Washington 1970, Rule 39, i, vi), the French Patent Act of 13th July 1978 [Article 6 (2) and (3)], the German Act of 2nd January 1968 as amended on 16th December 1980 (Articles 1, 2), the Italian Act, the British 1977 Patents Act, Swedish Act (1978) and the Finnish Act (1980) all exclude programs from their field of application. The same applies to Austria, Denmark, Norway, Spain, Turkey, Switzerland and New Zealand. In Japan, although there has been no law making programs ineligible for patentability, it is said in general that programs as such are hardly eligible for patentability, and there is currently an important debate on the question of the form of program protection. In *Australia,* the practice of the patent office is not to accept computer programs as such for patenting, but this does not mean that an invention which, inter alia, includes a computer program would not be patentable for this reason alone. In *Canada,* the courts have also tended to refuse patent protection for programs. In the *United States* the question has been under discussion for a long time.

Under patent law it is a basic principle that an invention, in order to be patentable, must be susceptible to industrial application. This concept implies that the invention is a solution to a technical problem using substance and energy according to the laws of nature. Consequently, schemes, rules and methods of performing mental acts have for a long time not been regarded as inventions under patent law. The exclusion from patentability of what is merely a computer program is in many countries considered to be in line with this well established principle. On the other hand, analysis of the creative activity involved in the formulation of a program is difficult and sometimes simply a matter of the skills of patent examiners. Moreover, under most national patent legislation, creative activity leads to a specific result, namely mastery of the laws of nature; if a program is seen as an algorithm or an equation, we are faced with a description of the laws of nature which in no way entails mastery of them and hence is not patentable. There has been much discussion on the nature of the change brought about in hardware through the use of different software between advocates and opponents of the patentability of software. What is the present state of opinion concerning the two conditions of patentability?

Although it is possible to lump together the program and the documents associated with it, this does not lead very far since the search for legal protection is concerned essentially with the programs themselves while related documents are merely accessory to the main creation of which they form a part. But this question arises again with the emergence of firmware and programs forming an integral part of a manufacturing process and which might for this reason come under legislation on process patents. Thus, paragraph 3 of Article 52 of the Munich Convention provides (like the French, Italian and United Kingdom enactments) that programs shall only be excluded insofar as the application for a European patent concerns only one of these components, considered in and of itself. The position is apparently similar in the Finnish and Swedish patent acts, but not in Germany whose domestic legislation does not include Paragraph 3 of the Munich Convention and whose courts have been refusing to patent such programs since 1974. The courts in some European countries have therefore recognised that:

"...a process shall not be ineligible for patenting solely because one or more of its phases are performed by a computer requiring to be controlled by a program."

This view was not, however, followed in Canada where the Federal Court has confirmed the dismissal of a claim by a party connected with the claimant in the French case referred to

160

above, on the ground that the invention consisted of the discovery that certain mathematical functions enabled the result sought to be achieved and that a mathematical formula had to be treated as a scientific principle which could not be protected by a patent.

In the United States the situation regarding computer program related patents is rather complex. In 1968, the U.S. Patent and Trademark Office adopted guidelines based on an interpretation of Section 101 of the 1952 Patent Law that totally excluded computer programs per se from patent protection. Case law in the Supreme Court confirmed that interpretation by denying patent protection to programs. [Gottschalk V. Benson, 409 U.S. 63 (1972) and Parker V. Flook, 437 U.S. 584 (1978)].

However, in 1981 the Supreme Court decided [Diamond V. Bradley, 450 U.S. 381 (1981) and Diamond V. Diehr, 450 U.S. 175 (1981)], cases that represented a new development in dealing with patent applications involving mathematical equations, algorithms and computer programs. Fundamentally, patent protection will be afforded to inventions that otherwise satisfy the patent law's requirements for novelty and non-obviousness even if they include computer programs. Clearly, the protection does not extend to the program per se, but only to the process of which the program is a part [(Diamond V. Diehr, 450 U.S. 175, 209 USPQ 1 (1981))] or to the process upon which the program is based so long as it is not exclusively a mathematical formula, calculation, or procedure for solving a mathematical problem. In [re Pardo, 684, P.2D 912, 214 USPQ 673 (CCPA 1972)]. Exactly how far these decisions go in protecting computer program related inventions remains to be determined, as no cases dealing with patent infringement of computer related inventions have so far been decided.

The United States Patent and Trademark Office includes in the Manual of Patent Examining Procedure (MPEP) its standards for the examination of patents relating to mathematical algorithms or computer programs (MPEP Section 2110, P. 2100-2). Those procedures are based on the case law discussed above.

Recent cases clearly demonstrate that both operating system and applications programs are protected by copyright even if they are fixed in read only memory (ROM) chips. In Apple V. Segimex, Tribunal de Grande Instance de Paris, 21/9/83, the court noted that as "technology leads more and more to the integration of operating system programs into memories, such programs have not, by this simple fact, changed their nature; whereas, when considering integrated circuits, one must recognise from the manner in which they and their components are manufactured (that they) are indeed industrial products, but, by contrast, their "contents" which make them original in relation to each other, are only the expression in advanced technology of the original creation of the program's author. This raises questions about the future for recent national precedents (Schlumberger and Diehr decisions) recognising the patentability of processes using programs and the practice (as in *Finland, Sweden* and *Switzerland)* of granting patent protection to software incorporated within hardware or chips designed to solve a particular problem. The fact remains that certain authors[27] argue that although the trend seems to be to protect all forms of programs (application or operating) by copyright, there is no reason why certain types of programs should not be patented under certain conditions, but that considerations limit recourse to this type of protection: its cost and the lead times between patent application and the grant of the actual patent (18 months in France) are the first two. Accordingly, the rapid evolution of computer technology makes the patent obsolete the day it is published. Another consideration is the great material difficulty in demonstrating the novelty of the program. Starting from the point that the program is inherently a procedure for processing information, it will be necessary to prove that it has never yet been employed in any industry and that it cannot be compared to a scientific principle ineligible for patent protection and in the public domain.

Establishing novelty is particularly difficult in a field where the intellectual component is the most important. How can a combination of logical instructions be proved to be novel? Just as it is easy to prove for a tangible object, it is hard to prove for an immaterial good. Another problem arises from the fact that the patent involves publicising the invention it protects, with the result of enabling parties other than its holder to copy the software or improve it. These considerations taken together explain why copyright is resorted to especially bearing in mind that copyright is universally applicable, not only to protect all forms of software, but also integrated circuits.

2. Copyright and Programs

Copyright appears for the time being to be the form of legal protection recognised by a great number of Member countries to protect both application and operating system software. This outcome is suggested by WIPO activities, country legislation on copyright specifically including software (Australia and the United States), and especially case law jurisprudence in Australia, Canada, France, Germany, Italy, Japan, the Netherlands, the United Kingdom and the United States.

It became clear at the second WIPO meeting of the Committee of Experts on software protection in June 1983 at Geneva, that the majority of the countries represented had opted to protect programs through copyright, although some voices were raised in favour of distinguishing the various types of programs, some questioned whether copyright was the preferred long term solution.

The Committee in June 1983 took note of the information given at the meeting on the increasing trend at the national level in a certain number of countries of granting protection under copyright law to computer software. It noted that this situation could have – thanks to the principle of national treatment – the consequence that the need for international protection may, between such countries, be satisfied to a considerable extent by means of the international copyright conventions. The Committee also noted that WIPO, jointly with UNESCO, suggests undertaking a study and convening a committee of governmental experts on the protection available for computer software under existing copyright laws and treaties. In view of the foregoing considerations and of the complexity of the problem, the Committee considers it premature to take, for the time being, a stand on the question of the best form for the international protection of computer software and recommends that the consideration of the conclusion of a special treaty as presented to it should not be pursued for the time being.

A meeting of a group of experts was held in WIPO/UNESCO in February 1985 to examine the copyright aspects of the protection of computer software at both the national and international levels. The discussions at this meeting reflected a general recognition of the pressing need for adequate protection of computer programs both nationally and internationally. Several participants expressed the view that the international copyright conventions protected computer programs and required no amendment to that effect. Other participants expressed their doubts as to the applicability of those conventions in their present form. A great number of participants at this meeting stated that computer programs were works protected by copyright provided that they were original productions constituting individual, creative expression of the set of instructions developed in them; they stated that computer programs may be assimilated to literary works. Delegations from countries where computer programs were protected by copyright said that, in general, copyright provided an effective means of protection. Several delegations said that in their countries the possibility of adopting sui generis protection was under consideration. Several participants said that the copyright law of their respective countries applied at present, without any amendment to the protection of programs. Several other participants stressed the importance of introducing special rules adapting copyright protection to particular features of computer programs or, at least, to make it clear, by means of legislation, that computer programs were works protected by copyright, since case law might change without a clear legislative basis.

Certain countries *(Australia, United States)* have already amended their copyright legislation while others *(Japan, Germany, Canada, Denmark, France, Spain, United Kingdom)* plan to do so. Commissions have been established to study the question in *The Netherlands, Sweden, Norway, Finland, Ireland, Italy* and *Portugal.* There have been several studies of this question in *Belgium* by the INSEA (Professional Association of Computer Service Companies) and the AICIPI (Association of Industrial Property Consultants). ECSA (European Computing Services Association) and ADAPSO (American Association of Data Processing Services Organizations) were very active also in this field. In some Member countries, it is in principle possible for programmers to take advantage of legislation for the protection of literary and artistic works *(Austria* and *Germany).* In Australia, although the copyright laws have just been amended to clarify the protection accorded to computer programs following uncertainties generated by recent litigation, the government has made it clear that this is to be regarded as a short term measure only, and that it will now move to a consideration of issues for the long term through an appropriate form of enquiry. In the *United States* the Act of 12th December 1980 amending the Copyright Act clarified that copyright protection was available for programs. The 1909 and 1978 Copyright Acts already gave programs copyright protection to the extent that they met the normal requirements for protection (original expression of an idea). Programs were treated as literary works. But the 1976 Act, in force from 1978 (1.1), because of the limitation of the original Section 117, did not allow for the special problems that might arise from the grant of copyright for programs. For example, the insubstantial nature of a program fed into the main memory of the computer without being recorded in tangible form (as in the case of computer networks) or the definition of the status of copies from the legal standpoint. The 1980 Act defines a computer program as "...a set of statements or instructions to be used directly or indirectly in a computer in order to bring about a certain result....". This definition has also been cited with approval by the courts and read expansively. Earlier criticism by the ADAPSO has been abandoned in view of the reading of the definition that has been applied by the courts. Under present law, copyright protects not only against copies but also against the development of a work by a third party, even if the work is not the exact replica of a work protected by copyright.

Some problems regarding simultaneous copyright and trade secrets protection have arisen in the United States with respect to the technical legal questions arising from the preemption provision of the U.S. Copyright Law and the U.S. copyright registration practices. However, the balance of legal opinion appears to support the simultaneous availability of copyright and trade secret protection. Arguments that the use of the copyright notice constitutes an admission that the work has been published have been unsuccessful [Technicon Medical Information Systems Corp versus Greenbay Packaging, Inc, 211 USPQ 343 (ED WIS 1980), AFFD 687 F 2D 1032 (7th CIR 1982) CERT, denied January 10, 1983]. It is also not clear that deposit and registration with the Copyright Office will result in a loss of trade secrecy [Warrington Associates versus Real Time Engineering Systems, Inc, 522-F SUPP 367 (ND ILL 1981)].

Country case law increasingly recognises copyright protection for programs. In Germany, following the 9th February 1983 decision of the Karlsruhe Court of Appeal, the Frankfurt decision of 13th June 1983 and the Federal Labour Court decision of September 1983, the possibility of protecting a program through copyright is generally recognised[27].

In *France,* the position has been the same since decisions by the Tribunal de Commerce de Paris (18th November 1980), the Cour d'Appel (2nd November 1982) and the Tribunal de Grande Instance de Paris of 21st September 1983. The position is similar in *New Zealand, Turkey* (although not widespread in that country) and *Denmark.* In *Australia* in *Apple computers V. Computer Edge,* the full Federal Court has ruled on appeal in favour of copyright protection for computer programs, but the case is on further appeal to the high court and will now involve a consideration of the effect of recent amendments to the copyright act. In *Japan,* there have been three Court decisions (6th December 1982 at the Tokyo District Court, 30th March 1979 at the Yokohama District Court and 26th January 1984 at the Osaka District Court) to the effect that computer programs constitute an intellectual work protected under the copyright law. On 13th January 1985, for the first time in a criminal case, the Tokyo District Court found the criminal law applicable to copyright infringement in computer programs. The situation is similar in Canada (Federal Court of Canada in Toronto 26th June 1984), in Italy (Tribunal of Turin, 14th July 1983), in the Netherlands (Assen District Court, 1981 and District Court of Hertogenbosch, 14th May 1982), in the United Kingdom (Thrustcode Ltd V. W.W. Computing Ltd, 1983 and Saga Enterprises V. Richards, 1983) and also in the United States.

Some difficulties appear when copyright protection is used for computer programs. The first problem derives from the fact that the author's monopoly relates to copying of the work rather than its use. Numerous legal theorists have asked whether a third party who feeds a program into a computer without authorisation is using the program or copying it. For some writers[28] the act is one of unlawful copying, since to the extent that the introduction of the medium into the machine causes physical changes inside the memory and that the instructions are stored there in some way, the user could "photograph" the memory at a given moment in time to obtain knowledge of its content. The WIPO working group on Technical questions Relating to the Legal Protection of Computer Software meeting held in Canberra in April 1984 reached the conclusion that it could not be said in all cases that the use of a computer program entailed its reproduction.

Another problem is whether the execution of a computer program might in any case be permissable when done in the private or domestic setting. Copying a program for the private use of the person making the copy is authorised by the law in some countries. In this case, the purpose of the copying must be examined and it must be considered whether reproduction of a program solely for use in a machine constitutes a private use.

The third problem concerns the extent of the protection. The copyright protects the form rather than the intellectual content of works. If in principle, it is impossible to own ideas, since this would constitute an intolerable restriction on the freedom of expression, however, it may happen that copyright can protect more than the pure expression of an idea by applying the test of composition (of French origin) or of internal form (of German origin). Protection covers the expression of the idea itself, but also the choice of subjects and the composition of the material, i.e. the arrangement of the subject (plan of the action, sequence of topics). Parallels may then be drawn between programs and a creative work, the flowchart being the composition of a program and the instructions being the expression of the program. It nevertheless remains that in scientific works the test of composition is narrower than in literary works since the sequence of operations is usually dictated by the subject matter and the monopoly can hence not extend beyond the "detailed layout". Applied to programs, this formula means that the criterion of protection should be that the program was not copied totally in or substantially from another work. Only a degree of complexity in the program evidencing original and ingenious work could be protected over and above a service reproduction. This rule might lead to a move towards "gratuitous sophistication" in programs in order to protect their use.

The recognition of an author's moral right under some countries' copyright legislation may also raise problems, for example, an author can object to modification of his work insofar as the moral right may override any transferral of his rights under an employment contract.

Furthermore, in some countries it is not certain that a legal person can be regarded as an author. Finally, some have suggested that the copyright protection terms (50 years or 70 years after the author's death in Berne Convention countries, 75 years in the United States) may be inappropriate to the protection of some programs which are very quickly renewed and, therefore, may soon become obsolete.

These issues have led some writers and experts to question copyright on certain points and to examine the solutions presented by the model software protection provisions of WIPO in 1978, prepared by the International Bureau of WIPO, which rely on elements of patent (the test to determine the scope of protection is that of use) and of copyright (criterion of personal intellectual work), but which have no formal value.

Since questions still remain in some countries about recognising a program as an intellectual creation within the scope of intellectual property laws, or for considering that existing patent and copyright can effectively protect them, such programs have been treated as "know-how" – intangible assets of an economic nature.

3. Programs and Know-How

Like know-how, a program can be protected contractually, or by proceedings for unfair competition, or through proceedings comparable to those for third party liability, or under industrial and commercial secrecy legislation.

Software not protected by an intellectual property right is a public good, but by remaining secret it may become the subject matter of a contract of sale constituting initial recognition of property rights in it. This is similar to the sale of know-how and is borne out by the practice of software licences which are similar to those for know-how.

It is in relation to contracts that the know-how aspect of software is most striking. The terms and practice of contracts are similar: a confidentiality and non-disclosure clause, ongoing control of the subject matter of the sale by the licensor, type of payments (royalties or lump sum), co-operation between the parties with the result of a long-term contract, or a succession of contracts between the parties for a long duration of time.

In several countries (for example, *France, United States, Sweden, Spain, Belgium, Turkey, Italy* and Germany) a contract is a means of protecting program secrecy at two levels:

- At the level of working relationships, through the employment contract;
- At the level of sales of the right to use the program to a person outside the enterprise.

This is the commonly used means of protection and because of uncertainties as to the status of program is also considered the most effective. It is based on the recognition of the property right of the supplier by user. Its importance explains why in certain countries (such as *Sweden*), software suppliers are in the process of developing contractual forms organising arrangements to guarantee confidentiality.

Parties are in principle free to determine the content of their contracts. Generally speaking, the subject of the contract is either the sale for use of a piece of software, or the sale of a copy of the program combined with restrictions as to its use, or the provision of software as an accessory to a sale of hardware, or the provision of a piece of software designed for a particular purpose, creating or transferring the use of exclusive rights. Sometimes, in order to guarantee program confidentiality, the supplier does not give the user access to the source programs. The installation of security systems is a necessary condition for the implementation of contractural program protection. One of the weaknesses of the protection of secrecy by contract stems from the "relative" character of the contract, binding only the parties to it, so that the secrecy obligation is not imposed on third parties. But if the right to use software is sold to several entities and if the duration of the contractual ties diminishes, and thus the technical control exercised by the supplier, the software has a tendency to take on the characteristics of a product, whereupon contractual protection becomes less effective. This often occurs to packaged software, even though it is often supplied subject to a restriction on transferability and non-exclusive utilisation. The tendency is to contrast packaged software with custom software, whose secrecy might be easier to protect because of the particular purpose it is assumed to pursue.

One of the responses to this problem on the part of programmers has been to seek protection through trademarks. Once the software becomes a "product" sold directly on the market it will qualify for this type of protection. The problem is that the aim of trademark protection is not to protect creation but to identify the origin of the product, protect the reputation of its creator and consequently guarantee certain quality standards. While the trademark does not directly protect the content of the software it may provide an additional element of protection by making visible the ownership link between the product (the software) and the programmer (or owner). Only to this extent can it provide protection, which has the advantage of being international and not impairing the secrecy of the content of the software since the deposit of the trademark does not require a full description (unlike patents or copyright).

Because of the staff rotation phenomen and the scarcity of software professionals, the problem of secrecy protection inside the company is acute. It should be settled by the employment contract, but there are always awkward borderline cases[29]. The fact remains that no secrecy clause can be so broad as to restrict the employee's freedom of work. Some countries have criminal sanctions for violation of professional secrecy under certain conditions[30].

Legislation on industrial and commercial secrecy may also be a recourse. The questionnaire shows that this is used by software producers in *Germany, Italy,* the *United States, Finland* and *France.* But these laws can only offer protection provided that the secret has not been divulged. In the United States, that condition which makes copyright protection incompatible with protection via the secrecy laws was discussed. Another point is that they give no protection, especially in the United States, against a user in good faith.

There are also forms of protection under civil law. Actions against unfair competition can now be brought in *France, Australia,* the *United States, Finland, Belgium, Norway* and *Germany.* In *Switzerland* the ongoing change in the Federal Act on unfair competition takes into account the software protection issue. Civil actions akin to third party liability actions can also be brought, but only subject to certain conditions, especially proof of good faith, possession of rights in the software and proof of novelty. So in order to identify the software precisely and establish a definite date of creation, it may be worth depositing with an approved body, lawyer or court officer in a country whose copyright law does not provide for depositing. Another point is that some proposals for "computer crime" legislation cover theft of software and would treat it as a criminal offence.

B. IMPLICATIONS OF THE UNCERTAINTIES AS TO SOFTWARE

Defining software as a product or a service will affect the definition of the subject in software supply contracts and consequently the definition of the rights and obligations of parties to such contract. They also affect the treatment of software for accountancy purposes.

1. Implications for Contract Law

The diversity, lack of precision or actual unsuitability of definitions for the subject of software supply contracts reveals the many different functions and contexts such contracts may serve. It is usual to distinguish packaged from custom software. A packaged software contract would be said to assign a non-exclusive and non-transferable right to use the package, while a custom software contract would be said to provide a service (enterprise contract). Accordingly, the law of sale ought not to apply, but this would be overlooking the fact that software has long been regarded as the (sometimes indissoluble) accessory of hardware and therefore sold at the same time as the hardware, while packaged software, being standardized, is akin to a product. This situation sometimes leads to a degree of confusion in the minds of those drafting contracts, using in one and the same contract elements in the law of sale and elements in the transfer of rights to use. The fact that software will no longer be regarded as inseparable from hardware will clarify such situations as well as the increased number of packaged software on the market.

Another problem arises out of the fact that custom and packaged software suppliers shun the contract of sale, because any program or package containing "bugs" or defects would immediately render them liable on the basis of the legal guarantee, in view of the presumption of bad faith weighing on every computer professional, that exists in some countries, but not in the United States where there is no such presumption of "bad faith" and where implied warranties may be disclaimed and liability limited. Moreover, suppliers of custom and packaged software, being obliged to use the contract as a way of recognising their property rights in programs in the case where there is no universal recognition under exclusive rights, are also obliged in the same contract to limit the scope of their own property rights, since they themselves have to specify the limits (transferability, exclusiveness, etc.) and realise that intellectual property rights have only a limited life over time, and also in their substantive and sometimes even their geographical coverage.

If exclusive rights over programs were recognised, these various problems would be cleared up. By assigning copyright, the supplier wards off liability under the legal guarantee against latent defects, and the contract would no longer serve for the preservations of proprietary rights and of trade secrets. That legal construction is well known and provides a more reliable framework. But in some instances a copyright assignment contract can have shortcomings, because if the software concerned is a means of achieving a predetermined result, it becomes akin to a technical means, whose use should be communicated through a patent licence contract since it is the right to use it that is being sold, not merely a right to reproduce it. This point brings us back to the discussion about the scope of copyright protection. So there is probably a need for legislators to intervene here, to clarify the position, and for the solutions adopted to be harmonised internationally, so as to facilitate international trade in software.

These uncertainties taken together do however raise the question of how far it may be possible to give the same kind of protection to all the programs on the market and of the disparate nature of computer programs. Some are regarded as intangible goods, eligible for appropriation, some as know-how and some even as hardware accessories.

2. Accountancy Practices

Here too, some uncertainties remain. In some countries (*Portugal, Italy, Turkey, Spain, Finland* and the *United Kingdom*), accountancy practice does not differentiate among aspects of software, or are not always the same. Software is treated as an operating cost rather than as an investement set out as balance-sheet asset (*Ireland, Denmark, Norway, New Zealand,* except for large-scale software development). The situation is similar in *Switzerland* where, however, because of the increasing volume of software packages on the market the question has arisen as to whether or not such software packages might be amortized.

Elsewhere (the *United States*) whether and when software can be treated as an intangible asset or, like R&D expenditures or overheads, is a subject of considerable discussion.

The practice both of suppliers and of users must be considered. In *Belgium* and *France,* if a software purchase is linked to a hardware purchase, it is entered as a fixed asset, to be amortized at the same rate and over the same term as the hardware.

In *Belgium,* for the software supplier, all design outlays were entered as operating costs and, on the assets side, as stock formation. This called for extreme caution, in view of the uncertainty as to the real value of the stock. In *France,* apparently, few precise accounting directives have to date been issued, or at least the solutions presented were tentative. Consultancies, software houses and computer manufacturing companies treated R&D expenditure as research expenditure, amortizing it over the year incurred (sometimes over two or three years). Non-computer companies showed software development costs as outlays. Packaged software royalties, and expenditures on outside software development were very often shown as assets, with amortization periods of between two and three years for management programs (longer for production programs). A bill is currently being prepared to clarify the situation.

In *Sweden,* there are as yet no standardized practices. But there are directives covering the accountancy treatment of software acquired by a user. No distinction is made between applications software and systems software. The position of a custom program user is the same from the accounting standpoint as that of the producer. They treat the software as an asset if the design and production costs represent an important proportion of their budgets for the years ahead. It has to be entered as an asset on an annual basis, for a reasonable amount of the investment[31]. Very large-scale software may be included on the assets side as "software" and be valued in accordance with the usual rules and practices for "works made assets" under which direct costs and a reasonable proportion of the indirect costs can be treated as assets. For user-ready packaged software, royalties paid to the supplier are entered as operating costs. But if the supplier requires a substantial lump sum at the end of the contract, and if the lifetime of the package is estimated as at least three years, the user can enter that sum as an asset over financial years corresponding to the package lifetime, provided that so entering it helps to give a better representation of the user's economic situation and results. In this case, the sum would be shown as "tenancy and similar rights", and on the asset side, as usufructuary right to computer software.

The Authorised Public Accountant's Association has established a working party to review the question of accountancy treatment for software.

In the *United States,* the main issue is how software R&D costs should be treated for accountancy purposes. In 1974[32], in a publication by the Financial Accounting Standards Board (FASB)[33], the principle was laid down that R&D outlays should be shown in the accounts for the financial year in which they are incurred, and that principle was applicable to software. But the publication stated that each case should be considered separately in terms of its own specific characteristics and the decision whether to expense or capitalise software development costs made accordingly. General confusion followed and in 1975 the FASB sought to clarify its position by publishing Interpretation No. 6[34]. The principle was laid down that while software development costs can in certain cases be treated differently from R&D costs, this did not mean that they should ipso facto be shown as assets; the special circumstances in each individual situation should be the basis for the accounting treatment of software development costs. This prompted software industry organisations to react that the accountancy profession was preventing the software industry from adopting an accounting pattern appropriate to the nature of its activities[35]. The principle of making a determination based upon the circumstances peculiar to each individual case was repeated in a technical bulletin published in 1979 by the FASB. In August 1983, a moratorium imposed by the Securities and Exchange Commission (SEC) prohibited firms under its authority from showing certain internal software development costs as intangible assets. The accountancy profession hopes that the FASB will clarify the problems during 1984 or 1985. Software producers would like to capitalise a proportion of software R&D costs in order to obtain bank credit more readily and make it easier to get stock exchange quotations. Computer software companies are proliferating and are increasingly going public. Financial analysts consider that since technological progress is so rapid, to capitalise certain software development costs may give a false picture of their probable economic lifetime. Software producers also criticise the FASB for classifying R&D outlays and defining the appropriate accountancy treatment for software too loosely, making it harder to compare the financial performances of similar companies with different accountancy policies. On the first point, a preliminary response may be given by the draft recommendation of the National Association of Accountants[36] of 5th October 1983 which broadly suggests that the only costs to be capitalised should be those relating to the production phase of the software as such, while costs upstream and downstream of production should be shown as debits for the year.

Accountancy practice and policy in Member countries is highly diversified and not yet stabilized, reflecting the difficulty of identifying software uniformly. It is sometimes regarded as an investment, sometimes as an expenditure, depending on what it does and what purpose it serves.

3. Tax Law

In the absence of stabilized accountancy practices, tax considerations can influence enterprises in drawing up their accounts. Yet in this field, too, uncertainty prevails. In *Ireland,* software is generally regarded as a service, except for the user-ready software packages. In *Finland,* the Revenue regards software development as an investment eligible for depreciation over three to five years. Custom software is considered as a service and as such does not attract tax, whereas the user-ready software package is regarded as a "product" subject to sales tax. In *Norway,* only a large-scale software development can be regarded as an investment, and amortized over three to five years.

In *France,* to date no tax instrument deals directly with software, but legislation is evolving. In practice, though, the Revenue currently applies the rule of showing all research costs as fixed assets and recognises the possibility of amortizing them. There has as yet been no legal trial of this point, but tax doctrine seems to consider that if software has an economic value to the firm it can be regarded as an industrial asset if acquired for a lump sum, but not if acquired against royalties. Notice that while software is regarded as an industrial asset, it is an intangible service, on which V.A.T. is not due in France whenever the recipient is abroad.

In this field again, everything depends on the context in which the software is being used, and on its functions and there are, so far, no definite rules. But divergencies between accountancy law and tax law in certain countries create problems for the development of a "software industry". In the United States, the Internal Revenue Service has ruled that tax accounting practices need not follow financial accounting practices, therefore this has not posed a problem for United States firms.

4. Software and Insurance Policies

There are practically no insurance policies directly for software. Generally speaking, an insurance policy covering tangibles (or products), designed to compensate for losses resulting from the partial or total destruction, disappearance or loss of value of a tangible or an intangible object because the risk has materialised, includes operating software in the concept of hardware. Application programs are treated as media or internal aids, and can be covered by supplementary policies covering costs of reconstituting programs or archives, where compensation arrangements are comparable to those for liability and loss insurance. The latter are designed to compensate the insured for losses incurred as the result of a successful claim for damages by a third party. In recent years this latter type of insurance has come to include new forms of policy treating software distinctly, and differently from earlier practice. Two types of policy can be mentioned: guarantees against loss of royalty on the leasing of software packages, for the contingency in which, for accidental reasons, a firm which has developed or distributed a software package receives no rental. The guarantee assumes that the packages form part of the assets of the firm concerned, and on reflection appears cognate with product insurance, in which the goods insured necessarily form part of the insured's assets. The second kind of policy provides legal cover against the risk of pirating. The insurers, starting from the principle that developing programs and software packages may require very heavy investment, whose value is to be treated as an asset belonging to the firm which has developed them, are marketing a guarantee for all the pecuniary consequences arising out of proceedings for pirating. In this way, the insurers have sought to compensate for the legal uncertainties surrounding program protection.

NOTES AND REFERENCES

1. In November 1981, the International Standards Organisation defined software as, "Intellectual creation comprising the programs, procedures, rules and any associated documentation pertaining to the operation of a data processing system. Software is independent of its carrier media". In June 1983 the World Intellectual Property Organisation suggested a set of more detailed definitions (see Annex II).

2. B. Boehm, "Software and Its Impact: A Quantitative Assessment", *Datamation*, May 1983. For an overview of the diverse uses of the results of this study, see Annex IV, Figure 1.

3. Delivered source instructions (DSIs): net, ready to use source instructions of a software product. Software output measured in DSIs includes the testing, integration and documentation work accompanying it.

4. CSA Briefing Note, *Software Quality Assurance.*

5. According to one estimate, the cost of a "state-of-the-art" software engineering tool was about $500 000 in 1978 and it needed a mainframe computer. In 1981, the average cost had fallen to $100 000 and most could already be used on microcomputers. In 1982 and 1983 costs continued to decline, to approach $50 000 in 1982 and $25 000 in 1983 (*Datamation*, February 1983).

6. Total expenditures on machinery and equipment of the United States economy in 1984: $240 billion.

7. According to Dataquest, between 55 and 60 per cent of computers installed in the United States will be part of a network by 1985.

8. IBM seems to have followed a similar strategy for its new MVS/XA operating system. Publishing the specifications of this highly complex software at the same time as putting it on the market, IBM confronts rivals with a formidable challenge: either they rapidly adapt their hardware and software to the new environment or they lose potential customers wishing to adopt MVS/XA.

9. For more detailed information about size, growth and classification of leading computer service firms in the United States, Europe and Japan, see Annex IV.

10. The publishing and distribution of software packages, especially for microcomputers, has become a highly profitable industry in itself. There are thought to be a great many software marketing companies now in the United States, most of them small (only about 100 having over 25 employees). According to an estimate by Future Computing, 1 per cent of package sales are through specialist software stores in the United States for 1984, but that share is expected to attain 25 per cent by 1987. Although the need for a degree of specialisation, together with a consultancy and after-sales service capability accounts for this "cottage industry" structure of distribution, the profits seem so high and so certain that newcomers are constantly entering and can be expected to transform its organisation. Several established software houses are now beginning to act, in effect, as "publishers" for the smaller firms and individual software creators (there are thought to be some 10 000 such small-scale creators in the United States), together with a number of very large firms not previously involved in the industry at all (American Express, McGraw-Hill, etc.).

11. See, *Venture Capital in Information Technology*, OECD, 1985.

12. Only embedded software is considered here. Computer and automation systems based on microprocessors but implementing non-embedded programs, of which the software organisation and requirements are very differently structured, are considered in Sections I and III.

13. This trend seems to be substantially altering the economics of the distribution industry, leading to further concentration. The top 10 distributors already accounted for 65 per cent of the industry's sales in 1983 as compared to 37 per cent in 1973.

14. This point is clearly made in two recent remarks from industry. The United States National Research Council's Committee on Computer-Aided Manufacturing, 1982 Report notes: "While most of the 'hard' technology for the realisation of integrated manufacturing systems already exists, much of the needed 'integratable' software for them does not". Professor N. Okino, Chairman of the Computer-Aided Manufacturing International's Robotics Software Group, said in 1982: "Great progress has been made in robotics hardware, but robotics software is lagging behind and is in a rather confused state, and a great deal of work is needed to be done". This does not mean that no hardware technology problems remain, but that software difficulties are preventing users from getting the best out of the hardware already available.

15. According to one of the main US experts on this question, "... the day when a portable part program is the norm instead of the exception is not here yet, but the publication of the EIA proposal will bring that day closer ... " (L. R. Herdon, Chairman, Vega Servo-Control, Inc.).

16. According to D. Ross, main author of the language. See, R.L. Wexelblat ed., *History of Programming Languages,* Academic Press, 1981.

17. Even in Sweden, one of the countries best endowed with advanced automation techniques, an expert commented recently: "We need more skilled production engineers out of our graduate schools and universities ... since the growth of robot applications in industry today is *people limited – not technology-limited*" (B. Weichbrodt, General Manager, Industrial Robot Division, ASEA).

18. In economics "public goods" are goods which, because they cannot be withheld from one individual without withholding them from all, must be supplied communally.

19. The National Software Centre, currently being established in Dublin, is intended to provide a research and technology transfer infrastructure for Irish industry. It will be staffed on opening by some 15 highly qualified specialists.

20. Italy's finalised computer project (PFI) is a national programme aiming:

    i) To develop advanced applied research in areas of common interest to Italy;
    ii) To integrate the understanding and skills of Italy's computer community into the industrial and social fabric of the country.

    Its public budget for 1979 to 1983 was L 49 billion (about $30 million) together with contributions from private industry from 1981. Several government, university and industrial research laboratories are participating in the programme.

21. Belgium's action programme on micro-electronics technologies, adopted by the Government in 1982, supports specific research projects. As far as software is concerned, research into software engineering and experts systems are to be promoted.

22. Even in the most recent French computer literacy plan, cited above, FF 1.7 billion of the total FF 2 billion will be devoted to hardware purchases, leaving compartively few resources for software development and purchases.

23. It is noted however, that most government personnel resources in the United States go to the maintenance of existing software and few to internal software development.

24. *Changing Market Structures in Telecommunications: Proceedings of an OECD Conference,* North-Holland Press, May 1984 and *Transborder Data Flows,* OECD Symposium, London, December 1983 – North-Holland Press, 1985.

25. An important recent initiative in this respect is that of the Australian Government. Custom duties on computers, electronic components and office equipment were lowered to "minimum" rates, in order that "... a number of distortions in the consumption and production of [computer and electronic] goods are overcome ... and industry competitiveness generally enhanced through the

availability at world prices of most products". (Australian Government Statement, 5th July 1984).

26. For example, see article by Mr. Bertrand in Expertises No. 55, October 1983.

27. See Dr. U. Sieber: Der urheberrechtliche Schutz von Computerprogramnen. Betriebs-Berater Heft No. 16-10.6.1983.

28. Professor Ulmer, *La protection par le droit d'auteur des œvres scientifiques en général et des programmes d'ordinateur en particulier,* RIDA 1982, LXXIV.

29. See for example the decision of the German Federal Court on industrial relations of 13th September, 1983 that defines the conditions under which an employee may maintain their copyright on the software he has created.

30. French Penal Code, Article 378, Article 418, paragraph 177 and 179.

31. Paragraph 17, Section 2 of the Swedish Accountancy Act.

32. From the paper by Mr. J. Cohen Scali to the Feduci Seminar on Legal Aspects of Software, Paris, November 1983.

33. Statement No. 2: Accounting for R&D Cost, Stanford, Connecticut, 1974.

34. Applicability of FASB Statement No. 2 to Computer Software, Connecticut, 1975.

35. J.R. Porter, Software Products Industry View of Financial Accounting.

36. Including financial directors, management controllers, the Association is very active in accountancy research.

LIST OF MEMBERS OF THE EXPERT GROUP

CHAIRMAN OF THE EXPERT GROUP

Mr. J.P. BRULÉ

Vice-Chairman of the Committee for Information, Computer and Communications Policy.

AUSTRALIA

Mr. M. LESTER

Counsellor, Permanent Delegation to the OECD, Paris.

BELGIUM

Mr. E. MILGROM

Lecturer, Université Catholique of Louvain.

CANADA

Mr. M. HARROP

Advisor, Government EDP Standards Supply and Services Canada, Ottawa.

FINLAND

Mr. I. PIETARINEN

Ministry of Finance, Helsinki.

FRANCE

Mr. R. ATTARD

Postes, Télécommunications et Télédiffusion, Direction Générale des Télécommunications, Direction des Affaires industrielles et internationales, Issy-les-Moulineaux.

Mr. B. PINCEMAILLE

Chargé de mission SSCI et logiciel, Direction de l'Industrie électronique et Informatique, Ministère de l'Industrie, Paris.

Ms. C. M. PITRAT

Mission à l'Informatique, Montrouge.

GERMANY

Mr. L. NEFIODOW

Researcher, Gesellschaft für Mathematik und Datenverarbeitung, St. Augustin

GRECE

Mr. N. MALAGARDIS

Counsellor, Ministry of Research and Technology. Director, Bureau for the Orientation of Computing Standardization, Paris.

IRELAND

Mr. R. COCHRAN

Head of Computing and Software Section, National Board for Science and Technology, Dublin.

ITALY

Mr. A. CAZZIOL

Consultant, ETMOTEAM SPA, Milan.

Mr. R. PETRUCCIANI

Training and Education Systemist, ENIDATA SPA (ENI Group), Rome.

JAPAN

Mr. K. TAKASAKI

Research Secretary, Ministry of International Trade and Industry, Tokyo.

Mr. H. IRISAWA

First Secretary, Permanent Delegation to the OECD, Paris.

NETHERLANDS

Mr. P. HOLDERT

Policy Officer, Ministry of Economic Affairs, The Hague.

Mr. P. KLINT

Researcher in Computer Science, Ministry of Science Policy, The Hague.

NORWAY

Mr. A. MAUS

Researcher in Computer Science, Norwegian Computing Centre, Oslo.

PORTUGAL

Mr. J. ALVES LAVADO

Director, Direccao-General da Organisacao Administrativa, Lisbon.

Mr. H. M. FERREIRA COELHO

Laboratorio Nacional de Engenharia Civil, Lisbon.

Mr. F. T. GOMES

Counsellor, Permanent Delegation to the OECD, Paris.

SPAIN

Mr. J. RUIZ RODRIGUEZ

Permanent Delegation to the OECD, Paris.

SWEDEN

Mr. K. HASHMI

Assistant Director, National Central Bureau of Statistics, Stockholm.

Mr. T. STROM

Director of R & D, DAFA, Stockholm.

SWITZERLAND

Mr. F. VUILLEUMIER

Information, Computer and Communications Desk Officer, Office fédéral des Affaires économiques, Berne.

TURKEY

Professor B. EPIR

Informatics Consultant, State Planning Organisation, Middle East Technical University, Ankara.

UNITED KINGDOM

Mr. N. BERNARD

Head of Technical Unit, Information Technology Division, Department of Trade and Industry, London.

UNITED STATES

Mr. W. R. ADRION

Director, Special Projects in Computer Science, National Science Foundation, Washington.

Mr. F. R. CRUPE

Director, Information Finance and Management Service Industries Division, US Department of Commerce, Washington.

Mr. R. O. MILES

Science & Electronic Sectoral Office, International Trade Administration, US Department of Commerce, Washington.

CEC

Mr. R. MEIJER

Administrator, Task Force Information Technologies, Brussels

YUGOSLAVIA

Mr. L. LENART

Software Project Manager, ISKRE-Automatike, Ljubljana.

WIPO DEFINITIONS FOR SOFTWARE

i) "Computer program" means a set of instructions capable, when incorporated in a machine-readable medium, of causing a machine having information-processing capabilities to indicate, perform or achieve a particular function, task or result.

ii) "Program description" means a complete procedural presentation in verbal, schematic or other form, in sufficient detail to determine a set of instructions constituting a corresponding computer program.

iii) "Supporting material" means any material, other than a compouter program or a program description, created for aiding the understanding or application of a computer program, for example problem descriptions and user instructions.

iv) "Computer software" means any or several of the items referred to in i) to iii).

TABLE: SELECTED EVENTS IN THE EVOLUTION OF SOFTWARE AND THE US INDUSTRY

1945	First electronic computer, the ENIAC, built at the University of Pennsylvania by John Mauchly and John Eckert. Its program instructions were soldered into its wiring. As a result rewiring was required to solve different problems.
Late 1940s	Concept of a general purpose, stored program computer developed by John von Neumann.
1951	First commercial computer, UNIVAC 1, delivered to Census Bureau with program instructions stored in high-speed memory. Stored program could be easily changed to solve a new problem.
1954 to 1955	First elementary operating system developed at General Motors Research Labs for IBM 701 computer.
	First assembly language and assembler, the Autocoder, introduced for IBM 705. Allowed programmer to use symbols and mnemonics as substitutes for the "1's" and "0's" of machine language. Assembler then converted symbols into machine language.
1956:	FORTRAN, first high-level programming language developed by John Backus at IBM for scientific and engineering users. However, program instructions written primarily in mathematical notation not English.
	First artificial intelligence (A1) program, the Logic Theorist, developed by Allan Newell and Herbert Simon at Carnegie Tech (now Carnegie-Mellon University). Programmed in Information Processing Language (IPL), it gave computers the power to process symbols rather than numbers.
1957	First English language compiler introduced for UNIVAC 1. Translated programs written in high level language into assembly language.
1958	Lisp, the major A1 programming language of the 1960s and the 1970s, developed by John McCarthy at the Massachusetts Institute of Technology (MIT).
	ALGOL, the first high-level algorithmic programming language introduced for IBM 709.
Late 1950s	First contract programming firms established to meet US Government programming needs, particularly Department of Defense (DOD) and NASA.
	COBOL, first programming language specifically for business data processing introduced.

Early 1960s	Report Program Generator (RPG) developed at IBM as a tool to allow programmers to specify format of system inputs, files and output reports. As a result, it became possible to "write programs" by filling out a set of forms.
1961	First experimental timeshared system launched at MIT under sponsorship of DOD's Advanced Research Project Agency (ARPA). Operating system allowed several users to access IBM 7094 concurrently.
1963	First operating system, the Master Control Program (MCP), introduced for the Burroughs B500 computer system, featuring multiprogramming, multiprocessing and virtual storage.
	First general-purpose programming language, PL/1, introduced by IBM as possible replacement for FORTRAN and COBOL.
	First conversational programming language, JOSS, developed at the Rand Corporation for timesharing users.
1964	First commercial on-line transaction processing operating system developed at IBM for American Airlines' SABRE reservation system.
	IBM introduced operating system (OS/360) for its new generation of computers. First attempt to create an operating system that could run on all computer systems in a family.
1965	Beginners All-Purpose Symbolic Instruction Code (BASIC) developed by John Kemeny and Thomas Kurtz at Dartmouth College. Easy-to-learn conversational programing language now used extensively on personal computers.
	First minicomputer, the PDP-8, introduced by Digital Equipment Corporation. Beginning of small computer usage.
	DENDRAL, first expert system program developed by Edward Fiegenbaum and Joshua Lederberg at Stanford University.
Mid-1960s	Firms attempt to modify certain programs for use by a wide range of users. Beginning of packaged software.
1967	Mathematica Products Group introduced RAMIS, first non-procedural language.
1968	Pascal, a programming language derived from ALGOL, developed in Zurich, Switzerland became a standard in university computing.
1969	IBM announced that it would price software separately from hardware. "Unbundling" stimulating growth of independent software suppliers and packaged software market.
	Bell Labs (AT&Ts research subsidiary) began development of UNIX operating system. An important multi-user, multi-tasking operating system, particularly for mini and personal computer users.
	IBM introduced new generation system 370 computers.
1972	Another important A1 programming language, PROLOG, jointly developed at University of Marseilles, France, and Imperial College of London, England.
	SMALL TALK, object-oriented A1 programming language and software development environment developed at Xerox Research. Forerunner of integrated software such as Lotus 1, 2, 3 and VisiOn.
	PL/M, first resident high-level language compiler developed for a microprocessor.

1975	Western Electric, AT&Ts manufacturing subsidiary, licenses UNIX to educational institutions and to commercial sector. Spawned substantial number of UNIX-derivatives.
	Development of ADA began, the standard programming language of DOD.
1977	CP/M-80, a non-proprietary operating system developed by Gary Kildall for 8-bit personal computers. Emerged as de facto standard for these machines.
1978	Radio Shack and Apple Computer introduced first commercially successful personal computers. Represented another important stimulant to growth of US software industry in early 1980s.
1979	DOD selected version of ADA from CII-Honeywell Bull (France) as standard.
	VisiCalc, first electronic spreadsheet developed for personal computers. Marked beginning of sophisticated applications packages for this market sector.
	RI (also known as X-CON), first expert system used routinely in an industrial environment, developed at Carnegie-Mellon for Digital Equipment Corporation.
1980	INTELLECT, first commercial natural language query system introduced by Artificial Intelligence Corporation.
1981	IBM introduced the PC. Microsoft developed version of its PC-DOS operating system, called MS/DOS, which became de facto standard for 16-bit personal computers. Had installed base of 650,000 units by 1983.
1982	Context Management and Lotus Development announced integrated applications software which allow concurrent use of several programs and transfer of data between these applications.
1983	Several US software firms announced products linking personal computers to mainframes.
	American National Standards Institute (ANSI) publishes an official description of ADA.

Source: US Department of Commerce, "Competitive Assessment of the US Software Industry", 1984.

Annex IV

TABLES AND FIGURES

Figure 1 **HISTORY OF A CURVE: HARDWARE/SOFTWARE COST RATIOS**

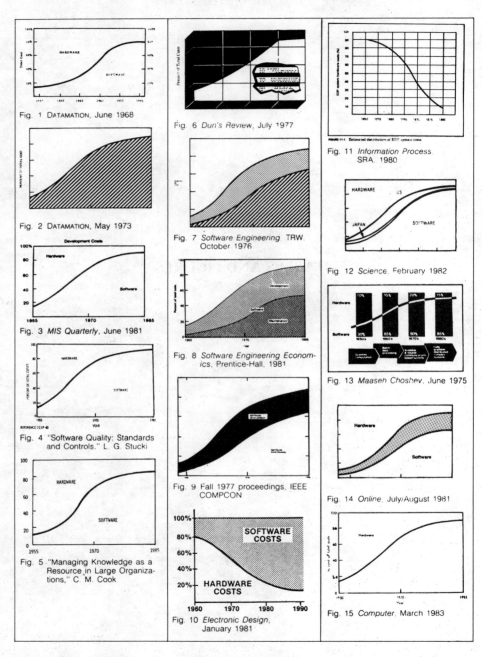

Fig. 1 DATAMATION, June 1968

Fig. 2 DATAMATION, May 1973

Fig. 3 *MIS Quarterly*, June 1981

Fig. 4 "Software Quality: Standards and Controls." L. G. Stucki

Fig. 5 "Managing Knowledge as a Resource in Large Organizations," C. M. Cook

Fig. 6 *Dun's Review*, July 1977

Fig. 7 *Software Engineering* TRW. October 1976

Fig. 8 *Software Engineering Economics*, Prentice-Hall, 1981

Fig. 9 Fall 1977 proceedings, IEEE COMPCON

Fig. 10 *Electronic Design*, January 1981

Fig. 11 *Information Process.* SRA. 1980

Fig. 12 *Science*. February 1982

Fig. 13 *Maasen Choshev*, June 1975

Fig. 14 *Online*. July/August 1981

Fig. 15 *Computer*. March 1983

Source : W. Frank, *Datamation*, 1983

184

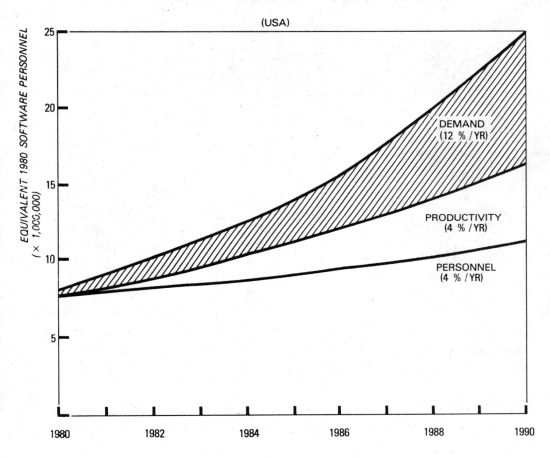

Figure 2 **CURRENT REPRESENTATION OF THE SOFTWARE "BOTTLENECK"
IN THE UNITED STATES**

(USA)

EQUIVALENT 1980 SOFTWARE PERSONNEL
(× 1,000,000)

DEMAND
(12 % / YR)

PRODUCTIVITY
(4 % / YR)

PERSONNEL
(4 % / YR)

25

20

15

10

5

1980   1982   1984   1986   1988   1990

Source: D.o.D. 1983.

185

Figure 3 CURRENT REPRESENTATION OF THE SOFTWARE DESIGN PROBLEM: METAMORPHOSIS OF A SYSTEM DURING ITS DEVELOPMENT

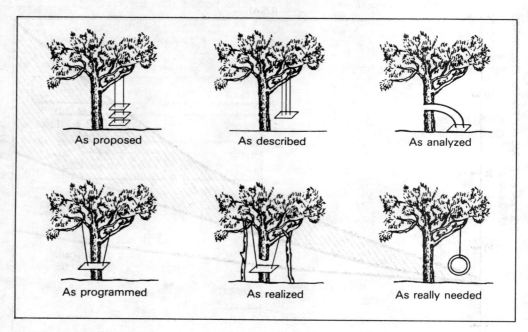

Source: Datalert/Bilisim.

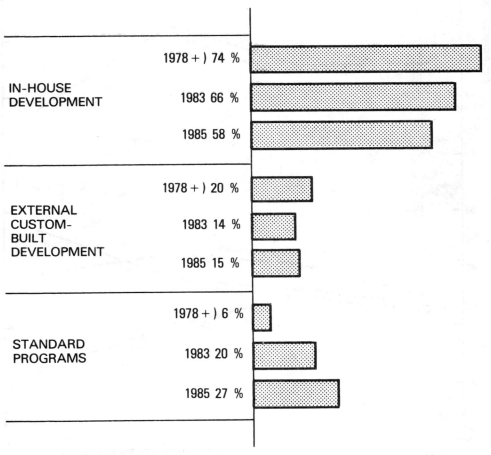

Figure 4 **ORIGINS OF SOFTWARE FOR BIG USERS (a) IN GERMANY, 1978 TO 1985 (b)**
New development of applications software

IN-HOUSE DEVELOPMENT
1978 +) 74 %
1983 66 %
1985 58 %

EXTERNAL CUSTOM-BUILT DEVELOPMENT
1978 +) 20 %
1983 14 %
1985 15 %

STANDARD PROGRAMS
1978 +) 6 %
1983 20 %
1985 27 %

+ . 1979 survey (the market for applications software in Germany).
a. Computer budgets of more than DM 1 million.
b. Forecasts.

Source: GMD.

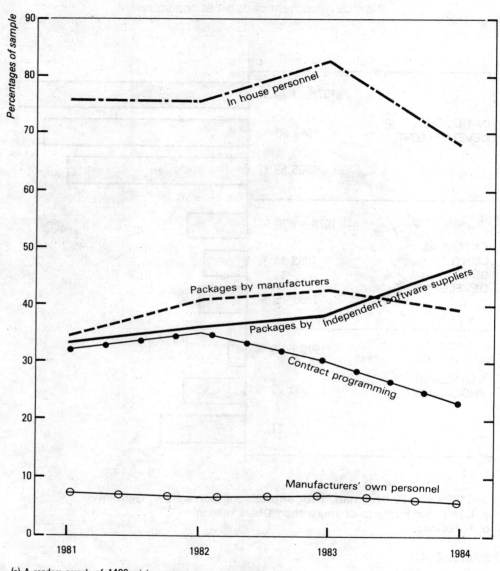

Figure 5 **ORIGINS OF APPLICATIONS SOFTWARE FOR MINICOMPUTER USERS (a) IN THE UNITED KINGDOM, 1981-1984**

In house personnel

Packages by manufacturers

Packages by   Independent software suppliers

Contract programming

Manufacturers' own personnel

(a) A random sample of 1400 minicomputer users.

Source : Computer Weekly/Datapro, 1985

Figure 6 EXPECTED GROWTH OF THE WORLD MARKET
FOR SOFTWARE PACKAGES 1982 AND 1987

SALES VALUE OF SOFTWARE PACKAGES BY HARDWARE
MANUFACTURERS AND INDEPENDENTS, 1982 AND 1987

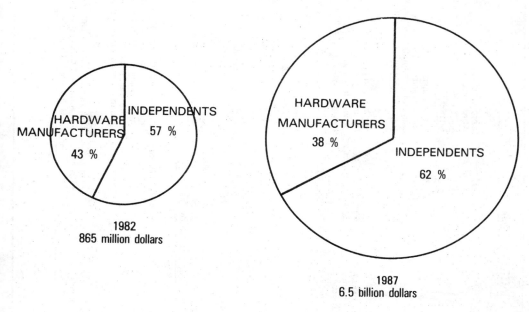

SHARE OF MICRO-COMPUTER SOFTWARE PACKAGES
IN TOTAL SOFTWARE PACKAGE SALES

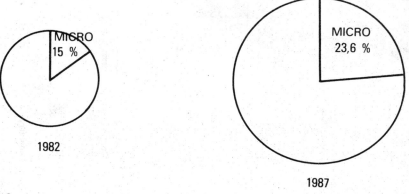

Source: IDC.

Table 1. **Best selling software in the United States, February 1984**

Name	Supplier	Price ($)	Task
APPLICATIONS SOFTWARE			
For personal computers:			
Wordstar	Micro-Pro International	495	Word processing
PPS-Write	Software Publishing	125–140	Word processing
1-2-3	Lotus Development	495	Spreadsheet, graphs and file management
Multiplan	Microsoft	275	Spreadsheet
VisiCalc	VisiCorp	250	Spreadsheet
VisiTrend/Plot	VisiCorp	300	Draws graphs
PFS-Graph	Software Publishing	125–140	Draws graphs
General Accounting	BPI Systems	195–595	Standard accounting functions
Peachtree Accounting Software	Peachtree	395	Standard accounting functions
For large computers:			
Human Resource System	Information Science	50 000 to 100 000	Personnel and payroll
MSA Human Resource System	Management Science America	80 000 to 130 000	Personnel and payroll
MAS General Ledger System/FICs	Management Science America	50 000 to 100 000	General ledger accounting
Policy Management System	Policy Management Systems	*	Insurance policy management
UTILITY SOFTWARE			
For personal computers:			
dBase II	Ashton-Tate	700	Data base management
PFS: File	Software Publishing	125–140	Data base management
Microsoft Basic	Microsoft	350–600	A compiler for writing Basic programs
Visi On	VisiCorp	95	An integrated "environment"
For large computers:			
Total	Cincom Systems	95 000	Data base management
Mark IV	Informatics General	78 000 to 98 000	Data base management
Adabas	Software AG	106 000 and up	Data base management
System 2000	Intel Systems	50 000 to 100 000	Data base management
Focus	Information Builders	66 000 to 120 000	Data base management
SYSTEMS CONTROL SOFTWARE			
For personal computers:			
Apple DOS	Apple Computer	Free with machine	Apple II and III operating system
CP/M	Digital-Research	150	Operating system for 3-bit computers
Concurrent CP/M-85	Digital-Research	350	Latest version of CM/M for 16-bit computers with windowing environment
MS/DOS	Microsoft	**	Operating system for IBM Personal Computer
For large computers:			
CA-Dynam	Computer Associates	24 750	Disk and tape catalog management
Datamanager	Manager Software Products	8 100	Keeps track of data in data base
SyncSort	SyncSort	***	Sorts and combines programs

* Price varies widely depending on size of installation and type of computer.
** Purchased through computer maker.
*** Leases for $6 200 a year on a three-year contract.
Source: ICP, Business Week, 27.2.1984.

190

Table 2. **Ranking of software selection criteria in the United States**

Percentage of responses in 1984

Selection criteria	Very important	Important	Not important
Documentation	73.7	25.9	0.4
Ease of use	72.3	27.0	0.7
Features/Performance	60.6	38.2	1.2
Support (service, training, maintenance)	51.9	42.4	5.7
Compatibility with other software already in use	42.0	44.4	13.6
Error handling	36.6	58.9	4.5
Portability/Compatibility with other hardware	19.7	44.4	35.9
Price	18.9	67.8	13.3
Vendor reputation, size, financial reputation	15.4	60.8	23.8

Note: Two thousand organisations participated in the survey including those in research, education, government and finance.

Source: "1984 Software User Survey", *Software News,* 1984/US Department of Commerce, 1984.

Table 3. **Top 25 software and service suppliers in the United States**

1983 rank	1982 rank	Company	Software products and services (SP&S) offered	Years in SP&S business	Fiscal year end	SP&S revenue (million)
1	1	International Business Machines Corporation	abceijlm	39	Dec. 31	2 813
2	3	Digital Equipment Corporation	abcdefghijklm	26	June 30	1 404
3	2	Control Data Corporation	abcdeghikjlm	26	Dec. 31	1 260
4	4	Burroughs Corporation	abce	27	Dec. 31	830
5	5	NCR Corporation	abcdeghijklm	31	Dec. 31	805
6	8	TRW, Inc.	abk	31	Dec. 31	790
7	6	Automatic Data Processing, Inc.	ghi	35	June 30	753
8	7	Computer Sciences Corporation	ghijklm	26	Mar. 31	695
9	9	Electronic Data Systems Corporation	abcghijklm	21	June 30	630
10	12	Hewlett-Packard Company	abce	17	Oct. 31	462
11	10	General Electric Information Services Company	abceghikm	20	Dec. 31	450
12	—	Computervision Corporation	e	15	Dec. 31	400
13	13	McDonnell Douglas Automation Company	aehikl	24	Dec. 31	376
14	14	Tymshare, Inc.	agikl	18	Dec. 31	289
15	15	Harris Corporation	bcde	24	June 30	250
16	19	Boeing Computer Services Company	ajlm	14	Dec. 31	250
17	16	Honeywell Inc.	abcem	28	Dec. 31	229
18	17	The Perkin-Elmer Corporation	abcejklm	10	July 31	214
19	18	General Instrument Corporation	abceghi	19	Feb. 28	213
20	22	Shared Medical Systems Corporation	ehij	15	Dec. 31	211
21	—	The Dun & Bradstreet Corporation	abceik	1	Dec. 31	210
22	20	Informatics General Corporation	abcik	22	Dec. 31	198
23	79	Cap Gemini DASD	bcklm	10	Dec. 31	173
24	32	First Data Resources Inc.	ai	15	Dec. 31	158
25	29	Martin Marletta Data Systems	abcehijklm	14	Dec. 31	154

Legend for software products and services business classes

a	Applications software supplier	h	Remote non-interactive processing firm
b	Systems software supplier	i	Interactive processing firm
c	Utilities software supplier	j	On-site processing firm
d	OEM distributor	k	Custom programming firm
e	Turnkey systems operator	l	DP consulting supplier
f	Software product retailer	m	Education/training supplier
g	Local batch processing firm		

Source: ICP Business Software Review, Special Edition 1984.

Table 4. **Top 25 independent software suppliers in the United States**

		Total corporate revenue ($ million)	Percentage software	Total software revenue ($ million)
1.	MSA (Management Science America, Inc.)	145	100	145
2.	Informatics General Corporation	198	51	101
3.	Softsel	88	100	88
4.	Applied Data Research, Inc.	89	92	82
5.	Cullinet Software, Inc.	79	100	79
6.	Cincom Systems, Inc.	71	100	71
7.	SEI Corporation	68	100	68
8.	Computer Associates International, Inc.	58	100	58
9.	Lotus Development Corporation	53	100	53
10.	Alpha Microsystems	52	100	52
11.	Microsoft Corporation	50	100	50
12.	MicroPro International Corporation	45	100	45
13.	Pansophic Systems, Inc.	43	100	43
14.	Visicorp	42	100	42
15.	Digital Research, Inc.	38	100	38
16.	SAS Institute, Inc.	32	93	30
17.	Candle Corporation	30	100	30
18.	Information Builders, Inc.	30	98	28
19.	Software AG of North America, Inc.	30	95	29
20.	Policy Management Systems Corporation	62	43	27
21.	ISSCO (Integrated Software Systems Corporation)	24	100	24
22.	Softeam, Inc.	27	80	22
23.	American Software, Inc.	21	100	21
24.	Boole & Babbage, Inc.	22	93	20
25.	The Continuum Company, Inc.	21	98	20

Note: Suppliers whose software business exceeds all other lines of business in terms of revenues generate.
Source: ICP, 1984.

Table 5. **Top 20 independent micro software suppliers in the United States**

$ million

		Total micro software revenue
1.	Softsel	88
2.	Lotus Development Corporation	53
3.	Alpha Microsystems	52
4.	Microsoft Corporation	50
5.	MicroPro International Corporation	45
6.	VisiCorp	42
7.	Digital Research, Inc.	38
8.	Softeam, Inc.	22
9.	Lifeboat Associates	22
10.	Micro D, Inc.	22
11.	Ashton-Tate	18
12.	Broderbund Software	13
13.	Sierra On-Line Inc.	13
14.	Software Arts, Inc.	12
15.	Sorcim Corporation	12
16.	Holland Automation	10
17.	Software Publishing Corporation	10
18.	Perfect Software, Inc.	10
19.	Multimate International Corporation	10
20.	Software Knowledge Unlimited	10

Note: Suppliers whose revenues are generated entirely from microcomputer software.
Source: ICP, 1984

Table 6. **Leaders in SP&S growth by percentage in the United States,**
1982-1983

		SP&S revenue ($ million)		Annual percentage growth
		1982	1983	
1.	Lotus Development Corporation	0*	53	3 042
2.	Softsel	34	88	159
3.	Softeam, Inc.	12	27	125
4.	VM Software, Inc.	2	5	122
5.	Micro D, Inc.	10	22	119
6.	Hogan Systems, Inc.	8	17	114
7.	Science Management Corporation	14	30	112
8.	MicroPro International Corporation	22	45	104
9.	Alpha Microsystems	26	52	100
10.	SAS Institute, Inc.	16	32	100
11.	Microsoft Corporation	26	50	92
12.	Goal Systems International, Inc.	5	9	86
13.	Affiliated Computer Systems	46	84	83
14.	Global Software, Inc.	3	6	83
15.	Data Architects, Inc.	13	24	81
16.	Precision Visuals	4	7	75
17.	SAGE Systems, Inc.	5	9	74
18.	T and B Computer, Inc.	6	10	73
19.	ComputerLand Corporation	25	43	72
20.	SEI Corporation	40	68	70

* Rounded from $174 226.
Source: ICP, 1984

Table 7. **Differences in employment growth by region**
in US computer services industry

Number of employees

	Computer services (SIC 737)		Annual change 1974-1981 %	1983	Annual change 1981-1983 %
	1974	1981			
Northeast	39 594	81 763	11	89 280	5
North Central	33 180	63 400	9	67 320	3
South	44 490	102 299	13	115 200	6
West	29 839	76 502	14	88 200	7
Total United States	148 539	323 967	12	360 000	5

Source: US Department of Commerce.

Table 8. Top 30 computer service companies in Western Europe, 1983[a]

	Company	Country of origin	Ownership	Packaged software	Custom software/ consultancy	System house	Processing services	Number of employees	Western european revenue ($ million)
1.	IBM	United States	Public Company	X			X	—	279.0
2.	SG2	France	Société Générale	X	X	X	X	4 200	144.7
3.	Cap Gemini Sogeti	France	Management/CGIP/BA	X	X		X	4 000	139.1
4.	GSi	France	CGE			X	X	2 400	128.8
5.	Geisco	United States	General Electric Co.	X			X	1 300	112.9
6.	Scicon Int.[b]	United Kingdom	British Petroleum			X	X	2 650	110.4
7.	Datev	Germany	Tax Advisors Co-op		X		X	1 788	108.9
8.	CiSi	France	CEA/BNP		X		X	2 800	98.0
9.	CCMC	France	CCMC/Société Générale				X	1 224	83.9
10.	Telesystemes	France	PTT	X	X	X	X	1 644	77.3
11.	Sligos	France	Crédit Lyonnais/Tymshare		X	X	X	1 800	74.9
12.	Sema	France	Paribas	X	X		X	2 110	71.9
13.	Kommunedata	Denmark	Local Government	X	X	X		1 447	66.8
14.	Thorn EMI	United Kingdom	Public Company	X	X			1 690	62.4
15.	Datema	Sweden	Nordstjernan AB	X	X	X		1 057	62.2
16.	SESA	France	CGE/Management		X		X	654	61.3
17.	Datacentralen	Denmark	Government				X	1 281	59.4
18.	Kommunedata	Norway	Local Government				X	1 100	55.8
19.	Steria	France	Staff/BNP/Total	X	X	X		1 342	51.6
20.	CDC[c]	United States	Public Company	X	X	X	X	720	51.2
21.	ADP	United States	Public Company			X	X	750	50.8
22.	ACI/UCC	Switzerland/United States	Wyly Corp.	X			X	500	48.6
23.	Kommundata	Sweden	Local Government	X	X	X	X	912	48.5
24.	NCR[d]	United States	Public Company		X	X	X	640	44.9
25.	CIG[e]	Belgium	Société Générale/AG Group		X			1 052	42.8
26.	Volmac	Netherlands	Private Company		X			680	42.3
27.	Hoskyns	United States/United Kingdom	Martin Marietta			X	X	955	38.9
28.	Logica	United Kingdom	Public Company	X	X	X		1 428	38.5
29.	IDA	Norway	Commercial Bank		X		X	330	36.7
30.	CMG	United Kingdom	Staff				X	670	36.5

Major services

a) Includes all third party vendors' software and services activities. Only the processing services activities of hardware vendors are included.
b) Comprised of GFI (France), Scicon (United Kingdom), SCS (Germany).
c) CDC includes Arbat.
d) NCR includes JDC.
e) CIG includes LA Computer Services (United Kingdom) and Rhein Main (Germany).
Note: The figures quoted for European and US companies represent revenues earned in Western Europe only. All captive revenues (revenues earned through work carried out for parent company) are excluded.
Source: ECSA/IDC, 1984.

Table 9. **Independent packaged software vendors in Europe, 1983**

	Country of origin	Revenue ($ million)	Market share (percentage)
Cincom	United States	26.0	2.6
Computer Associates	United States	22.1	2.2
MSA (including Peachtree Int. $5 million)	United States	18.2	1.9
ADR	United States	15.1	1.5
SEMA	France	14.1	1.5
MicroSoft	United States	14.0	1.4
Cullinet	United States	13.7	1.4
VisiCorp	United States	13.0	1.3
Steria	France	11.7	1.2
ADV/Orga	Germany	11.2	1.1
SAP	Germany	10.8	1.1
CGI	France	10.7	1.1
DRI	United States	10.5	1.1
Informatics	United States	10.4	1.1
Thomson CSF (includes Answare, CETT, Cima, Syseca, TITN)	France	9.9	1.0
ACI/UCC	Switzerland/United States	9.8	1.0
Software AG	Germany	9.1	0.9
SESA	France	9.0	0.9
Peterborough SW	United Kingdom	8.1	0.8
Boole & Babbage	United States	7.7	0.8
Data Management Group	Italy	7.5	0.8
Pansophic	United States	7.0	0.7
Softlab	Germany	6.7	0.7
Syntax	Italy	6.7	0.7
BIS	United Kingdom	6.6	0.7
Other		693.1	70.5
Total		983.0	100

Source: IDC, 1984.

Table 10. **Profitability of computer service firms in the United States, 1982**

Type of company	Number of companies	Non-captive US revenue	Employees	Public companies pretax profit margins
		$ million	Thousands	Percentage
Processing services	2 130	12 484	226	13.2
Software products	1 879	5 295	68	18.3
Professional services	1 348	5 329	110	5.7
Integrated systems	1 113	3 332	46	12.9
Total	6 470	26 430	450	11.8

Source: INPUT/ADAPSO.

Table 11. **Sensitivity of software firms' profits to the accountancy treatment of software investment**
1983 profits in dollars

Company	Reported earnings per share[a]	Assuming 50% deferral[b]
Applied Data Research	1.45	2.13
Computer Associates	0.83	1.12
Cullinet Software	1.00	1.26
Hogan Systems	0.29	0.42
Lotus Development	1.02	1.06
Policy Management Systems	0.63	0.80
SEI	0.89	1.30
Shared Medical Systems	1.11	1.29

a) Current practice: all software investment treated as current expenditure.
b) If 50 per cent of software investment is capitalized.
Source: Alex, Brown and Sons, *Business Week,* March 19, 1984.

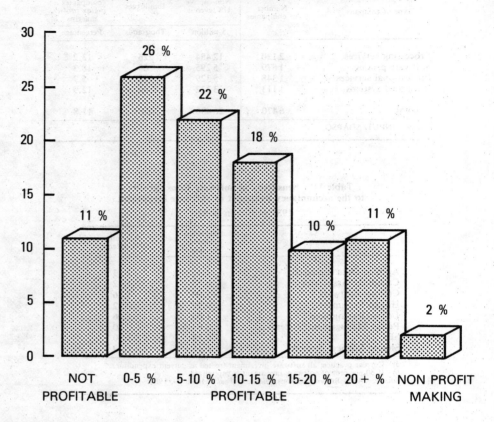

Figure 7 **PROFITABILITY OF COMPUTER SERVICE FIRMS IN EUROPE 1982**
pre-tax profits distribution of respondents to the survey

Source: Quantum Science/ECSA.

Table 12. **Top 25 information processing companies in Japan**[a]

Fiscal year 1982

		Total sales	Sales per individual	Sales growth over previous year
		Y million	Y 10000	Percentage
1.	NEC Software, Ltd.	26 129	2 216	10.9
2.	Nippon Business Consultations Co., Ltd.	22 987	1 371	14.5
3.	Computer Service Co., Ltd.	17 712	565	23.5
4.	Hitachi Software Engineering Co., Ltd.	14 829	706	27.5
5.	Nomura Computer Systems Co., Ltd.	14 677	2 754	15.4
6.	Japan Information Processing Service Co., Ltd.	14 648	1 355	18.1
7.	Japan Information Service Co., Ltd.	13 935	1 452	34.1
8.	Fujitsu FIP, Co., Ltd.	13 575	1 209	43.0
9.	Toyo Information System Co., Ltd.	13 023	1 470	35.0
10.	Intec Inc.	12 361	1 039	17.5
11.	Quotations Information Center K.K.	12 813	6 101	—
12.	NEC Information Service, Ltd.	10 752	1 955	12.8
13.	Century Research Center Co., Ltd.	10 255	1 163	16.0
14.	Japan Business Automation Co., Ltd.	9 346	1 923	11.6
15.	Kyoei Information Processing Service Center	8 851	1 125	8.3
16.	Central Systems Co., Ltd.	7 974	1 199	13.9
17.	TKC Co., Ltd.	7 128	3 198	9.3
18.	Daiko Electronic & Communication Co., Ltd.	7 040	1 709	12.4
19.	Mitsui Knowledge Industry Co., Ltd.	6 710	2 275	10.7
20.	Nippon Electric Development Co., Ltd.	6 572	1 027	—
21.	Marketing Intelligence Corp.	6 433	969	17.3
22.	Diamond Computer Service Co., Ltd.	6 168	2 345	23.8
23.	The Nikko Computer Systems Co., Ltd.	5 737	2 732	—
24.	Computer Engineers Co., Ltd.	5 525	910	15.1
25.	Nippon Time Share Co., Ltd.	5 719	974	34.3

a) "Information processing" sector cover computer services industry and on-line information providers.
Source: Computopia, November 1983/JIPDEC.

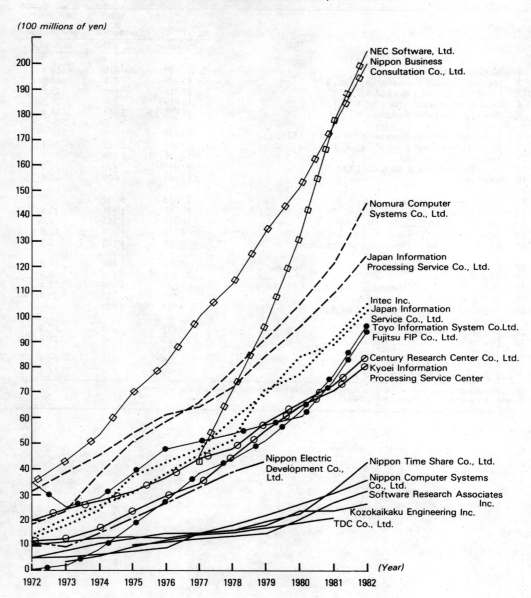

Figure 8   SALES OF MAJOR JAPANESE
INFORMATION PROCESSING FIRMS, 1972 TO 1982

Table 13. **Bestselling software packages in Japan, August 1983**

Product	Distributor	Remarks
Cumulative sales: Y 3-4 billion		
ADABAS (Database Management System)	Software AG of Far East	Imported
Cumulative sales: Y 2.5-3 billion		
EASYTRIEVE (Simplified business package for report preparation)	K. K. Ashisuto	Imported
Cumulative sales: Y 2-2.5 billion		
MARK IV (Applications Development System)	Computer Applications	Imported
Cumulative sales: Y 0.9-1 billion		
A-AUTO (Automatic Operation System)	Software AG of Far East	
Cumulative sales: Y 800-900 million		
JASPOL (Simplified Business Package)	Japan System Science	
Cumulative sales: Y 500-600 million		
PANVALET (Source Program Management System)	K. K. Ashisuto	Imported
FOCUS (Fourth Generation Language)	Focus	Imported
Cumulative sales: Y 400-500 million		
NATURAL (Four Dimensional Voice Input Programming Language)	Software AG of Far East	Imported
PC-PAL (Simplified Business Package for Totalling Data)	Personal Business Assist	Microcomputer package
MODEL 204 (Database Management System)	Mitsui Knowledge Industry	Imported
Cumulative sales : Y 300-400 million		
COM-PLETE (Three Dimensional Online Monitor)	Software AG of Far East	Imported
DCP (Data Compression Management Program)	Software Research Associates	
UCSD P-system (Software Development/Educational Language)	Japan Business Automation	Imported
Cumulative sales: Y 200-300 million		
JARS (Job Accounting Report System)	K. K. Ashisuto	Imported
UFO (CICS Online Applications Development Tool)	K. K. Ashisuto	Imported
DATAMANAGER (Data Dictionay)	Computer Applications	Imported
SORD-PIPS-III (General purpose Information Processing System)	Sord	Microcomputer package
DYANA (Comprehensive Test Evaluation Tool)	Software Research Associates	
PRIDE (System Management Methodology)	Nippon System Corp.	Imported
MASP (File Maintenance Summary Print-Out Program)	Japan Business Consultant	
Cumulative sales: Y 100-200 million		
ANSWER/2 (Report Writer)	Computer Applications	Imported
MARK V (Online Applications Development System)	Computer Applications	Imported
IFPS (Interactive Decision-Making Support System)	Computer Applications	Imported
SHRINK (File Compression System)	JMA Systems Corp.	Imported
SORD-PIPS-II (General-purpose Information Processing System)	Sord	Microcomputer package

Table 13 *(Continued)*

Product	Distributor	Remarks
Cumulative sales: Y 100-200 million		
BASIC-II (BASIC Programming Language)	Sord	Microcomputer package
PRO/TEST (Program Testing Tool)	Software Research Associates	Imported
Cumulative sales: Y 50-100 million		
UCC SEVEN (Computer Production Management System)	Computer Applications	Imported
DMS/OS (DASD Space Integrated Management System)	CEC	Imported
SYNCSORT (Sorting Program)	CEC	Imported
KBASIC-II (KANJI BASIC Programming Language)	Sord	Microcomputer package
SOAR (Data Retrieval Program)	Software AG of Far East	
ADAPT (General-Purpose File Editing Program)	TDC	
QUIKJOB	Nissho Electronics	Imported
PCOM (Communications Program)	Personal Business Assist Engineering	Microcomputer package
HIDOC (Automatic Hierarchical Document Preparation System)		
STAMPS (Standardized Business Data Processing System)	Hitachi Software	

Source: Software Ryutsu Magazine, October 1983/JIPDEC.

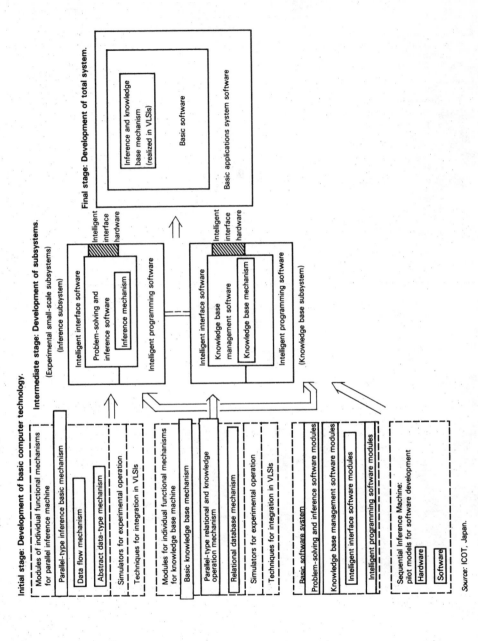

Figure 9 STAGES OF JAPANESE FIFTH GENERATION PROJECT 1980 TO 1990

Initial stage: Development of basic computer technology.

Modules of individual functional mechanisms for parallel inference machine

- Parallel-type inference basic mechanism
  - Data flow mechanism
  - Abstract data-type mechanism
- Simulators for experimental operation
- Techniques for integration in VLSIs

Modules for individual functional mechanisms for knowledge base machine

- Basic knowledge base mechanism
- Parallel-type relational and knowledge operation mechanism
- Relational database mechanism
- Simulators for experimental operation
- Techniques for integration in VLSIs

Basic software system

- Problem-solving and inference software modules
- Knowledge base management software modules
- Intelligent interface software modules
- Intelligent programming software modules

Sequential Inference Machine: pilot models for software development
- Hardware
- Software

Intermediate stage: Development of subsystems.
(Experimental small-scale subsystems)

(Inference subsystem)

Intelligent interface software

Problem-solving and inference software
- Inference mechanism

Intelligent programming software

Intelligent interface hardware

Intelligent interface software

Knowledge base management software
- Knowledge base mechanism

Intelligent programming software

Intelligent interface hardware

(Knowledge base subsystem)

Final stage: Development of total system.

Inference and knowledge base mechanism (realized in VLSIs)

Basic software

Basic applications system software

Source: ICOT, Japan.

203

OECD SALES AGENTS
DÉPOSITAIRES DES PUBLICATIONS DE L'OCDE

ARGENTINA – ARGENTINE
Carlos Hirsch S.R.L., Florida 165, 4° Piso (Galería Guemes)
1333 BUENOS AIRES, Tel. 33.1787.2391 y 30.7122

AUSTRIA – AUTRICHE
OECD Publications and Information Center
4 Simrockstrasse 5300 Bonn (Germany). Tel. (0228) 21.60.45
Local Agent/Agent local :
Gerold and Co., Graben 31, WIEN 1. Tel. 52.22.35

BELGIUM – BELGIQUE
Jean De Lannoy, Service Publications OCDE
avenue du Roi 202, B-1060 BRUXELLES. Tel. 02/538.51.69

CANADA
Renouf Publishing Company Limited/
Editions Renouf LimitéeHead Office/Siège social – Store/Magasin :
61, rue Sparks Street,
OTTAWA, Ontario K1P 5A6
Tel. (613)238-8985. 1-800-267-4164
Store/Magasin: 211, rue Yonge Street,
TORONTO, Ontario M5B 1M4
Tel. (416)363-3171
Regional Sales Office/
Bureau des Ventes régional :
7575 Trans-Canada Hwy., Suite 305,
SAINT-LAURENT, Québec H4T 1V6
Tél. (514)335-9274

DENMARK – DANEMARK
Munksgaard Export and Subscription Service
35, Nørre Søgade
DK 1370 KØBENHAVN K. Tel. +45.1.12.85.70

FINLAND – FINLANDE
Akateeminen Kirjakauppa
Keskuskatu 1, 00100 HELSINKI 10. Tel. 65.11.22

FRANCE
Bureau des Publications de l'OCDE,
2 rue André-Pascal, 75775 PARIS CEDEX 16. Tel. (1) 524.81.67
Principal correspondant :
13602 AIX-EN-PROVENCE : Librairie de l'Université.
Tel. 26.18.08

GERMANY – ALLEMAGNE
OECD Publications and Information Center
4 Simrockstrasse 5300 BONN Tel. (0228) 21.60.45

GREECE – GRÈCE
Librairie Kauffmann, 28 rue du Stade,
ATHÈNES 132. Tel. 322.21.60

HONG-KONG
Government Information Services,
Publications (Sales) Office,
Beaconsfield House, 4/F.,
Queen's Road Central

ICELAND – ISLANDE
Snaebjörn Jónsson and Co., h.f.,
Hafnarstraeti 4 and 9, P.O.B. 1131, REYKJAVIK.
Tel. 13133/14281/11936

INDIA – INDE
Oxford Book and Stationery Co. :
NEW DELHI-1, Scindia House. Tel. 45896
CALCUTTA 700016, 17 Park Street. Tel. 240832

INDONESIA – INDONÉSIE
PDIN-LIPI, P.O. Box 3065/JKT., JAKARTA, Tel. 583467

IRELAND – IRLANDE
TDC Publishers – Library Suppliers
12 North Frederick Street, DUBLIN 1 Tel. 744835-749677

ITALY – ITALIE
Libreria Commissionaria Sansoni :
Via Lamarmora 45, 50121 FIRENZE. Tel. 579751/584468
Via Bartolini 29, 20155 MILANO. Tel. 365083
Sub-depositari :
Ugo Tassi
Via A. Farnese 28, 00192 ROMA. Tel. 310590
Editrice e Libreria Herder,
Piazza Montecitorio 120, 00186 ROMA. Tel. 6794628
Costantino Ercolano, Via Generale Orsini 46, 80132 NAPOLI. Tel. 405210
Libreria Hoepli, Via Hoepli 5, 20121 MILANO. Tel. 865446
Libreria Scientifica, Dott. Lucio de Biasio "Aeiou"
Via Meravigli 16, 20123 MILANO Tel. 807679
Libreria Zanichelli
Piazza Galvani 1/A, 40124 Bologna Tel. 237389
Libreria Lattes, Via Garibaldi 3, 10122 TORINO. Tel. 519274
La diffusione delle edizioni OCSE è inoltre assicurata dalle migliori librerie nelle
città più importanti.

JAPAN – JAPON
OECD Publications and Information Center,
Landic Akasaka Bldg., 2-3-4 Akasaka,
Minato-ku, TOKYO 107 Tel. 586.2016

KOREA – CORÉE
Pan Korea Book Corporation,
P.O. Box n° 101 Kwangwhamun, SÉOUL. Tel. 72.7369

LEBANON – LIBAN
Documenta Scientifica/Redico,
Edison Building, Bliss Street, P.O. Box 5641, BEIRUT.
Tel. 354429 – 344425

MALAYSIA – MALAISIE
University of Malaya Co-operative Bookshop Ltd.
P.O. Box 1127, Jalan Pantai Baru
KUALA LUMPUR. Tel. 577701/577072

THE NETHERLANDS – PAYS-BAS
Staatsuitgeverij, Verzendboekhandel,
Chr. Plantijnstraat 1 Postbus 20014
2500 EA S-GRAVENHAGE. Tel. nr. 070.789911
Voor bestellingen: Tel. 070.789208

NEW ZEALAND – NOUVELLE-ZÉLANDE
Publications Section,
Government Printing Office Bookshops:
AUCKLAND: Retail Bookshop: 25 Rutland Street,
Mail Orders: 85 Beach Road, Private Bag C.P.O.
HAMILTON: Retail: Ward Street,
Mail Orders, P.O. Box 857
WELLINGTON: Retail: Mulgrave Street (Head Office),
Cubacade World Trade Centre
Mail Orders: Private Bag
CHRISTCHURCH: Retail: 159 Hereford Street,
Mail Orders: Private Bag
DUNEDIN: Retail: Princes Street
Mail Order: P.O. Box 1104

NORWAY – NORVÈGE
J.G. TANUM A/S
P.O. Box 1177 Sentrum OSLO 1. Tel. (02) 80.12.60

PAKISTAN
Mirza Book Agency, 65 Shahrah Quaid-E-Azam, LAHORE 3.
Tel. 66839

PORTUGAL
Livraria Portugal, Rua do Carmo 70-74,
1117 LISBOA CODEX. Tel. 360582/3

SINGAPORE – SINGAPOUR
Information Publications Pte Ltd,
Pei-Fu Industrial Building,
24 New Industrial Road N° 02-06
SINGAPORE 1953. Tel. 2831786, 2831798

SPAIN – ESPAGNE
Mundi-Prensa Libros, S.A.
Castelló 37, Apartado 1223, MADRID-28001. Tel. 275.46.55
Libreria Bosch, Ronda Universidad 11, BARCELONA 7.
Tel. 317.53.08, 317.53.58

SWEDEN – SUÈDE
AB CE Fritzes Kungl Hovbokhandel,
Box 16 356, S 103 27 STH. Regeringsgatan 12,
DS STOCKHOLM. Tel. 08/23.89.00
Subscription Agency/Abonnements:
Wennergren-Williams AB,
Box 30004, S104 25 STOCKHOLM.
Tel. 08/54.12.00

SWITZERLAND – SUISSE
OECD Publications and Information Center
4 Simrockstrasse 5300 BONN (Germany). Tel. (0228) 21.60.45
Local Agents/Agents locaux
Librairie Payot, 6 rue Grenus, 1211 GENÈVE 11. Tel. 022.31.89.50

TAIWAN – FORMOSE
Good Faith Worldwide Int'l Co., Ltd.
9th floor, No. 118, Sec. 2,
Chung Hsiao E. Road
TAIPEI. Tel. 391.7396/391.7397

THAILAND – THAILANDE
Suksit Siam Co., Ltd., 1715 Rama IV Rd,
Samyan, BANGKOK 5. Tel. 2511630

TURKEY – TURQUIE
Kültur Yayinlari Is-Türk Ltd. Sti.
Atatürk Bulvari No : 191/Kat. 21
Kavaklidere/ANKARA. Tel. 17 02 66
Dolmabahce Cad. No : 29
BESIKTAS/ISTANBUL. Tel. 60 71 88

UNITED KINGDOM – ROYAUME-UNI
H.M. Stationery Office,
P.O.B. 276, LONDON SW8 5DT.
(postal orders only)
Telephone orders: (01) 622.3316, or
49 High Holborn, LONDON WC1V 6 HB (personal callers)
Branches at: EDINBURGH, BIRMINGHAM, BRISTOL,
MANCHESTER, BELFAST.

UNITED STATES OF AMERICA – ÉTATS-UNIS
OECD Publications and Information Center, Suite 1207,
1750 Pennsylvania Ave., N.W. WASHINGTON, D.C.20006 – 4582
Tel. (202) 724.1857

VENEZUELA
Libreria del Este, Avda. F. Miranda 52, Edificio Galipan,
CARACAS 106. Tel. 32.23.01/33.26.04/31.58.38

YUGOSLAVIA – YOUGOSLAVIE
Jugoslovenska Knjiga, Knez Mihajlova 2. P.O.B. 36. BEOGRAD
Tel. 621.992

Les commandes provenant de pays où l'OCDE n'a pas encore désigné de dépositaire peuvent être adressées à :
OCDE, Bureau des Publications, 2, rue André-Pascal, 75775 PARIS CEDEX 16.

Orders and inquiries from countries where sales agents have not yet been appointed may be sent to:
OECD, Publications Office, 2, rue André-Pascal, 75775 PARIS CEDEX 16.

68837-08-1985

OECD PUBLICATIONS, 2, rue André-Pascal, 75775 PARIS CEDEX 16 - No. 43297 1985
PRINTED IN FRANCE
(93 85 04 1) ISBN 92-64-12755-0